HUME
PRECURSOR OF MODERN
EMPIRICISM

HUME

PRECURSOR OF MODERN EMPIRICISM

An analysis of his opinions on
Meaning, Metaphysics, Logic
and Mathematics

by

FARHANG ZABEEH

Second revised edition

THE HAGUE
MARTINUS NIJHOFF
1973

Library of Congress Number 72-84848

PRINTED IN THE NETHERLANDS

Preface To Second Edition

In the ten years that have passed since *Hume, Precursor of Modern Empiricism* was first published, I have come to see that to do full justice to the title I should have included in this book other enduring aspects of Hume's thoughts.

Modern empiricists are continuing their research not only on such issues as the nature of meaning, reference and truth, but also on other Humian problems, i.e., the logic of induction, prediction and explanation, the causal account of action, innate ideas and innate disposition, and the logic of factual, conceptual and optative assertions.

In this revised edition I take care to discuss these issues and others under a new chapter, i.e., "The Domain of Inductive Reason" The in-depth discussion is both expository and critical. I shall try to show that the Myth of the Given, which was propagated by the classical empiricists and is unquestioned by Hume, is the core of his unsolved problems of the Justification of Induction, of the Existence of the External World and of Personal Identity.

Moreover, I shall address myself to those aspects of his thoughts which have permanently influenced the course of modern philosophy.

There is added an Appendix on the controversy concerning Hume's view on geometry and a minor rearrangement of chapters.

CONTENTS

In the inquiry that follows, I have kept to three fundamental principles:

always to separate sharply the psychological from the logical, the subjective from the objective;

never to ask for the meaning of a word in isolation, but only in the context of a proposition;

never to lose sight of the distinction between concept and object.

GOTTLOB FREGE
The Foundations of Arithmetic

Introduction

David Hume is the most influential precursor of modern empiricism. By modern empiricism, I intend a belief that all cognitive conflicts can be resolved, in principle, by either appeal to matters of fact, via scientific procedure, or by appeal to some sets of natural or conventional standards, whether linguistic, mathematical, aesthetic or political. This belief itself is a consequent of an old apprehension that all synthetic knowledge is based on experience, and that the rest can be reduced to a set of self-evident truths. In this broad sense, Modern Empiricism encompasses classes, such as Logical Empiricism, Logical Atomism and Philosophical Analysis, and unique individuals such as Russell and Moore. It excludes, thereby, the present day continental philosophies, such as Thomism, Existentialism, and Dialectical Materialism.

Modern empiricists, to be sure, are influenced by many other philosophers. Locke, Berkeley, and Mill, among the classical empiricists, and Leibniz and Kant, among the rationalists (the former especially on the logico-mathematical side) in one way or other are responsible for the appearance of empiricism in its new form. But none of them were as influential as Hume.

This, by itself is not news. Weinberg, in his well-known book, *An Examination of Logical Positivism*, observes that:

> Many, if not all, of the principal doctrines of contemporary positivism derive from Hume. In almost all respects Hume is intellectually closer to the philosophy of the Viennese Circle than is the author of the *Cours de Philosophie Positive* [Auguste Comte]. The empiricistic trend of Logical Positivism may safely be traced, I believe, to Hume.[1]

Likewise, Einstein in *Remarks on Bertrand Russell's Theory of Knowledge*, writes:

---

[1] Julius Rudolph Weinberg, *An Examination of Logical Positivism*, London,, 1950, p. 3.

If one reads Hume's books, one is amazed that many and sometimes even highly esteemed philosophers after him have been able to write so much obscure stuff and even find grateful readers for it. Hume has permanently influenced the development of the best philosophers who come after him. One senses him in the reading of Russell's philosophical analysis, whose acumen and simplicity of expression have often reminded me of Hume.[1]

Indeed, Einstein acknowledges his own indebtedness to Hume, when in reference to Hume's non-Newtonian view of time he states that:

The type of critical reasoning which was required for discovery of this central point [the arbitrary character of the axiom of the absolute character of time...] was decisively furthered, in my case, especially by the reading of David Hume's and Ernst Mach's philosophical writings.[2]

Immanuel Kant, himself a hybrid of empiricism and rationalism, readily admits that Hume's writings changed his entire philosophical view point.

I honestly confess that my recollection of David Hume's teaching was the very thing, which many years ago first interrupted my dogmatic slumber, and gave my investigations in the field of speculative philosophy quite a new direction.[3]

Kant thought that the life or death of metaphysics hinges upon Hume's verdict that the causal maxim, i.e. whatever begins to exist must have a cause, is neither an analytic nor synthetic truth. He observes that Hume's analytic-synthetic dichotomy leaves no place for any metaphysical principle. Cognizant that metaphysics consists altogether of statements similar to the causal principle, he remarks that "since the origin of metaphysics so far as we know its history nothing has ever happened which might have been more decisive to the fortunes of the science than the attack made upon it by David Hume."[4]

Kant concludes that either the synthetic-a priori judgment (a new category invented by him) is possible, or everything which we call metaphysics must turn out to be mere delusion of reason.

It is argued, however, that Hume's influence on Kant did not last long. For in spite of Kant's cognizance that in the absence of any criteria for settling the dispute, there can be "no polemic in the field of pure reason," and despite his assertions that our under-

[1] The Philosophy of Bertrand Russell, The Library of Living Philosophers, ed. Paul Arthur Schilpp, volume V, Evanston, Illinois, 1946, p. 285.
[2] Albert Einstein, The Library of Living Philosophers, ed. Paul Arthur Schilpp, New York, 1951, p. 53.
[3] Kant, Prolegomena to Any Future Metaphysics, John P. Mahaffy translation, London, 1889, p. 7.
[4] Ibid., p. 3.

standings are confined within the field of possible experience, and for all his endeavour to show the fallaciousness of arguments from purely conceptual premises to existence conclusions, he himself did not hesitate to ontologize concepts which transcend human experience.

Kant, using Hume's ammunition, demolished the illusory "dialectical metaphysics," so goes the rumour, only to erect his own "Metaphysics of Nature." In this vein Passmore remarks that "Hume woke Kant from his 'dogmatic slumber' only so far as to inspire him to construct the very kind of philosophical system to which Hume most objected."[1]

True as such remarks may be, it should be also mentioned that those non-Humian aspects of Kant's system are the very ones which were the target of much Humian type criticism, by both Humian and non-Humian philosophers. The Humian elements of Kant, I hold, still remain intact; and these are the very elements which, in fact, disturb any architectonic metaphysics.

Of late, in the literature, attempts have been made to bring into focus the resemblances of Hume's philosophy to modern empiricism. Here and there similarities between the principles and the methods of the precursor and the successors are observed. Yet, no attempt has been made to give special attention to those enduring aspects of his philosophy by disentangling them from the bulk of his writings.

The present work is a systematic and critical examination of those fundamental aspects of Hume's philosophy which make him the acknowledged precursor of modern empiricism.

In what follows, a coherent account of Hume's fundamental principles, which we call "the principle of meaning" and "the principle of analyticity," will be given. Devised as chief weapons against rationalistic metaphysics, these principles still serve those who discern a deep cleavage between meaningful and meaningless judgments and between analytic and synthetic truths.

In the course of the inquiry we shall observe that Hume does not only explore the bankruptcy of theologio-metaphysical systems, but also the dogmas of the scientific systems of his time, namely, the Cartesian and Newtonian sciences. Not only is the significance of mental substance, immortal ego, the most perfect Being,

---

[1] J. A. Passmore, *Hume's Intentions*, Cambridge, 1952, p. 153.

the final cause, "those barren vestal virgins of medieval theology," on trial, but also the status of pseudo-scientific entities e.g., *vis inertia*, the inherent qualities of matter, the force of gravity – and in an oblique way, Absolute Time and Space which are supposed to have a sort of existence independent of passing events and the terrestrial denizens that occupy them – the very concepts which were later dogmatized by Kant despite Newton's warning.

Finally, the attempt will be made to make clear the relationship of Hume's empirical principles to those neglected and controversial parts of his work which are concerned with the nature of demonstrative reason and deductive science, such as logic, geometry and arithmetic.

Hume is a philosopher without a synoptic system. He sees himself primarily as an experimental philosopher; readily admits his mistakes; disclaims his former ideas, and even points out to others the paradoxical position which sometimes issues from the application of his own principles without ever trying to remove the difficulty by an *ad hoc* solution. But though Hume is not a system-builder, he is not like those piecemeal engineers who believe that any use of a general principle in such inquiries is doomed to failure inasmuch as the significance of any concept and the truth of any judgment are determinable only under heterogeneous conditions. Throughout his work, Hume makes use of certain principles which seem to him well-founded and on many occasions when he finds that certain usages of language lead him to some unexpected difficulty, he alters the expression of his principle. In this respect, Hume is more like the Logical Empiricists than the Philosophical Analysts, more like Russell than Moore.

It is often said that Hume's excessively microscopic and pseudo-psychological method should not be confused with the new method of philosophical analysis.

However, it has to be admitted that questions such as: How do we know...? and, What do we mean...? or How do we use a symbol, are not entirely unconnected questions. There is a point where philosophical investigation of natural syntactics should give way to an inquiry into the relation between language and fact; and this is a point where the modern analyst, should ask the very old epistemological questions.

Furthermore, we should remember that when Hume speaks of: Relations of Ideas and Matters of Fact, Simple and Complex Ideas, independency of all perceptions, Bundle of Impressions, the limit of human knowledge and the genesis of concepts – where modern empiricists talk about: Analytic-Synthetic statements, Atomic and Complex propositions, logical construction, the limit of intelligible discourse and meaningfulness or meaninglessness of expressions, he is using only the philosophical language of his time, and since that time some changes have occurred in philosophy, if not a revolution. So let us not be deluded by the form, it is the content which counts.

However, in the following chapters no attempt will be made to conceal or justify Hume's mistakes. On the contrary, every effort will be made to show the shortcomings of his method, and his failure to give a true account of deductive science, a defect which is due to his preoccupation with psychologism.

In the last part some other enduring aspects of Hume's philosophy will be discussed. Hume says many illuminating things on the nature of induction and the logic of causal reasoning – on the problems of free will and determinism – on miracles – on the relation between ethics and science; similar to things said by modern empiricists.

CHAPTER ONE

The Principle of Meaning

1. THE CRITIQUE OF METAPHYSICS

Hume in his philosophical writings held that the philosopher and the vulgar often entertain opinions which are in principle unverifiable; and a large part of what is called "metaphysics" consists of such opinions, the truth or falsehood of which, in principle, cannot be ascertained. Hume's anxiety over metaphysical speculation is reflected throughout most of his writing. Already, at the age of twenty-three, he expresses in a letter opinions concerning the state in which philosophy then appeared to him, and speaks of some new method by which philosophical puzzles could be untangled.

> Every one, who is acquainted either with the Philosophers or Critics, knows that there is nothing yet establisht in either of these two Sciences, and that they contain little more than endless Disputes, even in the most fundamental Articles. Upon Examination of these, I found a certain Boldness of Temper, growing in me, which was not enclin'd to submit to any Authority in these Subjects, but led me to seek out some new Medium, by which Truth might be establisht.[1]

In the *Introduction* to the *Treatise*, Hume again reflects upon the lamentable state of philosophy.

> Principles taken upon trust, consequences lamely deduced from them, want of coherence in the parts, and of evidence in the whole, these are every where to be met with in the systems of the most eminent philosophers, and seem to have drawn disgrace upon philosophy itself. (T. xvii).[2]

In reading Hume, we notice many examples of *Principles taken upon trust* and chosen by eminent philosophers as axioms for their systems (e.g., Law of Causation, or *Ex nihilo, nihil fit*, "that impious maxim of the ancient philosophy"). We also notice Hume's endeavor to establish sometimes the vacuity of these principles, and sometimes the lack of validity of inferences made from them.

Hume observes that the sound and fury of philosophical disputes

[1] David Hume, *The Letters of David Hume*, J. T. Greig, ed., Oxford, 1932, Vol. I, p. 13.

[2] All references to Hume's *A Treatise of Human Nature* are to Selby-Bigge, First Edition, Oxford, reprinted 1951. I refer directly to the pages of this edition, by giving the number of the page, after the letter T. All references to Hume's *Enquiries Concerning The Human Understanding And Concerning the Principles of Morals* are to Selby-Bigge, Second Edition, Oxford, impression of 1951. I refer directly to the pages of this edition by giving the number of the page, after the letter E. *Italics mine*, in Hume's quotations, are to be identified by "i.m."

might arouse even the layman's suspicion that something is wrong with the entire philosophical enterprise. "Nor is there requir'd such profound knowledge to discover the present imperfect condition of the sciences, but even the rabble without doors may judge from the noise and clamour, which they hear, that all goes not well within." (T. xvii).

That every philosophical problem appears to hang in the air is further backed by the fact that even the experts can not come to a-greement on any issue. "There is nothing which is not the subject of debate, and in which men of learning are not of contrary opinions. The most trivial question escapes not our controversy, and in the most momentous we are not able to give any certain decision." (T. xviii).

Since philosophical disputes seem to be undecidable, Hume observes that in this domain one who appeals to emotion, rather than to reason, wins public approval. "Amidst all this bustle 'tis not reason, which carries the prize, but eloquence; and no man needs ever despair of gaining proselytes to the most extravagant hypothesis, who has art enough to represent it in any favourable colours." (T. xviii).

As a consequence of the state in which philosophy appears to the public, there arises in them (the laymen), according to Hume, "that common prejudice against *metaphysical reasonings of all kinds*." (T. xviii). He observes that the public, in general, "by metaphysical reasonings, do not understand those on any particular branch of science, but every kind of argument, which is in any way abstruse, and requires some attention to be comprehended." (T. xviii). However, Hume takes care to comment that this aversion to metaphysics, if by that we mean "every kind of argument, which requires some attention to be comprehended" is totally unjustifiable; since, according to him, "if truth be at all within the reach of human capacity, 'tis certain it must lie very deep and abstruse; and to hope we shall arrive at it without pains, while the greatest geniuses have failed with the utmost pains, must certainly be esteemed sufficiently vain and presumptuous." (T. xix).

It is of interest to note that Hume distrusts philosophical argument which appears too obvious and transparent. In the *Introduction* he writes: "I pretend to no such advantage in the philosophy I am going to unfold, and would esteem it a strong presumption against it, were it so very easy and obvious." (T. xix).

It seems that for Hume the proper function of philosophers, whatever it is, is not laboring the obvious by reporting the ordinary discourses of the vulgar. We find that in his essay *Of Commerce* he divides mankind into two classes: "Shallow Thinkers who fall short of the truth," and "Abstruse Thinkers who go beyond it." A shallow thinker is one who labors the obvious. "An author is little to be valued, who tells us nothing but what we can learn from every coffee house conversation"; whereas abstruse thinkers are "by far the most rare; and I may add, by far the most valuable... at most, what they say is uncommon; and if it should cost some pains to comprehend it, one has, however, the pleasure of learning something that is new."[1]

Philosophical issues cannot be easily expressed in ordinary language, since "common language," according to Hume, being crude and vague, is unable to reflect the complexities of life.[2]

> I must not conclude this subject without observing, that 'tis very difficult to talk of the operations of the mind with perfect propriety and exactness; because *common language* has seldom made any very nice distinctions among them, but has generally call'd by the same term all such as nearly resemble each other." (T. 105 – i.m.).

In this regard I think Hume would be in full agreement with the opinion of "the very ingenious author, Dr. Berkeley," that:

> In the ordinary affairs of life, any phrases may be retained, so long as they excite in us proper sentiments, or dispositions to act in such manner as is necessary for our well being, how false soever they may be, if taken in a strict and speculative sense. Nay, this is unavoidable, since propriety being regulated by custom, language is suited to receive opinions, which are not always the truest; that therefore "in such things we ought *to think with the learned, and speak with the vulgar.*"[3]

Hume, in the *Treatise*, speaks of two kinds of philosophies. A True Philosophy is one which deals with what is within reach of the human mind; whereas False Philosophy seeks to explain what is beyond human understanding. Comparing false philosophers with Sisyphus and Tantalus, he says of them:

---

[1] David Hume, *Essays Moral, Political and Literary*, T. H. Green and T. H. Grose, eds., London, 1875. Vol. I, p. 287.

[2] This opinion of Hume, though, is in conflict with the cult of the ordinary language (if such a cult exists) jibes with the view of a modern empiricist who referring to the members of this cult wrote: "They are persuaded that common speech is good enough, not only for daily life, but also for philosophy. I, on the contrary, am persuaded that common speech is full of vagueness and inaccuracy, and that any attempt to be precise and accurate requires modification of common speech both as regards vocabulary and as regards syntax. Everybody admits that physics and chemistry and medicine each require a language which is not that of everyday life. I fail to see why philosophy, alone, should be forbidden to make a similar approach towards precision and accuracy." Bertrand Russell, *My Philosophical Development*, New York, 1959, p. 241.

[3] George Berkeley, *The Works of George Berkeley*, A. A. Luce and T. E. Jessop, eds., Volume II, pp. 62–63. (Italics mine).

At present they [false philosophers] seem to be in a very lamentable condition, and such as the poets have given us but a faint notion of in their descriptions of the punishment of *Sisyphus* and *Tantalus*. For what can be imagin'd more tormenting, than to seek with eagerness, what for ever flies us; and seek for it in a place, where 't is impossible it can ever exist? (T. 223).

The false philosopher torments his mind by seeking what is unattainable and thus misleads us. Yet sheer common sense is not enough to keep us from error. We need certain kinds of philosophy, namely a true philosophy, if for no other reason than to liberate us from the horrors of superstition; and in this vein Hume prescribes philosophy as a substitute for religion. In the end of Book One of the *Treatise*, he writes:

'Tis certain, that superstition is much more bold in its systems and hypotheses than philosophy; and while the latter contents itself with assigning new causes and principles to the phaenomena, which appear in the visible world, the former opens a world of its own, and presents us with scenes, and beings, and objects, which are altogether new. Since therefore 'tis almost impossible for the mind of man to rest, like those of beasts, in that narrow circle of objects, which are the subject of daily conversation and action, we ought only to deliberate concerning the choice of our guide, and ought to prefer that which is safest and most agreeable. And in this respect I make bold to recommend philosophy, and shall not scruple to give it the preference to superstition of every kind or denomination. (T. 271).

In the *Enquiries*, Hume more explicitly distinguishes between true and false philosophy. Here true and false philosophy are identified with True and False Metaphysics. Hume maintains that "the generality of mankind [is] contented to prefer the *easy philosophy to the abstract and profound*." But, he also says that "as the matter is often carried farther, even to the absolute rejecting of all profound reasonings, or what is commonly called *metaphysics*, we shall now proceed to consider what can reasonably be pleaded in their behalf." (E. 9).

Then, he states that in fact, there are two kinds of Metaphysics. "We must cultivate true metaphysics with some care, in order to destroy the false and adulterate." (E. 12).

Metaphysics when appearing profound and abstruse is often obscure and confused, and "this obscurity in the profound and abstract philosophy, is objected to, not only as painful and fatiguing, but as the inevitable source of uncertainty and error." (E. 11). He says, for example,

It is easy for a profound philosopher to commit a mistake in his subtle reasonings; and one mistake is the necessary parent to another, while he pushes on his consequences, and is not deterred from embracing any conclusion, by its unusual appearance, or its contradiction to popular opinion. (E. 7).

Furthermore, abstruse philosophy has no "influence over our conduct and behavior." Philosophy, "if just," he says, "can present us only with mild and moderate sentiments; and if false and extravagant, its opinions are merely the objects of a cold and general speculation." However, Hume tells us that "the justest and most plausible objection against a considerable part of metaphysics" lies in the fact "that they are not properly a science." (E. 11).

This frontal attack against metaphysics does not satisfy Hume. He goes on to find the causal factors which led philosophers to engage in such activities. Metaphysics, according to Hume, either

... arise from the fruitless efforts of human vanity, which would penetrate into subjects utterly inaccessible to the understanding, or from the craft of popular superstitions, which, being unable to defend themselves on fair ground, raise these intangling brambles to cover and protect their weakness. Chaced from the open country, these robbers fly into the forest, and lie in wait to break in upon every unguarded avenue of the mind, and overwhelm it with religious fears and prejudices." (E. 11).

"True metaphysics," in contrast to false metaphysics, which is often mixed with superstition, consists of "an accurate scrutiny into powers and faculties of human nature" and "accurate and just reasoning," according to Hume,

is the only catholic remedy, fitted for all persons and all dispositions; and is alone able to subvert that abstruse philosophy and metaphysical jargon, which, being mixed up with popular superstition, renders it in a manner impenetrable to careless reasoners, and gives it the air of science and wisdom. (E. 12).

Once again, Hume seems to indicate that metaphysics, is an ally to religion, and a correct method of philosophical investigation is badly needed if we are to be saved from the horrors of superstition. "Happy, if, reasoning in this easy manner, we can undermine the foundations of an abstruse philosophy, which seems to have hitherto served only as a shelter to superstition, and a cover to absurdity and error!" (E. 16).

In the famous statement which appears at the end of *An Enquiry Concerning Human Understanding*, Hume clearly states his opinion concerning metaphysics and theology.

If we take in our hand any volume; of divinity or school metaphysics, for instance; let us ask,: *Does it contain any abstract reasoning concerning quantity or number?* No. *Does it contain any experimental reasoning concerning matter of fact and existence?* No. Commit it then to the flames: for it can contain nothing but sophistry and illusion. (E. 165).

Thus, it seems that metaphysics and theology for Hume, being subjects which fall under neither the experimental sciences nor the mathematical sciences, are worthless subjects. However, for Hume philosophy is not identical with metaphysics, and hence it does not seem that he wants to commit his own books to the flames. Hume describes his work, *A Treatise of Human Nature*, as "Being an Attempt to introduce the experimental Method of Reasoning into Moral Subjects," and at the end of *An Enquiry concerning the Principles of Morals*, he distinguishes between his own method of philosophical investigation and metaphysical speculation truly so called. He maintains that his own philosophical inquiry into principles of morals is in fact nothing but scientific investigation, whereas the hypotheses of his opponents, being abstruse and unintelligible, in reality, are nothing more than metaphysical speculation.

All this is metaphysics, you cry. That is enough; there needs nothing more to give a strong presumption of falsehood. Yes, reply I, here are metaphysics surely; but they are all on your side, who advance an abstruse hypothesis, which can never be made intelligible, nor quadrate with any particular instance or illustration. The hypothesis which we embrace is plain. It maintains that morality is determined by sentiment... We then proceed to examine a plain matter of fact, to wit, *what actions have this influence?* We consider all the circumstances in which actions agree, and thence endeavour to extract some general observations with regard to these sentiments. *If you call this metaphysics, and find anything abstruse here, you need only conclude that your turn of mind is not suited to the moral sciences.* (E. 289, i.m.).

2. THE LIMIT OF HUMAN KNOWLEDGE

A. An Exposition

To rescue the human mind from the tyranny of False Metaphysics, to rectify the logical geography of knowledge, and to deprive religion of its rational supports, Hume, following Descartes[1] and Locke in procedure, invites us "to enquire seriously into the nature of human understanding, and show, from an exact analysis of its powers and capacity, that it is by no means fitted for such remote and abstruse subjects." (E. 12).

In the *Treatise*, Hume declares that his intention is to study the Science of Man; for he believes that it is the study of this science

[1] Descartes claims that: "No more useful inquiry can be proposed than that which seems to determine the nature and the scope of human knowledge ... nothing seems to me more futile than the conduct of those who boldly dispute about the secrets of nature, the influence of the heavens on these lower regions, the predicting of future events and similar matters, as many do, without yet having ever asked even whether human reason is adequate to the solution of these problems." *Rules*, p. 26, Vol. I, *The Philosophical Works of Descartes*, trans. Haldane. This way of speaking is still with us. Consider, for example, the title of Russell's later work viz., *Human Knowledge, its Scope and Limits.*

which might provide an answer to the questions concerning the proper province of human knowledge.

For my part, my only hope is, that I may contribute a little to the advancement of knowledge, by giving in some particulars a different turn to the speculations of philosophers, and pointing out to them more distinctly those subjects, where alone they can expect assurance and conviction. Human Nature is the only science of man; and yet has been hitherto the most neglected. (T. 273).

What is this Science of Man, which, according to Hume, could determine the limits and extent of human knowledge, and in doing so could give us insight into the nature of *subjects where alone we can expect assurance*, and subjects which are remote and obscure and thus beyond our reach? As we observed in the title of the *Treatise*, Hume describes his work: "An Attempt to Introduce the Experimental Method of Reasoning into Moral Subjects." Moral subjects, as shown in the introduction to this book, consists of Ethics, Criticism, Politics and Logic or the art of reasoning. Ethics and Criticism, he says, deal with tastes and sentiments, and politics considers man as a member of society; while "The sole end of logic is to explain the principles and operations of our reasoning faculty, and the nature of our ideas." Thus it seems that Hume wants to consider the whole Book I of the *Treatise* as a work on logic. We shall see later that this identification of logic with psychology and what we now call epistemology causes considerable difficulty for Hume.

The study of what Hume calls "Logic" and what we may describe to be, in fact, epistemology and semantics, was considered by him to be the basic study for all sciences. "Even *Mathematics, Natural Philosophy, and Natural Religion,* are in some measure dependent on the science of Man." "The capital or center of all sciences," he says, "is human nature itself," and, "There is no question of importance, whose decision is not compriz'd in the science of man; and there is none, which can be decided with any certainty, before we become acquainted with that science." (T. xx).

The science of logic, then, for Hume is part of the science of man, and it is the study of logic which may give us insight into the limit and the scope of human knowledge.

Knowing the proper province of human knowledge, according to Hume, constitutes a cure for philosophical perplexities.

When we see that we have arrived at the utmost extent of human reason, we sit down contented; tho' we be perfectly satisfied in the main of our ignorance, and perceive that we can give no reason for our most general and most refined principles, beside our experience of their reality. (T. xxii).

And this freedom from philosophical perplexities and mental agitation is the best thing that philosophy can offer. "When this mutual contentment and satisfaction can be obtained betwixt the master and scholar," Hume says, "I know not what more we can require of our philosophy." (T. xxii).

In the *Enquiries* Hume asserts that

... no inconsiderable part of science [of man is] to know the different operations of the mind, to separate them from each other, to class them under their proper heads, and to correct all that seeming disorder, in which they lie involved, when made the object of reflexion and enquiry.... And if we can go no farther than this mental geography, or delineation of the distinct parts and powers of the mind, it is at least a satisfaction to go so far. (E. 13).

"The airy sciences" such as metaphysics, which contain unintelligible questions, should be replaced by the science of human nature, since the statements contained in the body of the latter science, Hume insinuates, are meaningful. "...that there is a truth and falsehood in all propositions on this subject, and a truth and falsehood, which lie not beyond the compass of human understanding." (E. 14).

The chief advantage of the science of man lies in its power to map out the extent of our knowledge and indeed one of the advantages of *mitigated scepticism* lies in acknowledging that only what is in the province of man's understanding can be investigated. "Another species of *mitigated* scepticism which may be of advantage to mankind, and which may be the natural result of the Pyrrhonian doubts and scruples, is the limitation of our enquiries to such subjects as are best a-dapted to the narrow capacity of human understanding." E.(162).

Common sense tends to believe that there are no limits to man's thinking, but as we shall see later in detail, Hume is convinced that this is a mistaken view. "Nothing, at first view, may seem more unbounded than the thought of man.... But though our thought seems to possess this unbounded liberty, we shall find, upon a nearer examination, that it is really confined within very narrow limits...." (E. 18).

To the question: What, then is the limit of human understanding? a passage in the *Treatise* gives an explicit answer:

Let us fix our attention out of ourselves as much as possible: Let us chace our imagination to the heavens, or to the utmost limits of the universe; we never really advance a step beyond ourselves, nor can conceive any kind of existence, but those perceptions, which have appear'd in that narrow compass. This is the universe of the imagination, nor have we any idea but what is there produc'd. (T. 67).

In the *Treatise, Enquiries* and the *Dialogues concerning Natural Religion,* Hume provides us with abundant examples of the types of questions and problems which he regards to be beyond the reach of human understanding. Here we only mention some:

In the *Treatise* he says, "I am afraid, that such an enterprize (an attempt to explain the cause of sense-data) is beyond the reach of human understanding, and that we can never pretend to know body otherwise than by those external properties, which discover themselves to the senses." (T. 64). "As to those *impressions,* which arise from the *senses,* their ultimate cause is, in my opinion, perfectly inexplicable by human reason, and 'twill always be impossible to decide with certainty, whether they arise immediately from the object, or are produc'd by the creative power of the mind, or are deriv'd from the author of our being." (T. 84).

"'Tis universally allow'd, that the capacity of the mind is limited, and can never attain a full and adequate conception of infinity: And tho' it were not allow'd, 'twou'd be sufficiently evident from the plainest observation and experience." (T. 26).

In the *Enquiries* the same contention is expressed. He says: "It is true, if men attempt the discussion of questions which lie entirely beyond the reach of human capacity, such as those concerning the origin of worlds, or the economy of the intellectual system or region of spirits, they may long beat the air in their fruitless contests, and never arrive at any determinate conclusion." (E. 81).

"While we cannot give a satisfactory reason, why we believe, after a thousand experiments, that a stone will fall, or fire burn; can we ever satisfy ourselves concerning any determination, which we may form, with regard to the origin of worlds, and the situation of nature, from, and to eternity?" (E. 162).

B. An Interpretation

Hume's statements on the scope and the limits of human understanding, at first sight, seem unintelligible. Taken at their face value, any one of Hume's assertions, such as: "... though our thought seems to possess this unbounded liberty, we shall find, upon a nearer examination, that it is really confined within very narrow limits," or, "If men attempt the discussion of questions which lie entirely beyond the reach of human capacity... they may long beat the air... and never arrive at any determinate conclusion" may be objected to by questions such as: How do we ever know that something is entirely

beyond the reach of human capacity? or how can one draw a limit
to the human mind, if our mind, as Hume himself describes it, is nothing but a congeries of impressions and ideas?

We shall maintain here, that though Hume's manner of expressing his thought on what could not be thought is obscure and confused, so much so that it has in fact misled some of his important critics (i.e., Kant and Laird), his intention is quite clear and obvious.
In drawing a limit to man's thought, Hume, in fact, was drawing a
limit not to thinking (whatever that might mean), but only to
expression of thought. Hume was drawing our attention to what
could be said significantly and what could be mere talk without
sense. The intention to draw a limit to man's expressions was a conscious result of Hume's observation that "'tis usual for men to use
words for ideas, and to talk instead of thinking in their reasonings."
(T. 61).

Many of Hume's statements, though they at first sight seem to express some thought about persons and objects in the world, actually
amount to saying something about words and meaning. Indeed,
Hume, on many occasions, explicitly employs his theory of the limit
of man's mind quite in line with our interpretation.

As we observed, Hume constantly maintains that the truth or falsity of certain philosophical issues cannot be established. For example, "It will *always* be impossible to decide" the question concerning
the ultimate causes of our perception. Likewise, he believes that
questions "such as those concerning the origin of worlds, or the economy of the intellectual system or region of spirits" are in principle
undecidable. Metaphysicians, he says, "may long beat the air in
their fruitless contests, and never arrive at any determinate conclusion." By saying that certain issues *never* can be decided, Hume was
saying, in effect, that these issues are *in principle* unverifiable, as
distinct from hypotheses which are not subject to examination *in
practice*. Thus, in spite of Hume's language, when he, like Locke, invites us *to sit down in quiet ignorance and be satisfied with what we have*, he
is not saying that we should stop investigating matters of fact or
matters of logic, but rather that we should not ask questions which
in principle defy answer.

We also maintain that a very important part of what Hume calls
"The Science of Man" is concerned with finding conditions for significant discourse, and thereby excluding as being devoid of cognitive meaning any statements which do not satisfy these conditions.

To say this is not to say that Hume was consciously aware that he was explicating language and not the human mind, nor is it to say that there are no psychological statements, either true or false, in Hume's epistemology. We do not regard, for example, The Laws of Association, which enter into Hume's philosophy, as linguistic theory.

However, we insist that to make sense of the great body of Hume's arguments we should translate them (following Carnap's recommendation) from the *Material Mode of Speech* into the *Formal Mode*.

Hume envisages himself as describing the geography of our mind, whereas what he is actually doing is not fundamentally different from what modern epistemologists, such as Ryle, practice. Ryle, in the *Introduction* to the *Concept of Mind*, announces that, "The philosophical arguments which constitute this book are intended not to increase what we know about minds, but to rectify the logical geography of the knowledge which we already possess."[1]

Indeed, it is Ryle's claim that his research is in line with the practices of great epistemologists like Locke, Hume, and Kant, even though these epistemologists were not aware that their psychology and epistemology were concerned more with the analysis of language than with generalizations concerning the human mind. Ryle says:

> The great epistemologists, Locke, Hume and Kant, were in the main advancing the Grammar of Science when they thought they were discussing parts of the occult life-story of persons acquiring knowledge. They were discussing the credentials of sorts of theories, but they were doing this in para-physiological allegories.[2]

Ryle's statement requires some clarification. Hume's activity, though it may in part be described as "advancing the Grammar of Science," may not be properly described as "advancing the Grammar of language." Hume sees himself chiefly as an experimental philosopher, and not as a grammarian. In the *Enquiry* he says that, "Nothing is more usual than for philosophers to encroach upon the province of grammarians; and to engage in disputes of words, while they imagine that they are handling controversies of the deepest importance and concern." (E. 312).

The business of our experimental philosopher, according to Hume, is to advance general principles, and "general principles, if just and

[1] G. Ryle, *The Concept of Mind*, New York, 1949, p. 7.
[2] *Ibid.*, p. 318.

sound, must always prevail in the general course of things, though they may fail in particular cases; and it is the chief business of philosophers to regard the general course of things."[1]

Thus we may say with Ryle that Hume was in the main advancing the Grammar of Science only in the sense that he was making some generalizations, not specifically about the way people talk (which is the proper function of the grammarians), but about the nature of significant discourse, or rules by which to judge causes and effects, etc.

Of course, we should admit that Hume's language is often ambiguous. The analogical expressions used by him, such as "mental geography," "power of mind," "the limit of understanding," etc., are in fact responsible for the often unwarranted arguments (*ignoratio elenchi*) against his doctrines.

Thus Kant's comments on Hume's method seem to me quite misleading. Kant writes that "the celebrated David Hume was one of those geographers of the human reason who supposed that all these questions (metaphysical) were sufficiently disposed of by being relegated outside that horizon, which, *however, he was not able to determine*."[2]

Even a contemporary Hume scholar, no less than John Laird, is seduced by Hume's language. Laird says that:

> It seemed to Hume that, if human nature were thoroughly explored, the master-key to every science would have been found. He did not so much consider the obvious objection that the human mind might be primarily a sort of tool, and that if it were a tool, the nature of its objects might no more be inferable from its own nature than the character and disposition of the stars are inferable from the composition of a telescope.[3]

One cannot help imagining Hume smiling at this "obvious objection." It seems that it was never Hume's intention to claim that by exploring the human mind we may know the structure of the stars, but rather that by exloring the universe of discourse we might be able to formulate significant questions about the world.

Not all of Hume's students were misled by his language. For example, G. E. Moore, I think, correctly interprets Hume's statements concerning the limitation of knowledge as a proposal about the nature of propositions which "we cannot know to be true." He says that Hume

---

[1] David Hume, T. H. Green, ed., *op. cit.*, p. 288.
[2] Kant, *Critique*, Max Muller, *op. cit.*, p. 609 (italics mine).
[3] John Laird, *Hume's Philosophy of Human Nature*, London, 1932, p. 351.

... wished to point out what characteristics are possessed by those of our opinions which we *can* know to be true, with a view of persuading us that any opinion which does *not* possess any of these characteristics is of a kind which *cannot* be known to be so. He thus tries to lay down certain rules to the effect that the *only* propositions which we can, any of us, know to be true are of certain definite kinds. It is in this sense, I think, that he tries to define the limits of human understanding....[1]

And

... This, I think, was clearly one of Hume's views. He meant to fix the limits of our knowledge at a point which would *exclude* most religious propositions and a great many philosophical ones, as incapable of being known; but which would *include* all the other kinds of propositions, which are most universally accepted by common sense, as capable of being known.[2]

Here, Moore's usage of "*cannot*" and "*can*" is significant. He italicizes these terms with the intention of indicating that the impossibility of knowing the truth, or, we may add, the falsehood of certain statements is not a physical, but rather a logical impossibility. Moore is, in effect, saying that for Hume, since most religious and a great many philosophical propositions defy verification or falsification, they are, strictly speaking, cognitively meaningless.

In the light of our interpretation, we also agree with Passmore's analysis, when he states that Hume

... supposed that he was engaging in 'mental geography'... he thought he was confronted by a set of 'internal' objects, which could be classified just in the kind of way we classify geographical regions, when he was actually discussing what it means to be real, or in what the evidence for a scientific proposition consists.[3]

So far, in our discussion of *The Critique of Metaphysics* and *The Limit of Human Knowledge* we have arrived at the following conclusions:

To Hume, many philosophical issues are in principle undecidable. These issues are called by him False Philosophy or simply Metaphysics.

True Philosophy, on the other hand, deals with issues which can be settled. We need a true philosophy in order to destroy the false one. However, true philosophy is neither easy nor necessarily compatible with common sense.

There are many objections against metaphysical systems. They are a source of uncertainty and error; they exert no influence upon our behavior; since metaphysical statements often are part of a syn-

[1] G. E. Moore, *Philosophical Studies*, London, 1922, p. 147.
[2] *Ibid.* p. 151.
[3] J. A. Passmore *Hume's Intentions* Cambridge, 1952, p. 157.

optic system, one mistake in our inference is enough to destroy the whole structure. But the most important objection against metaphysics is that it is not science. Moreover, metaphysics is often used in support of religion.

To free mankind from the tangle of metaphysics and superstition we should study the Science of Man. No inconsiderable part of this science is the science of logic. The end of logic is to explain the principles of our reasoning faculty and the nature of our ideas. The study of this science may give us insight into the limit and the scope of human knowledge. At first sight, it seems that there are no limits to human knowledge, but actually, there is a limit to thinking. Many philosophical arguments deal with issues that, in fact, bypass the limit of our thought, and for this reason the truth or falsity of such issues can never be determined.

We have interpreted Hume's theory regarding the limitation of man's thought as a theory concerning the limit of meaningful expression of thought. We have also interpreted Hume's statements concerning the impossibility of thinking what is not given to one's senses to mean impossibility not in the physical but only in the logical sense.

We have observed that Hume's language is often ambiguous, and this ambiguity is responsible for some of the misunderstandings of Hume's critics. We have also suggested a method of interpretation for removing these misunderstandings.

Now I think we are in a position to ask our main question, namely: What are the exact conditions under which we may determine the issues which can be significantly denied or asserted? What are the tests which indicate what lies within the universe of significant discourse and what lies beyond this universe? The search for these rules will lead us directly to Hume's main criterion of meaning.

3. THE PRINCIPLE OF THE PRIORITY OF IMPRESSIONS TO IDEAS

Hume's *Critique of Metaphysics* is based upon the belief that certain expressions, lacking certain specific credentials, are devoid of cognitive significance, while other expressions, enjoying those credentials, can be the subject of intelligent dispute. That is, Hume believes that judgments concerning the truth or the falsity of any statement presuppose a prior judgment concerning the meaningfulness of the elements which constitute that statement. Hence, a considerable part of Hume's work is an endeavor to establish, not the falsehood of metaphysical theories, but rather their lack of significance.

Let us take, for example, the metaphysical problem of the nature of the soul. Hume, after careful examination of the nature of the problem, expressly condemns the whole issue as utterly unintelligible. He argues, for reasons that we shall see later, that he has a "sufficient reason for abandoning utterly that dispute concerning the materiality and immateriality of the soul, and makes me absolutely *condemn even the question itself.*" (T. 234 - i.m.).

Since the subject of materiality or immateriality of the soul is devoid of significance, he concludes that the issue of the truth or the falsity of such theories, from the point of logic, can not be raised. "What possibility then of answering that question *Whether perceptions inhere in a material or immaterial substance*, when we do not so much as understand the meaning of the question?" (T. 234).

Now, the important question to raise is how are we to determine that expressions are significant or unintelligible, or to use Hume's expressions, are within the scope of man's understanding or beyond the limit of human mind?

To answer this question we have to examine in detail Hume's Principle of the Priority of Impressions to Ideas. Throughout the *Treatise* the principle of the priority of impressions to ideas is mentioned at least twelve times and made use of on sixteen occasions. The same Principle appears many times in *An Enquiry, An Abstract*, and also in *The Dialogues concerning Natural Religion*.[1]

Hume, in the opening of the *Treatise*, is concerned with the problem of perception. He divides all perceptions of the mind into two classes of Impressions and Ideas, and then explains the nature of the relation between these classes.

Hume's main interest in the problem of perception lies in the belief that perception and thought, or better, sense data and expression of thought, are intimately connected with each other. He is mainly interested in the relation between the expression of thought

---

[1] Thomas Reid, in one of his letters to Hume calls himself "your Disciple in Metaphysics." He was ready to accept Hume's principles, but having realized, more than anyone, the disastrous consequence which the application of these principles might have upon theologio-metaphysical systems, he wrote: "Your system appears to me not only coherent in all its parts, but likeways justly deduced from principles commonly received among Philosophers: Principles which I never thought calling in question, until the conclusions you draw from them in the Treatise of human Nature made me suspect them. If these principles are solid your system must stand." *The Letters of David Hume*, edited by J. Y. T. Greig, Oxford, 1932, p. 376.

and the data of experience, and not with the physiological explanation of veridical perception or the causes of perceptual anomalies. "The examination of our sensations," he says, "belongs more to anatomists and natural philosophers than to moral." (T. 8). He clearly defines the term "impression" as those perceptions which "make their first appearance in the mind with most force and violence." By "impression" he intends "not the manner in which our lively perceptions are produced, but merely the perceptions themselves." Impressions are simply the given (not the derivative), the original data (not the copy) of our feeling (not of our thinking or imagining), no matter from what sources they originate. A pang of pain, a muscular tension, a feeling of love or hate, are as much entitled to the name "impression" as a bitter taste or a purple shade.

On the other hand, Hume says many different things about the denotation of the term "Idea." "Idea" is defined as "the faint images of (impression) in thinking and reasoning." "Everyone of himself," he says, "will readily perceive the difference betwixt feeling and thinking." By saying this, I think he implies that to have a feeling is to have an impression, and to think is to have an idea. In the footnote to his definition of "idea," Hume writes that he hopes, by so defining this term, "to restore the word, idea, to its original sense, from which Mr. Locke had perverted it, in making it stand for all our perceptions." (T. 2). It is safe to assume that here Hume wants to keep the ordinary sense of "Idea" as used in common discourse to stand for Thought or Concept.

And in the *Enquiries*, he actually uses the terms "Ideas" and "Thought" interchangeably. "The less forcible and lively (Perceptions) are commonly denominated Thoughts or Ideas." (E. 18). "The most lively *thought* is still inferior to the dullest *sensation*.... If you tell me, that any person is in love, I easily understand your meaning,... but never can mistake that conception for the real disorders and agitations of the passion." (E. 17 – i.m.). "When we reflect on our past sentiments and affections, our *thought* is a faithful mirror, and copies its objects truly." (E. 18 – i.m.).

Hume also uses the term "Idea" to stand for meanings of linguistic expressions. He often identifies *meaning* with *ideas* and *talking without meaning* with *talking without ideas*. However, careful examination will reveal that, by this identification, he intends to say that Ideas or Thoughts are meanings only when they are conveyed and expressed through symbols. That is, ideas or thoughts are the meaning of words, when words are attached to such entities. Thus Hume says:

...When we entertain, therefore, any suspicion that a philosophical *term* is employed without any *meaning* or *idea* (as is but too frequent), we need but enquire *from what impression is that supposed idea derived?* And if it be impossible to assign any, this will serve to confirm our suspicion. (E. 22).

... as we can have no idea of any thing which never appeared to our outward sense or inward sentiment, the necessary conclusion *seems* to be that we have no idea of connexion or power at all, and that these words are absolutely without any meaning, when employed either in philosophical reasonings or common life. (E. 74).

... that when we say we desire to know the ultimate and operating principle, as something, which resides in the external object, we either contradict ourselves, or talk without a meaning. (T. 267).

Both impressions and ideas are divided into Simple and Complex. An idea or impression is simple if and only if it "admits of no distinction nor separation." Ideas and impressions are complex if they admit of distinction and separation into parts.

Hume, after these classifications, makes some important observations concerning the relation between impressions and ideas, and as a result of these observations, he arrives at his general theory, i.e., The Principle of the Priority of Impressions to Ideas. Hume states that it seems to him, at first glance, that his thoughts or ideas are the images of his impressions. "The one seem to be in a manner the reflexion of the other." (T. 2). But soon he modifies his statement by discovering that neither are all his complex ideas replicas of complex impressions, nor is there a correspondent set of complex ideas for every set of complex impressions in his mind. Therefore, he says, "the rule is not universally true, that they are exact copies of each other." (T. 3).

However, the simple ideas are different in this respect; "after the most accurate examination," he ventures to affirm "that the rule here holds without any exception, and that every simple idea has a simple impression which resembles it; and every simple impression a correspondent idea." (T. 3).

This statement again is modified and appears in the following form: "*That all our simple ideas in their first appearance are deriv'd from simple impressions, which are correspondent to them, and which they exactly represent.*" (T. 4).

At this point Hume cites some evidence in support of his general-
zation. He finds that, as a matter of fact, all that he sees in his own
mind is caused by his own impressions. He further challenges his
would-be-opponent "to show a simple impression, that has not a
correspondent idea, or a simple idea, that has not a correspondent
impression." Then he says that "If he does not answer this challenge,
as 'tis certain he cannot, we may from his silence and our own observation establish our conclusion." (T. 4).

The inquiry has yet to be continued. He next considers the question of the order of succession of impressions and ideas and finds
"by constant experience" that temporally impressions are prior to
ideas, "that the simple impressions always take the precedence of
their correspondent ideas, but never appear in the contrary order."
(T. 5).

The generalizations about the priority of impressions to ideas is
supported by reference to the processes of ostensive definition. According to Hume, learning the meaning of simple ideas is to have
some acquaintance with simple impressions. For example, if we want
to teach a child what "scarlet" or "orange" means, we have to point
out to him instances of scarlet or orange colors. "To give a child
an idea of scarlet or orange, of sweet or bitter, I present the objects,
or in other words, convey to him these impressions; but proceed not
so absurdly, as to endeavor to produce the impressions by exciting the ideas." (T. 5). By saying that "it is absurd to produce
the impressions by exciting the ideas," Hume means that it is empirically impossible to give the meaning of a simple idea by verbal
definitions. This claim, however, is not made concerning complex
ideas. He says he can understand the meaning of a sentence: "There
is a city such as *New Jerusalem*, whose pavement is gold and walls
are rubies, tho' [he] never saw any such." (T. 3). But this is only
because he is already acquainted with such things – gold, rubies,
walls, etc. All simple ideas are originated from simple impressions
and all complex ones are ultimately, according to Hume, reducible
to simple ones.

Hume provides some other evidence for this belief. A major defect
in our sense organ will deprive us, not only from having the proper
impression, but also from having the idea of that impression. A
man born blind cannot understand the meaning of color-words.
Restore the organ and you will open an inlet for the ideas. Yet it
is not sufficient to have a proper organ in order to have impressions,

but also "we have to put [the organs] in action." We cannot form for ourselves a just idea of the taste of a pineapple without having actually tasted it. "A Laplander or Negro," Hume assures us, "has no notion of the relish of wine...; nor can a selfish heart easily conceive the heights of friendship and generosity." (E. 20).

After citing all this evidence in support of his principle, Hume admits that:

> There is however one contradictory phaenomenon, which may prove, that 'tis not absolutely impossible for ideas to go before their correspondent impressions. I believe it will readily be allow'd, that the several distinct ideas of colours, which enter by the eyes, or those of sounds, which are convey'd by the hearing, are really different from each other, tho' at the same time resembling. Now if this be true of different colours, it must be no less so of the different shades of the same colour.... Suppose therefore a person to have enjoyed his sight for thirty years, and to have become perfectly well acquainted with colours of all kinds, excepting one particular shade of blue, for instance, which it never has been his fortune to meet with. Let all the different shades of that colour, except that single one, be plac'd before him, descending gradually from the deepest to the lightest; 'tis plain, that he will perceive a blank where that shade is wanting.... Now I ask, whether 'tis possible for him, from his own imagination, to supply this deficiency, and raise up to himself the idea of that particular shade, tho' it had never been conveyed to him by his senses? I believe there are few but will be of the opinion that he can; and this may serve as a proof, that the simple ideas are not always derived from the correspondent impressions; tho' the instance is so particular and singular, that 'tis scarce worth our observing, and does not merit that for it alone we should alter our general maxim. (T. 5–6).

The general maxim is, of course, "That our simple ideas proceed either mediately or immediately from their correspondent impressions."

Hume is quite aware of the importance of this maxim. "This," he says, "is the first principle I establish in the science of human nature; nor ought we despise it because of the simplicity of its appearance." (T. 7). Again he says that "no discovery cou'd have been made more happily for deciding all controversies concerning ideas, than that the above mention'd, that impressions always take the precedency of them, and that every idea, with which the imagination is furnish'd, first makes its appearance in a correspondent impression." (T. 33). Hume hopes by application of this maxim to resolve philosophical controversies.

> ... it is impossible for us to *think* of any thing, which we have not antecedently *felt*, either by our external or internal senses. I have endeavoured to explain and prove this proposition, and have expressed my hopes, that, by a proper application of it, men may reach greater clearness and precision in philosophical reasonings, than what they have hitherto been able to attain. (E. 62).

The principle of the priority of impression to idea in the *Enquiry* says that "all the materials of thinking are derived either from our outward or inward sentiment" (E. 19). Again, the claim is made that "here, therefore, is a proposition, which not only seems, in itself, simple and intelligible; but, if a proper use were made of it, might render every dispute equally intelligible, and banish all that jargon, which has so long taken possession of metaphysical reasonings, and drawn disgrace upon them." (E. 21).

The same principle, though, in different wording is expressed in *The Dialogues concerning Natural Religion*. "Our ideas reach no farther than our experience," and, "Every event, before experience, is equally difficult and incomprehensible, and every event, after experience, is equally easy and intelligible."[1]

The principle of the priority of impressions to ideas functions in Hume's work as a razor which cuts the significant concepts from the meaningless ones. Hume proclaims that his maxim serves as "a new microscope" such that "by a proper application of it, men may reach a greater clearness and precision in philosophical reasonings, than what they have hitherto been able to attain." (E. 62). He invites us to produce the impressions or original sentiments from which the ideas are copied.

These impressions are all strong and sensible. They admit not of ambiguity. They are not only placed in a full light themselves, but may throw light on their correspondent ideas, which lie in obscurity. And by this means, we may, perhaps, attain a new microscope or species of optics, by which, in the moral sciences, the most minute, and most simple ideas may be so enlarged as to fall readily under our apprehension, and be equally known with the grossest and most sensible ideas, that can be the object of our enquiry. (E. 62).

After the application of the criterion, we may know, for sure, whether any expression is meaningful or not:

When we entertain, therefore, any suspicion that a philosophical term is employed without any *meaning or idea* (as is but too frequent), we need but enquire, *from what impression is that supposed idea derived?* And if it be impossible to assign any, this will serve to confirm our suspicion. By bringing ideas into so clear a light we may reasonably hope to remove all dispute, which may arise, concerning their nature and reality. (E. 22 – i.m.).

The main difficulty with philosophical reasoning, according to Hume, is lack of communication between the disputants, and the way to remove this difficulty is to fix the meaning of expressions by the use of the criterion. "The chief obstacle, therefore, to our

---

[1] *Hume's Dialogues concerning Natural Religion*, edited by N. Kemp Smith, Oxford, 1935, p. 176.

improvement in the moral or metaphysical sciences is the obscurity of the ideas, and ambiguity of the terms.... We shall, therefore, endeavour, in this section, to fix, if possible, the precise meaning of these terms." (E. 61–62).

Not only in the *Enquiries* does Hume state clearly that his criterion is in fact to function as a principle of meaning, but the same belief is expressed in *An Abstract* and also in the *Treatise*.

'Tis impossible to reason justly, without understanding perfectly the idea concerning which we reason; and *'tis impossible perfectly to understand any idea*, without tracing it up to its origin, and examining that primary impression, from which it arises. The examination of the impression bestows a clearness on the idea; and the examination of the idea bestows a like clearness on all reasoning. (T. 74 – i.m.).

The application of the criterion of priority of impression to ideas, Hume claims, "will immediately cut off all loose discourses and declamations, and reduce us to something precise and exact." (T. 456).

In *An Abstract*, Hume writes concerning the author of *The Treatise*:

Accordingly, wherever any idea is ambiguous, he has always recourse to the impression, which must render it clear and precise. And when he suspects that any philosophical term has no idea annexed to it (as is too common) he always asks, *from what impression that idea is derived?* And if no impression can be produced, he concludes, that *the term is altogether insignificant.* 'Tis after this manner he examines our idea of *substance* and *essence*; and it were to be wished that this rigorous method were practised in all philosophical debates.[1]

Hume applies the principle of the priority of impressions to ideas, often with the intention of showing that certain important metaphysical concepts, i.e., material or mental substances, ultimate cause, unsensed mathematical entities, some ideas of future state, or of Deity, etc., strictly speaking, are meaningless.

Hume maintains, however, that we can make sense of these concepts, if by using them we describe what we experience or even what we could experience.[2] This general theory of meaning could be paraphrased in the following manner.

We can make significant use of linguistic expressions if these expressions represent ideas (ideas in turn are caused by impressions).

---

[1] Hume, *An Abstract of A Treatise of Human Nature*, Introduction by J. M. Keynes and P. Sraffa, Cambridge, 1938, p. 10 (italics mine).

[2] I take Hume's statement that sound reason convinces us that there are "bodies *vastly* more minute than those, which appear to the senses," but not "bodies *infinitely* more minute," to mean that we may, in future, be able to sense what it does not appear to our senses now, provided "we have instruments and art to make." (T. 48).

The linguistic expression, however, may signify complex ideas. In that case, we should look into its definition; but definition is, according to Hume, "nothing but an enumeration of these parts or simple ideas," (E. 62) which compose the complex idea. And as we know, the question whether there are some specific simple ideas can be settled, if one can "produce the impressions or original sentiments" from which the ideas are derived. Here is the end of our search for meaning, and Hume says that "these impressions are all strong and sensible. They admit not of ambiguity." (E. 62).

4. THE APPLICATION OF THE PRINCIPLE

Having established the principle of the priority of impressions to ideas, Hume soon takes care to examine the significance of the fundamental metaphysical concepts. First to be attacked is the concept of material substance. He asks the metaphysician what the term "substance" stands for, and he finds out that the term "substance," defined as that "unknown *something*, in which they (the particular qualities) are supposed to inhere," is not a name for any of our external or internal perceptions.

I wou'd fain ask these philosophers, ...whether the idea of *substance* be deriv'd from the impressions of sensation or reflection? If it be convey'd to us by our senses, I ask, which of them; and after what manner? If it be perceiv'd by the eyes, it must be a colour; if by the ears, a sound; if by the palate, a taste; and so of the other senses. But I believe none will assert, that substance is either a colour, or sound, or a taste. The idea of substance must therefore be deriv'd from an impression of reflexion, if it really exists. But the impressions of reflexion resolve themselves into our passions and emotions; none of which can possibly represent a substance. (T. 16).

As a result of this inquiry Hume arrives at the following conclusion: that the term "substance" used by metaphysicians is strictly speaking a meaningless expression. "We have therefore no *idea* of substance, distinct from that of a collection of particular qualities, nor have we any other *meaning* when we either talk or reason concerning it." (T. 16 – i.m.).

But Hume is not satisfied to point out that we do not have any evidence for the existence of metaphysical ghosts. He goes on later to explain why we believe in such ghosts. In fact, Hume, in most cases, after demonstrating the vacuity of certain concepts, tries to explain, often in psychological terms, the causes which led philosophers to take these concepts to be significant.[1] He also tells us that all these concepts, provided we satisfy certain conditions, still could be used quite meaningfully.

Concerning substance, he states, in effect, that since we need proper names in language, we assign a particular name to the collections of sense-data, despite their diversity. "The idea of a substance as well as that of a mode, is nothing but a collection of simple ideas, that are united by the imagination, and have a particular name assigned them, by which we are able to recall, either to ourselves or others, that collection." (T. 16).

So far, so good, but here the *imagination* or *fancy* carries us beyond our sense-data and *feigns* something unknown, in which sense-data are supposed to inhere. "... the imagination is apt to feign something unknown and invisible, which it supposes to continue the same under all these variations; and this unintelligible something it calls a *substance*, or *original and first matter*." (T. 220).

Nonetheless, by the light of our *understanding* we may be able to destroy the figment of *our imagination*. "Whenever it (the understanding) views the object in another light, it finds that all these qualities are different, and distinguishable, and separable from each other." (T. 221).

In so doing, Hume concludes that "substance" is actually a class-name which stands for a bundle of sense data. We may significantly use a class-name, and in fact we do, but we should not imagine that there is such a thing as a class, besides its members.

The *Second* occasion for the application of the criterion is on the subject of mental substance. The concept of mental substance is examined by Hume almost in the same manner as the concept of material substance. According to Hume, "the endless cavils" on this subject could be settled, provided that we examine the meaning of the terms employed in the materialistic or the mentalistic hypotheses.

These philosophers are the curious reasoners concerning the material or immaterial substances.... In order to put a stop to these endless cavils on both sides, I know no better method, than to ask these philosophers in a few words, *What they mean by substance and inhesion?* And after they have answer'd this question, 'twill then be reasonable, and not till then, to enter seriously into the dispute. (T. 232).

Once again in order to determine *what* philosophers mean by

---

[1] Consider Hume's anthropological work, *Essay on the Natural History of Religion*, in which an attempt is made to show the origin of religious beliefs: "They are any thing," he says, "but sick men's dreams."

"mental substance" Hume employs his criterion. "I desire those philosophers, who pretend that we have an idea of the substance of our minds, to point out the impression that produces it." (T.233). But since "we have no perfect idea of anything but a perception" and since "a substance is entirely different from a perception," it follows that the term "mental substance" so used is meaningless. Now having no idea of substance, we find also that it makes no sense to attribute any property to such concepts. "[We] can never tell in what sense perceptions are actions of that substance. The use, therefore, of the word, *action*, unaccompany'd with any meaning,... makes no addition to our knowledge." (T. 245). As a result of such inquiry, Hume concludes that "to pronounce, then, the final decision upon the whole: the question concerning the substance of the soul is absolutely unintelligible." (T. 250). Yet the expressions "self" or "mental substance," like "material substance," may be used significantly if these expressions are understood to be class-names and not something "to which our several impressions and ideas are suppos'd to have a reference." (T. 251).

Hume compares the mind to a 'kind of theatre,' where perceptions make their appearance, but he warns us that "the comparison of the theatre must not mislead us" to imagine, that apart from perceptions, there is *a place* in which perceptions take place. Since to speak of *having ideas in the mind*, is to use 'in' metaphorically, we have not "the most distant notion of the place, where these scenes are represented." (T. 253). A better simile is comparing the soul or the mind to a republic or commonwealth. A republic, Hume says, "not only changes its members, but also its laws and constitutions; in like manner the same person may vary his character and disposition, as well as his impressions and ideas, without losing his identity." (T. 261). Thus Hume teaches us that as in talking about the British Commonwealth, we do not assume that there exists something beside or behind the different things which make up this commonwealth – likewise in talking about the self, we should not imagine that there exists something like a class besides its elements. In both cases of mental and material substances, we may make use of class-expressions, provided we remember that classes are fictitious concepts.[1]

[1] For the restatement of such Humian analysis in a non-Humian language see Ryle's *The Concept of Mind*, especially his metaphor of 'the dogma of the Ghost in the Machine'

The *third* important topic examined by Hume under the micro-scope of his principle is the dispute over the nature of *the ultimate and original qualities of mind or of matter.* Already, Hume in the *Introduction* to the *Treatise* informs us that:

... the essence of the mind being equally unknown to us with that of external bodies, it must be equally impossible to form any notion of its powers and qualities otherwise than from careful and exact experiments ... and any hypothesis, that pretends to discover the ultimate original qualities of human nature, ought at first to be rejected as presumptuous and chimerical. (T. xxi).

In the *Enquiries,* Hume announces his intention to fix the precise meaning of the much disputed expressions, i.e., "the ultimate cause," "energy," "power," when these expressions are used to refer to the essential properties of mental or material substances.

There are no ideas, which occur in metaphysics, more obscure and uncertain than those of *power, force, energy* or *necessary connexion.* ... We shall, therefore, endeavor, in this section, to fix, if possible, *the precise meaning of these terms,* and thereby remove some part of that obscurity, which is much complained of in this species of philosophy. (E. 61 – i.m.).

Here the conclusion soon is established:

... as we can have no idea of any thing which never appeared to our outward sense or inward sentiment, the necessary conclusion *seems* to be that we have no idea of connexion or power at all, and that these words are absolutely *without any meaning,* when employed either in philosophical reasonings or common life. (E. 74 – i.m.).

In the *Treatise,* Hume goes farther with regard to this topic. He points out that metaphysicians surely cannot avoid the issue by giving verbal definitions for such expressions. No verbal definition in itself could help us to understand such concepts, unless, of course, the definition denotes impressions. He says that since

... the terms of *efficacy, agency, power, force, energy, necessity, connexion;* and *productive quality,* are all nearly synonymous; ... 'tis an absurdity to employ any of them in defining the rest. By this observation we reject at once all the vulgar definitions, which philosophers have given of power and efficacy; and instead of searching for the idea in these definitions, must look for it in the impressions, from which it is originally deriv'd. If it be a compound idea, it must arise from compound impressions. If simple, from simple impressions. (T. 157).

But there are no impressions corresponding to these ideas, and therefore, "these principles of substantial forms, and accidents, and faculties, are not in reality any of the known properties of bodies, but are perfectly unintelligible and inexplicable." (T. 158).

and his theory of 'category mistake,' e.g. the mistake of supposing that 'the University' stands for an extra member of the class of which other units are members, analogous to a mistake in supposing that besides intelligent behaviour there exists a mind, which is the cause of such behaviour.

And finally the usual method of challenge is employed. "If any one think proper to refute this assertion, he need not put himself to the trouble of inventing any long reasonings; but may at once shew us an instance of a cause, where we discover the power or operating principle. This defiance we are oblig'd frequently to make use of, as being almost the only means of proving a negative in philosophy." (T. 159).

Hume's microscopic examination of such ideas as the inherent qualities of matter, the operating principle, the ultimate force, and his verdict on their fictitious status are actually directed against those of Newton's disciples who ontologized some of Newton's concepts. Newton employed four fundamental concepts: absolute space and time and matter and force in the framework of his theory, and explained certain uniformities of planetary motion by using the laws of motion together with the law of gravitation. Believing in a space composed of points, and in a time composed of instants, which had an existence independent of the things and events that occupied them, he then postulated something like a universal force acting between sun and planets across empty space. It is argued that since it is possible to observe acceleration a, and the mass of the moving particle M, it is necessary to postulate a force causing acceleration of strength Ma. However 'force' itself was defined as mass times acceleration, and 'inertia' as how a body behaves if there were no force acting upon it.

But soon it was realized that *vis gravitatis* and *vis inertia* are non-empirical concepts (to say nothing of absolute space and time). Bodies can be seen moving in a perceptual space and their acceleration may be measured with reference to a time standard, but the gravitational force which is supposed to be the cause of the acceleration of bodies by definition is nothing else than mass times acceleration.

Newton himself had some misgivings with regard to the ontological status of certain concepts used in his system. In his famous Querry he writes:

> To tell us that every Species of Things is endow'd with an occult specifick Quality by which it acts and produces manifest Effects, is to tell nothing... But to derive two or three general principles of motion from phaenomena... though the causes of these principles were not yet discovered.[1]

However, despite such assertions and others which indicate that Newton took his theory to be only a mathematical description of the

[1] Newton, *Opticks*, 4th (1730) ed., New York, 1952, p. 400.

relation which had been found to exist between bodies of matter, he also talked as if gravitational force were an effect that had to be caused by God. Thus he writes:

All these things being consider'd, it seems probable to me, that God in the Beginning form'd Matter in solid, massy, hard, impenetrable, moveable Particles, of such Sizes and Figures, and with such Properties, and in such Proportion to Space, as most conduced to the End for which he form'd them... It seems to me farther, that these Particles have not only a *Vis inertiae*, accompanied with such passive Laws of Motion as naturally result from that Force, but also that they are moved by certain active Principles, such as is that of Gravity.[1]

Hume, notwithstanding his great admiration for Newton,[2] could neither accept Newton's resort to that ancient asylum of ignorance, i.e. the concept of the ultimate cause, for the explanation of natural events, nor the Newtonians' attempts to explain gravity in terms of the occult but inherent primary quality of matter.

To speak of the Final Cause or the Active Power working at a distance, Hume indicates, is to be deceived in supposing that in giving our ignorance a name we do actually provide an explanation. (How different is the attitude of Kant towards Newton's laws when in his *Metaphysical Elements of Natural Science* he tried to demonstrate the self-evidency of Newton's laws, e.g. the law of inertia, by deriving them from pure reason!)

With reference to the Newtonians' use of concepts such as inertia or gravity, Hume writes in the Enquiries:

... when we call this *vis inertiae*, we only mark these facts, without pretending to have any idea of the inert power; in the same manner as, when we talk of gravity, we mean certain effects, without comprehending that active power. It was never the meaning of Sir Isaac Newton to rob second causes of all force or energy; though some of his followers have endeavoured to establish that theory upon his authority. (E. 73).

Also he says that:

We are ignorant, it is true, of the manner in which bodies operate on each other: Their force or energy is entirely incomprehensible: But are we not equally ignorant of the manner or force by which a mind, even the supreme mind, operates either on itself or on a body? (E. 72).

---

[1] *Ibid.*, p. 401.

[2] "In Newton this island may boast of having produced the greatest and rarest genius that ever rose for the ornament and instruction of the species." *The History of England*, Vol. V, Philadelphia, p. 433.

In a letter to a lady friend Hume writes in a jocular manner: "Sir Isaac Newton himself, who cou'd measure the courses of the Plantes, and weigh the Earth as in a pair of scales, even he had no Algebra enough to reduce that amiable Part of our species to a just equation: and they are the only heavenly bodies, whose orbits are as yet uncertain." *The Letters of David Hume*, J. T. Greig, ed., Oxford, 1932, Vol. I.

Again hinting at the Newtonian controversies on the position of bodies in a vacuum or plenum, he writes:

Nothing is more suitable to that philosophy [the Newtonian], than a modest
scepticism to a certain degree, and a fair confession of ignorance in subjects, that
exceed all human capacity. (T. 639).

In the *History of England*, Hume, after giving great tribute to the
genius of Newton, writes:

While Newton seemed to draw off the veil from some of the mysteries of nature,
he showed at the same time the imperfections of the mechanical philosophy, and
thereby restored her ultimate secrets to that obscurity in which they ever did
and ever will remain.[1]

It is important to see how Hume employs on such occasions his
principle of meaning in conjunction with his theory of causation. If
by cause and effect we intend to describe only certain regularities
among our experiential data, then to explain the cause of motion by
reference to a barren concept such as the ultimate cause is to
violate, not only his principle of meaning, but also his rules of
judging cause and effect. Thus to speak of the ultimate cause of
gravitation in the manner of the Newtonians is to mix up different
categories, i.e. the category of the experiential concepts with the
category of concepts which forever did and "forever will remain"
obscure.

The *fourth* occasion for the use of the criterion is in the field of
theology, i.e. concerning questions of the immortality of the soul
and the existence of God. Hume, with much caution and care, argues
that no significant hypothesis can be formulated about such issues.
He is careful not to say that expressions such as "God," "Deity," etc.,
are meaningless; rather he first questions the significance of the properties attributed to God, and then he simply wonders how one can
talk about anything which is deprived of any property!

In the *Treatise*, with the reference to the Cartesians' attempt to
have *recourse to a supreme spirit or deity* as the only active being in the
universe, Hume again appeals to his criterion in order to show that
we do not have any idea of God's powers, although he does not equally say that we have no idea of deity itself.

He states first, "For if every idea be deriv'd from an impression,
the idea of a deity proceeds from the same origin"; then he states the
result of the search for such an impression by saying that "'tis equally impossible to discover or even imagine any such active principle
in the deity." (T. 160). However, this does not mean that we do not

[1] *Ibid.*

have any idea of deity itself but rather that we do not have any idea of God's power.

In the *Appendix* Hume, with reference to the idea of ultimate force, maintains that "we shou'd in vain hope to attain an idea of force by consulting our own minds." (T. 633). In the footnotes to this passage, he states cautiously that "the same imperfection attends our ideas of the Deity; but this can have no effect either on religion or morals. The order of the universe proves an omnipotent mind; that is, a mind whose will is *constantly attended* with the obedience of every creature and being. Nothing more is requisite to give a foundation to all the articles of religion...." Yet Hume in the same book, on another occasion, does not hesitate to undermine this very foundation.

As we observed in the above footnote, "God" is defined as a mind whose will is constantly attended with the obedience of every creature and being. But Hume also maintains, in another passage, that in fact this definition is a mere tautology, since

... in saying, that the idea of an infinitely powerful being is connected with that of every effect, which he wills, we really do no more than assert, that a being, whose volition is connected with every effect, is connected with every effect; which is an identical proposition, and gives us no insight into the nature of this power or connexion. (T. 249).

Thus for Hume, only an anthropomorphic concept of God is intelligible. "The idea of God, as meaning an infinitely intelligent, wise, and good Being, arises from reflecting on the operations of our mind, and augmenting, without limit, those qualities of goodness and wisdom." (E. 19.). "We have no idea of the Supreme Being but what we learn from reflection on our own faculties." (E. 72).

Yet Hume never hesitates to ridicule this anthropomorphic notion of the Supreme Being. First, he mentions that "every supposed addition to the works of nature makes an addition to the attributes of the Author of nature; and consequently, being entirely unsupported by any reason or argument, can never be admitted but as mere conjecture and hypothesis." (E. 145).

Second, as in the case of belief in substance, we must be aware of the tricks of the imagination. "The great source of our mistake in this subject, and of the unbounded license of conjecture, which we indulge, is, that we tacitly consider ourselves as in the place of the Supreme Being, and conclude, that he will, on every occasion, observe the same conduct, which we ourselves, in his situation, would have embraced as reasonable and eligible." (E. 145).

In the *Dialogues* Cleanthes wonders whether given Demea's principle, it does not follow also that the name "God" is without denotation and hence significance. He asks, "Is the name, *without any meaning*, of such mighty importance? Or how do you Mystics, who maintain the absolute incomprehensibility of the Deity, differ from Sceptics or Atheists, who assert, that the first cause of all is unknown and unintelligible?"

But Demea's conviction is similar to that of Wittgenstein that, "Whereof one cannot speak, thereof one must be silent." He already answered Cleanthes by saying that:

... it would, in such a case, be *an abuse of terms* to apply to it the name of thought or reason. At least, if it appear more pious and respectful (as it really is) still to retain these terms, when we mention the Supreme Being, we ought to acknowledge, that *their meaning* in that case, is totally *incomprehensible*; and that the infirmities of our nature do not permit us to reach any ideas, which in the least correspond to the ineffable sublimity of the divine attributes.[1]

Finally, the concept of immortality or a future state, according to Hume, despite all the indoctrination (his term is "education") which is imposed on us, is a concept without meaning.

A future state is so far remov'd from our comprehension, and we have so obscure an idea of the manner, in which we shall exist after the dissolution of the body, that all the reasons we can invent, however strong in themselves, and however much assisted by education, are never able with slow imaginations to surmount this difficulty,... I rather choose to ascribe this incredulity to the faint idea we form of our future condition, deriv'd from its want of resemblance to the present life, than to that deriv'd from its remoteness. (T. 114).

We thus observe that Hume, on the occasions mentioned above, employs his principle of the priority of impression to idea as a criterion of meaning. From the many applications which Hume makes of his principle we come to the following conclusions. Significant words are those which are conjoined to ideas caused by impressions. An idea which is not caused by an impression is a dubious entity and a word which expresses such a dubious entity is a word without meaning. Some expressions denote simple ideas and others denote complex ideas. But since complex ideas are ultimately analyzable into simple ones, all expressions, if they are significant, can be linked to simple ideas.

This theory, despite its simplicity, is very much like theories of meaning once expounded by such modern empiricists as Russell and Schlick. Both Russell and Schlick, in an early stage of their

[1] Hume's *Dialogues, op. cit.*, pp. 194–195 (italics mine).

work, following Hume, sought to explain the relation between language and experience in terms of a one to one correspondence between words and the data of experience.

Thus Russell once suggested that "every proposition which we can understand must be composed wholly of constituents with which we are acquainted."[1] And on another occasion he wrote that "we must attach some meaning to the words we use if we are to speak significantly and not utter mere noise, and the meaning we attach to our words must be something with which we are acquainted."[2]

Likewise, Schlick in an early attempt to construct a theory of meaning, writes: "In order to find the meaning of a sentence we have to transform it by the introduction of successive definitions until finally it contains only words that are not further defined, but whose meanings can be given by direct ostension."[3]

However, both Russell and Schlick, realizing the inadequacy of their theories,[4] modified the criterion.

The attempt to present a more adequate theory of meaning, without diverging from the Humian conviction that meaning and experience are closely connected, led Schlick to formulate his famous criterion of verifiability that "a sentence is significant if and only if it is possible to specify the circumstances under which the sentence is true."[5] Thus Schlick, seeing the shortcomings of his early formulation of the criterion, which is similar to Hume's principle, substitutes a theory which seeks to explain not the meaning of the words but the meaning of sentences.

I claim that Hume also, on many occasions, moves towards a more sophisticated theory of meaning without abandoning his main principle. Let us now consider some of Hume's statements which indicate his awareness that, besides true and false hypotheses, there are some theories which are unverifiable in principle.

We observe that in the *Enquiries*, Hume, when discussing the *religious hypothesis* (the theory of design), neglects to use his usual criterion of meaning, and instead employs (in effect) a criterion similar

---

[1] Bertrand Russell, *Mysticism and Logic*, Longmans, Green and Co., 1921, p. 219.
[2] *Ibid.*, p. 91.
[3] Quoted from Paul Marhenke, "The Criterion of Significance," Presidential Address, Pacific Division of A.P.A., 1949.
[4] Paul Marhenke in reference to this criterion writes: "That the criterion as it stands is only a necessary condition of significance becomes obvious when we consider that Russell's nonsense sentence "Quadruplicity drinks procrastination" can easily be transformed into a sentence that contains only ostensively defined terms. But this sentence is not thereby transformed into a significant sentence." *Ibid.*
Ibid.

to Schlick's verifiability principle. Here, and also in the *Dialogues*, Hume argues that "the religious hypothesis" is vacuous (not because the terms employed in the theory do not stand for any sense-data) but because the theory lacks any observable consequences, in so far that no present or even future evidence could ever confirm or disconfirm the theory, or in the words of Schlick, because it is logically impossible to specify the circumstances under which the sentence is true. Hume thus states that "no new fact *can ever be inferred from the religious hypothesis;* no event foreseen or foretold, no reward or punishment expected or dreaded, beyond what is already known by practice and observation." (E. 146 - i.m.).

The theory of design, like the statement: every object in the universe is an inch longer at the end of each month, is an unverifiable statement. Since any change in the course of nature is compatible with the Providential theory, such a theory, Hume says, "is both uncertain and useless," though he would not say with the later empiricists that it is *meaningless.* He says:

> While we argue from the course of nature, and infer a particular intelligent cause, which first bestowed, and still preserves order in the universe, we embrace a principle, which is both uncertain and useless. It is uncertain; because the subject lies entirely beyond the reach of human experience. It is useless; because our knowledge of this cause being derived entirely from the course of nature, we can never, according to the rules of just reasoning, return back from the cause with any new inference, or making additions to the common and experienced course of nature, establish any new principles of conduct and behaviour. (E. 142).

5. MEANING AND COMPLEX IDEAS

We leave here the application which Hume makes of his main principle of meaning and will explicate those parts of his writings in which he shows though quite unsystematically, his keen awareness, that his principle, though adequate in stating the necessary conditions for the meaningfulness of words, is inadequate in stating the conditions which have to be satisfied for the meaningfulness of statements which express complex ideas.

Hume, after explaining the relation of simple ideas and simple impressions in terms of the derivability of the former from the latter, gives some account of the nature of the relation of complex ideas and complex impressions.

According to Hume, our thought is composed of certain complex ideas, and complex ideas *commonly* mirror the course of complex impressions, i.e., the course of nature. There is usually a one to one correspondence between "the succession of our ideas" and "the course of nature." In the *Enquiries* Hume states that:

> Here, then, is a kind of pre-established harmony between the course of nature and the succession of our ideas.... our thoughts and conceptions have still, we find, gone on in the same train with the other works of nature. ... As nature has taught us the use of our limbs ...; so has she implanted in us an instinct, which carries forward the thought in a correspondent course to that which she has established among external objects.... (E. 54).

The connection of our thoughts and objects is so intimate that on hearing or reading any expression of thought, we tend to believe that these expressions truly picture the order of events.

But Hume warns us that it is a mistake to believe that necessarily the order of ideas and the order of facts are the same. In the *Treatise*, he says that though "the words or discourses of others have an intimate connexion with certain ideas in their mind; and these ideas have also a connexion with the facts or objects, which they represent," we should not exaggerate this connection, since "this latter connexion is generally much over-rated, and commands our assent beyond what experience will justify; which can proceed from nothing beside the resemblance betwixt the ideas and the facts." (T. 113).

As a consequence of such resemblance, we show a remarkable propensity to believe what we hear, that is, since our ideas often represent the course of nature, we take the words of others as if they also represented such an order. "We seldom regulate ourselves entirely by it [experience]; but have a remarkable propensity to believe whatever is reported, even concerning apparitions, enchantments, and prodigies, however contrary to daily experience and observation." (T. 113).

Not only may we take words of others to represent the course of nature, but we may take all our own words as signs for something real. "'Tis usual for men to use words for ideas, and to talk instead of thinking in their reasonings. We use words for ideas, because they are *commonly* so closely connected, that the mind easily mistakes them." (T. 61 - i.m.).

Since our thought *commonly* is a faithful mirror and copies its objects truly, the expression of thought, i.e. words, phrases, sentences, bring to our mind their correspondent objects. "Thus because such a particular idea is commonly annex'd to such a particular word, nothing is requir'd but the hearing of that word to produce the correspondent idea;... The imagination of itself supplies the place of this reflection, and is so accustom'd to pass from the word to the idea." (T. 93).

Hume observes that on hearing words, we may not call the ideas to our attention. We might omit the idea and preserve only a disposition, and call up the idea if we desire to do so. But this omission of ideas, Hume warns us, is a dangerous thing, since the imagination, being accustomed to supply ideas for words, may look for ideas whenever a linguistic expression is uttered.

Thus we may be led to assume that every linguistic expression ought to have a hidden meaning. Because most words are attached to ideas, and because we may bring ideas to our attention when we use words, we may imagine that every expression stands for some entity, even though we never had known and experienced these entities.

For it being usual, after *the frequent use of terms, which are really significant and intelligible*, to omit the idea, which we wou'd express by them, and to preserve only the custom, by which we recal the idea at pleasure; so it naturally happens, that *after the frequent use of terms, which are wholly insignificant and unintelligible*, we fancy them to be on the same footing with the precedent, and to have a *secret meaning*, which we might discover by reflection. (T. 224 – i.m.).

We may ask, why does Hume suppose that our thoughts regularly follow a certain order? To answer this question, we should turn to Hume's psychological account of the association of our ideas. We habitually join our ideas in such a way that they follow the correspondent order of nature. We join the idea of a wound and the idea of pain; the idea of a leg with the idea of a body; the idea of a portrait and the idea of the owner of that portrait, simply because that is how we find them in nature. Thus when we close our eyes and begin to reflect, "the gentle force of association" deploys our thoughts in the same manner in which impressions appear to us. "The chief exercise of the memory is not to preserve the simple ideas, but their order and position." (T. 9).

The hypothesis that in general the order of our thought and the order of nature are the same is further supported by the argument from the similarity of the structure of different languages. In the *Treatise*, Hume says that since, "among other things, languages so nearly correspond to each other," this may demonstrate "nature in a manner pointing out to every one those simple ideas, which are most proper to be united into a complex one." (T. 10). The same point is more carefully made in the *Enquiries*:

> Among different languages, even where we cannot suspect the least connexion or communication, it is found, that the words, expressive of ideas, the most compounded, do yet nearly correspond to each other: a certain proof that the simple ideas, comprehended in the compound ones, were bound together by some universal principle, which had an equal influence on all mankind. (E. 23).

Thus it appears that for Hume the similarity of the structure of different languages is evidence for the similarity of the way people associate and link ideas together, and the latter fact is evidence that our thought is a mirror of nature. That is, for Hume, the fact that the sentence, "Das Feuer ist warm," is translatable into "The fire is warm" is evidence for the belief that the idea of fire naturally brings to our mind the idea of warmth; and if the idea of fire usually is associated with the idea of warmth, it is because as a matter of fact fire is warm.

Hume cites other evidence in support of the theory that in general our complex ideas appear in certain order. "In our most serious thinking or discourse" (but not, he implies, in our fantasies and day dreams) "this is so observable that any particular thought, which breaks in upon the regular tract or chain of ideas, is immediately remarked and rejected." (E. 23).

Hume, however, is quite aware that our thought, though usually reflecting the course of nature, may also distort this order. We may sometimes, in our reveries, day dreams, and dreams, combine or disjoin many sets of complex ideas, despite the fact that the impressions corresponding to these ideas do have their natural order. Though "memory preserves the order and position" of our complex ideas, the imagination may free us from this bondage and combine different ideas, "for nothing is more free than that faculty."

But Hume warns us that we should be aware of the flight of the imagination when we deal with philosophy and science. "Nothing is more dangerous to reason than the flights of the imagination, and nothing has been the occasion of more mistakes among philosophers." (T. 267).

Poets and children may indulge in fancy, but for a philosopher, the flight of the imagination is an unforgivable sin. "We must pardon children, because of their age; poets, because they profess to follow implicitly the suggestions of their fancy: But what excuse shall we find to justify our philosophers in so signal a weakness?" (T. 225).

The imagination, though, may conjoin or disjoin any sets of the simple ideas, and poets and children may think about "winged horses" and "fiery dragons"; nonetheless, there are two limits to the power of imagination. First, we cannot think or imagine a simple idea which is not derived from a simple impression: "it is impossible for us to *think* of any thing, which we have not antecedently *felt*, either by our external or internal senses." (E. 62). Second, we cannot conceive a complex idea which contains a contradiction, "nor is any thing beyond the power of thought, except what implies an absolute contradiction." (E. 18).

The first condition, as we observed, is the consequence of the principle of the priority of impressions to ideas, and this principle is a necessary condition for the meaningfulness of an expression stating a simple idea.

Now I claim here that sometimes the second condition is used by Hume as a criterion for the meaningfulness of a certain class of statements which express complex ideas, namely, the class of analytic statements. For Hume, though it is necessary that each component of a statement describing complex ideas should denote a simple impression, this is not a sufficient restriction. We may have a statement which expresses a complex idea, each component of which denotes a simple impression, and yet the whole expression may lack significance. The criterion which Hume in effect uses to determine the meaningfulness (or according to him, "the truth") of analytic statements is the absence of contradiction. (However, Hume finds himself in difficulty with regard to the meaningfulness or the truth of synthetic statements.)

Hume, like Berkeley, uses terms like "absurd" and "nonsense" with reference to contradictory statements, and "intelligible" and "conceivable" with regard to synthetic statements.[1] He maintains that to determine the significance of statements of complex ideas, we do not call to our attention all the corresponding simple impressions from which these ideas are derived. However, we may avoid *talking nonsense* by noticing whether there is any contradiction or repugnance among complex ideas. To find a repugnance or a contradiction in a sentence is a sure sign that the sentence in question is meaningless, even though each component separately has significance.

---

[1] Berkeley, *Philosophical Commentaries*, A. A. Luce, *op. cit.* "Extension being a perception and perception not perceived is contradiction, nonsense, nothing," p. 31. "To say the mind exists without thinking is contradiction, nonsense, nothing," p. 80.

I believe every one, who examines the situation of his mind in reasoning, will agree with me, that we do not annex distinct and compleat ideas to every term we make use of, and that in talking of *government, church, negotiation, conquest,* we seldom spread out in our minds all the simple ideas, of which these complex ones are compos'd. 'Tis however observable, that notwithstanding this imperfection we may avoid talking nonsense on these subjects, and may perceive any repugnance among the ideas, as well as if we had a full comprehension of them. Thus if instead of saying, *that in war the weaker have always recourse to negotiation,* we shou'd say, *that they have always recourse to conquest,* the custom, which we have acquir'd of attributing certain relations to ideas, still follows the words, and makes us immediately perceive the absurdity of that proposition. (T. 23).

Hume is aware that the criterion of the absence of contradiction can be used only with regard to "propositions that are prov'd by intuition or demonstration" and not with regard to synthetic propositions. But he neglects to point out that not all synthetic statements are meaningful, though of course none of them is self-contradictory. One can easily construct a bona fide synthetic statement whose terms pass Hume's test of meaningfulness by being caused by an impression, and yet the whole sentence lacks any significance.

In the *Treatise* he raises the question: why do we believe that a certain proposition is true or false?

The answer is easy with regard to propositions, that are prov'd by intuition or demonstration. In that case, the person, who assents, not only conceives the ideas according to the proposition, but is necessarily determin'd to conceive them in that particular manner, either immediately or by the interposition of other ideas. *Whatever is absurd is unintelligible; nor is it possible for the imagination to conceive any thing contrary to a demonstration.* But as in reasonings from causation, and concerning matters of fact, this absolute necessity cannot take place. (T. 95 – i.m.).

According to Hume, we can recognize a contradiction by asking ourselves whether or not certain combinations of ideas are conceivable, and if we can conceive clearly certain ideas then it is possible that such ideas may exist. In saying that whatever is clearly conceiv'd may exist, Hume is referring to conceivability of complex ideas. He expressly says that we can conceive of a golden mountain, since there is no repugnance between the idea of gold and the idea of mountain, but we cannot conceive of a mountain without a valley. The statement "There is a mountain without a valley," like the statements "There is an effect without a cause" or "There is a husband without a wife" is a logically impossible statement.

'Tis an establish'd maxim in metaphysics, *That whatever the mind clearly conceives includes the idea of possible existence,* or in other words, *that nothing we imagine is absolutely impossible.* We can form the idea of a golden mountain, and from thence conclude that such a mountain may actually exist. We can form no idea of a mountain without a valley, and therefore regard it as impossible. (T. 32).

For Hume, all synthetic propositions, in contrast to analytic propositions, are meaningful no matter how incredible they may seem.
The statements that "no one has ever seen a man with wings, called
'Gabriel,'" that "Caesar died in his bed" are all meaningful, though
they may be false. "Suppose a person present with me, who advances propositions, to which I do not assent, *that Caesar dy'd in his
bed, that silver is more fusible than lead, or mercury heavier than gold,* 'tis
evident, that notwithstanding my incredulity, I clearly understand
his meaning." (T.95).
In the *Enquiries,* Hume says that false statements in the body of
deductive sciences, are in fact unintelligible, but false synthetic
statements are perfectly meaningful and conceivable.

> Every proposition, which is not true, is there (in the deductive sciences) confused
> and unintelligible. That the cube root of 64 is equal to the half of 10, is a false
> proposition, and can never be distinctly conceived. But that Caesar, or the angel
> Gabriel, or any being never existed, may be a false proposition, but still is per-
> fectly conceivable, and implies no contradiction. (E. 164).

Passmore, in reference to this statement, says, "But if to conceive
a thing is to conceive it as existing then it would 'imply a contradiction' to conceive the non-existence of Gabriel."[1] However, we
observed that for Hume the existence or non-existence of Gabriel
is conceivable, if we realize, that we can conceive any arrangement
of complex-ideas, except contradiction, though we cannot conceive
any simple idea without having a simple impression.
Finally, let us turn our attention to some of Hume's remarks
about the propriety of the use of linguistic expressions. We observed in the previous discussion that Hume is convinced it never
follows from the fact that we use linguistic expressions, either in
common discourse or in philosophy, that they have meaning. He
says that:

> As to the frequent use of words, Force, Power, Energy, &c., which everywhere occur
> in common conversation, as well as in philosophy; that is no proof, that we are
> acquainted, in any instance, with the connecting principle between cause and
> effect, or can account ultimately for the production of one thing to another. These
> words, as commonly used, *have very loose meanings* annexed to them; and their ideas
> are very uncertain and confused. (E. 77 – i.m.).

To fix the very loose meanings annexed to the words, we should
always look for the original impressions which gave rise to the ideas,
and if the statement containing the expression of complex ideas still

---
[1] Passmore, *op. cit.,* p. 98.

seems to be unintelligible, Hume implies we should also see whether
or not these expressions are properly used.

The artificial use of linguistic expressions by philosophers and the-
ologians, Hume complains, has warped reasoning and even language
from their natural course.

In later times, philosophy of all kinds, especially ethics, have been more closely
united with theology than ever..., and as this latter science admits of no terms
of composition, but bends every branch of knowledge to its own purpose, without
much regard to the phenomena of nature, or to the unbiassed sentiments of the
mind, *hence reasoning, and even language*, have been warped from their natural course.
(E. 322 – i.m.).

Of course, Hume judiciously says: "Philosophers, or rather divines
... every one may employ *terms* in what sense he pleases"; but Hume
wants to say, we should not misuse words and distort the *natural* relation of words and their denotation, "but this, in the meantime,
must be allowed, that... a blemish, a fault, a vice, a crime; *these expressions seem to denote* different degrees of censure and disapproba-
tion." (E. 322).

In a passage in the *Treatise* Hume indicates that we should not
dismiss, at first sight, expressions which seem to lack denotations.
Rather, we should be patient and try to discover the proper place in
which such expressions may be used, and this may also help us in
discovering their denotations.

He says, for example, that the expression "necessary connection,"
if used in a sentence, "Two objects are necessarily connected," at
first sight appears to be meaningless, since we do not have any impression of such connection when we observe objects. But "it is more
probable" that the expression "necessary connexion" loses its "true
meaning by being wrongly apply'd." Hence, he suggests, that we
find the proper usage of these expressions, which may lead us to their
original impressions.

Thus upon the whole we may infer, that when we talk of any being, whether
of a superior or inferior nature, as endow'd with a power or force, proportion'd
to any effect; when we speak of a necessary connexion betwixt objects, and suppose, that this connexion depends upon an efficacy or energy, with which any of
these objects are endow'd; *in all these expressions, so apply'd, we have really no distinct
meaning, and make use only of common words, without any clear and determinate ideas. But
as 'tis more probable, that these expressions do here lose their true meaning by being wrong
apply'd, than that they never have any meaning;* 'twill be proper to bestow another consideration on this subject, to see if possibly we can discover the nature and origin
of those ideas, we annex to them. (T. 162 – i.m.).

Hume, as a reward for his patience, finally discovers both the proper context in which the term "necessity" may appear and also the

impression which causes the idea of necessity. "Necessity, then... is
nothing but an internal impression of the mind, or a determination
to carry our thoughts from one object to another." (T. 165).

Up to this point we see that for Hume, though it is necessary that
linguistic expressions denote impressions, it is possible that such expressions be employed in a context without meaning. Hence, to use
meaningfully expressions which designate impressions, Hume implies,we should avoid self-contradictory constructions or any construction which deviates from proper usage. But now we come to a lengthy
passage in Hume's ethics (though his ethics is not our concern) where
he seems to imply that the criterion of denotation of words is not even
a necessary condition of significance. In this passage it seems that
Hume tries to establish the precise meaning of a certain expression,
knowing meanwhile that no original impression could constitute the
meaning for this type of expression.

In discussing the subject of promises, Hume first observes that
though an expression such as "virtuous action" is a name for some
pleasing sentiments, the expression "I promise" does not point to
any of our feelings. He concludes, therefore, that keeping a promise
is not "a natural virtue." For, "If promises be *natural* and *intelligible*,"
Hume says, "there must be some act of the mind attending these
words, *I Promise;* and on this act of the mind must the obligation depend." (T. 516).

Then comes Hume's customary challenge: "Let us, therefore, run
over all the faculties of the soul, and see which of them is exerted in
our promises." (T. 516). The result of this inquiry is, however, negative; there is no distinct sentiment attached to the expression, "I
promise," and hence Hume concludes that"... therefore I venture
to conclude, that promises are human inventions." (T. 519).

Secondly, we find that, on this occasion, Hume does not say, as
one might expect, that the expression of a promise is meaningless,
because it does not stand for any feeling and sentiment.

Thirdly, we see, on the contrary, that Hume is at pains to establish some important conditions under which the expression of promises can be properly used. Thus he believes, I take it, that though
the expression of promise is *not natural*, it is nonetheless *intelligible*. According to Hume the expression "I promise" is used in cases where
we want to express our resolution to perform certain actions.

In order, therefore, to distinguish those two different sorts of commerce, the
interested and the disinterested, there is a *certain form of words* invented for the

former, by which we bind ourselves to the performance of any action. This form of words constitutes what we call a *promise*, which is the sanction of the interested commerce of mankind. When a man says *he promises any thing*, he in effect expresses a *resolution* of performing it. (T. 521).

But though the expression of a promise is a sign for certain feelings of resolution, the two expressions, "I promise to do P" and "I am resolved to do P," are not synonymous, since no obligation is violated in *resolving* to do P and then *declining* to do so.

A resolution is the natural act of the mind, which promises express: But were there no more than a resolution in the case, promises wou'd only declare our former motives, and wou'd not create any new motive or obligation... the expression of a resolution is not commonly suppos'd to be obligatory; and we cannot readily conceive how the making use of a *certain form of words* shou'd be able to cause any material difference. (T. 522–3 – i.m.).

A mere expression of resolution does not make a promise a promise. One who expresses this *form of words* should also know what is involved in his utterance. "...along with that, by making use of this *form of words*, [he] subjects himself to the penalty of never being trusted again in case of failure." (T. 522).

But these conditions are not enough. In order that one use the expression of a promise quite properly, one also should be aware that if he uses this expression in jest, or we may add on stage, or in a class for demonstration, he is not thus bound by his expression.

But tho' the expression makes on most occasions the whole of the promise, yet it does not always so; and one, who shou'd make use of any expression, of which he knows not the meaning, and which he uses without any intention of binding himself, wou'd not certainly be bound by it. Nay, tho' he knows its meaning, yet if he uses it in jest only... he wou'd not lie under any obligation of performance. (T. 523).

In this way, Hume seeing that the expression "I promise" has no descriptive use, recognizes its "performative" function.

6. SUMMARY OF THE CHAPTER

We began our analysis of Hume's principle of meaning by demonstrating his dominating passion to wage a never-ending war against metaphysics and theology with the pronounced intention to free the human mind from the tyranny of superstition and dogma "of every kind or denomination." To do this, Hume expresses metaphorically that we should know the limit and extent of the human mind; and this can be accomplished by the study of the Science of Man. We saw that an important part of this science is what Hume calls "Logic," and logic for Hume consists mainly of what we now call Epistemology and Semantics. We interpreted Hume's inquiry into the scope and limit of the human mind to be in reality an investigation into the nature of the expression of thought. We noted that Hume's critique of metaphysics is based mainly on his application of the principle of the priority of impressions to ideas. This maxim, itself, is not intended to be an article of faith as alleged by Reid, but rather should be regarded as a generalization from experience, open to revision and weakened by exceptions. We then carefully examined both the nature and the usage of this principle, and showed the occasions on which Hume applies his maxim. We demonstrated how the concepts of material and mental substances, or the theories of the ultimate qualities of mind and matter, together with the suppositions of Deity and A Future State, went under Hume's "new microscope" and were cut to pieces by his razor.

But the search for a criterion of meaning led us to discover, besides the known principle of priority so frequently used by Hume, other criteria employed to determine the significance of philosophical concepts. We found that on some occasions Hume uses a principle akin to the verifiability criterion of meaning. We also discovered that Hume, when dealing with expressions of complex ideas, uses, in addition to the principle of priority of impression to idea, without warning, two other implied principles, namely the criterion of the absence of contradiction and the criterion of the propriety of usage. He maintains, in effect, that an expression of complex ideas is not meaningful if it is self-contradictory. That is to say, besides the fact that every term in our expression of complex ideas should denote a particular entity, they should also be used properly in the statement, and one thing which may guarantee the propriety of usage is lack of contradiction. Then, to our surprise, we discovered in Hume's ethics an occasion on which he abandons his search for the denotation of a word and rather tries to provide its meaning by establishing some rules for the proper use of the term, knowing at the same time that the expression does not stand for any impression. This was the case of promises.

Upon the whole we can say that there is no systematic theory of meaning in Hume's writings. However, Hume does say, as we observed, many interesting things concerning linguistic expressions, the meaning of such expressions, and their relation to experience. In the following I will conclude what I believe to be Hume's main contentions about the nature of meaning:

In general, significant words are only those which can be linked to ideas caused by impressions. An idea which is not caused by an impression is a dubious entity and a word which expresses such a dubious entity is a word without meaning. Some expressions denote simple ideas and others denote complex ideas. But since complex ideas are ultimately analyzable into simple ones, all expressions, if they are significant, could be linked to simple ideas. However, the expression of promises is an exception to the rule, insofar as no impression corresponds to such words. Yet we can use such an expression meaningfully if we know the conditions under which it is actually used in the language.

Aside from the fact that words should denote ideas, they should also be employed in accordance with the rules of language. Otherwise, their improper usage would lead to the utterance of meaningless sentences. Hume does not indicate what are the rules which determine propriety of usage. However, he does refer to a rule which should govern the proper usage of words in the context of analytic statements, i.e., "with regard to propositions, that are prov'd by intuition or demonstration," by saying that in such contexts the usage of words which produces a self-contradictory statement is to be avoided. No rule is given by Hume for determining the meaningfulness of synthetic statements besides indicating that certain seemingly synthetic expressions are vacuous, since it is impossible to specify the circumstances under which the sentence is true.

CHAPTER TWO

Evaluation of Hume's Principle

1. INTRODUCTION

We are now in a position to make a survey of the principle of the priority of impressions to ideas: to examine both the nature of the principle and the use which Hume makes of it as a criterion of meaning. To do the latter task completely, we must give a full account of Hume's theory of knowledge. We have to see, for example, given the principle, how successful is Hume's treatment of the nature of space, time, abstract ideas, etc. However, we are concerned with Hume's principle only in so far as it has direct bearing upon his treatment of demonstrative knowledge. In this part, we shall only touch upon some of the major difficulties inherent in Hume's principle. A full evaluation of the principle will be given in the chapter following the detailed examination of Hume's account of knowledge properly so called.

As we tried to establish, Hume actually employs four different criteria of meaning in his writing, though he mentions explicitly only one criterion.

The principle of the priority of impressions to ideas, or derivability of the latter from the former, is generally believed to be the only criterion which Hume made use of in his books. Reid, in reference to Hume's constant use of the principle expressed in questions like: Does the expression refer to an impression or an idea? If it refers to an idea, from what impression is that idea copied? says:

> These questions may seem trivial or impertinent to one who does not know that it is a tribunal of inquisition erected by certain modern philosophers, before which everything in nature must answer. The articles of inquisition are few indeed, but very dreadful in their consequences. They are only these: Is the prisoner an Impression or an Idea? If an idea, from what impression copied? Now if it appears that the prisoner is neither an impression, nor an idea copied from some impression, immediately, without being allowed to offer anything in arrest of judgment, he is sentenced to pass out of existence, and to be, in all time to come, *an empty unmeaning sound, or the ghost of a departed entity.*[1]

[1] Thomas Reid, *The Works of Thomas Reid*, edited by William Hamilton, Third Edition, p. 144 (italics mine).

No doubt the numerous repetitions and the numerous applications of the principle are responsible for Reid's allegations. However, as we have already observed, Hume employs other criteria for separating the significant from the nonsignificant concepts. We shall also see that neither is Hume's criterion an "article of inquisition," nor is the principle that ideas *have* to be copies of impressions, as alleged by Reid, though I think that Reid is right in recognizing that Hume's principle is used as a test for determining the meaningful concepts from "the unmeaning sound."

The interpretation of Hume's principle as a criterion of meaning is not unfamiliar to contemporary philosophers. Thus Austin writes that "Hume's theory about the 'derivation of our ideas' really amounts to the theory that a word, X, can only have meaning provided that I can know, on at least one occasion, that 'this is an X' where 'this' denotes something sensible."[1]

Passmore writes: "In Hume's view an expression is meaningless unless it refers to ideas which have been derived from past experience."[2]

Many other commentators recognize that Hume's principle, though it sounds like a statement that belongs to psychology, is in fact a semantic principle; and by saying this, they do not mean to imply that Hume was actually conscious that his principle was in fact a semantic criterion in disguise.

Since the view of these commentators on the nature of Hume's principle amounts to no more than what we quoted, I think a detailed examination of the principle may be of service to Hume's admirers.

In the following, I shall first examine the psychological problem of the relation between impressions and ideas, then endeavor to explain the semantic problem of the relation between linguistic expressions and impressions or ideas.

2. ON THE RELATION OF IMPRESSIONS AND IDEAS

The psychological issue of the relation between impressions and ideas is indeed a puzzling problem in Hume's epistemology. Hume quite carelessly describes the relation between the members of the two classes of impressions and ideas in terms of the exact resem-

---

[1] J. L. Austin, *Aristotelian Society*, Supp. Vol. XVIII, p. 97. "Are there A Priori Concepts?"
[2] Passmore, *op. cit.*, p. 68.

blance – copying, derivability of ideas from impressions, priority of impressions to ideas, constant conjunction of the two, etc.

Take, for example, the relation of impressions and ideas expressed in terms of exact resemblance. Hume says: "That all our simple ideas... are deriv'd from simple impressions, which are correspondent to them, and which they exactly represent." (T. 4). "An idea is by its very nature weaker and fainter than an impression; but being in every other respect the same." (T. 73). "Our ideas are copy'd from our impressions, and represent them in all their parts." (T. 96). "Ideas always represent their objects or impressions; and *vice versa.*" (T. 157). "An idea is a weaker impression; and as a strong impression must necessarily have a determinate quantity and quality, the case must be the same with its copy or representative." (T. 19). "*The mind cannot form any notion of quantity or quality without forming a precise notion of degrees of each.*" (T. 18).

Hume also makes the following statements: "many of our ideas are so obscure, that 'tis almost impossible even for the mind, which forms them, to tell exactly their nature and composition." (T. 33). "All ideas, especially abstract ones, are naturally faint and obscure: ... they are apt to be confounded with other resembling ideas; and when we have often employed any term, though without a distinct meaning, we are apt to imagine it has a determinate idea annexed to it. On the contrary, all impressions ...are strong and vivid." (E. 21).

Taking them at their face value, the assertions that simple ideas exactly copy their simple impressions and represent them in all their parts, that for every determinate impression there is a determinate idea, and the statements that many of our ideas are obscure and indeterminate seem to be incompatible.

William James, in reference to Hume's statement that the mind cannot form any notion of quantity or quality without forming a precise notion of degrees of each, asserts that this is an obviously false opinion. He says: "The slightest introspective glance will show to anyone the falsity of this opinion. Hume surely had images of his own works without seeing distinctly every word and letter upon the pages which floated before his mind's eye."[1]

Laird, on this issue, indeed goes farther than James, and accuses Hume of uttering inconsistent statements. He says: "According to Berkeley and Hume images and sensa plainly exist, and therefore

[1] William James, *Principles of Psychology*, Part I, Vol. II, p. 46.

must be completetely determinate, on pain of controvening the law of Excluded Middle. Yet Hume inconsistently admitted many ideas are obscure....[1]

However, a careful study of Hume will prove that both James and Laird are guilty of asserting hasty judgments. What Hume wants to assert is not that ideas exactly resemble their impressions *whenever* we reflect upon ideas, but only that ideas exactly resemble impressions *in their first appearance*. Not that the recurring idea *always* represents all the qualities of its impression, but that only when there occurs an impression then there occurs an idea which exactly resembles it.

Now then let us read Hume more carefully. Hume says that "*all our simple ideas in their first appearance are deriv'd from simple impressions, which are correspondent to them, and which they exactly represent.*" (T. 4). That "*every idea... first makes its appearance* in a correspondent impression." (T. 33). He considers "the order of their *first appearance*" (of idea and impression) and italicizes the expression "*their first appearance.*" (T. 5). And then he explicitly says that, though every impression is constantly followed by an idea, the contrary is not the case. Indeed, we would be in a sad predicament if thinking about an idea would be the same as having its correspondent impression.

> Our ideas upon their appearance produce not their correspondent impressions, nor do we perceive any colour, or feel any sensation merely upon thinking of them. On the other hand we find, that any impression either of the mind or body is constantly followed by an idea. (T. 5).

I think that Hume would be in complete agreement with his critics. He would say to James that he surely had images of his own works without seeing distinctly every word and letter upon the pages which floated before his mind's eye. He would probably point out to James that previously he had said in the early pages of the *Treatise* "that many of our complex impressions never are exactly copied in ideas...· I have seen *Paris;* but shall I affirm I can form such an idea of that city, as will perfectly represent all its streets and houses in their real and just proportion?" (T. 3).

I think that Hume would also answer Laird's objection by saying that the statement that an idea, like its impression, has a determinate quantity and quality and represents it in all its parts, and the statement that many of our ideas are so obscure... are not contradictory, provided we remember that simple ideas only in their first appearance exactly represent their simple impressions.

[1] Laird, *op. cit.*, p. 78.

However, Hume's statement that any impression is constantly followed by an idea cannot be accepted without some modification. I do not know whether or not Hume wants to admit that there are vague impressions as well as vague ideas. There are some statements in the *Treatise*, which might indicate that Hume was fully aware of the fact that some impressions may be *faint* and *unsteady*. Hume says: "On the other hand it sometimes happens, that our impressions are so faint and low, that we cannot distinguish them from our ideas." (T. 2).

But he also says "that no impression can become present to the mind, without being determin'd in its degrees both of quantity and quality. The confusion, in which impressions are sometimes involv'd, proceeds only from their faintness and unsteadiness, not from any capacity in the mind to receive any impression which in its real existence has no particular degree or proportion. That is a contradiction in terms." (T. 19).

It is difficult to make a clear appraisal of the above statement. This much can be said however: if Hume admits that there are vague impressions, then it is quite dubious that we are *constantly* or even sometimes aware of all our impressions, i.e., a dim view of the Bay Area or a clear view of all the particles in a ray of light observed in broad daylight, or even fears and pleasures which strike our minds in nightmares. Then let us say that if by "impression," Hume always means "those perceptions, which enter with most force and violence" (T. 1), provided that the mind pays its due attention to such impressions, then we may accept his statement that impressions are constantly followed by their corresponding ideas. Granting this modification, we may assert the following conclusions:

1. That ideas *on their first appearance occur* with their corresponding impressions.
2. That provided we are conscious of the appearance of *strong impressions*, ideas have all the properties of their impressions except that ideas are weaker than their impressions.
3. That ideas when they appear in the absence of their corresponding impressions may appear vague and obscure.

Now, if we accept the above interpretation, we shall see that the problem of the missing shade can be explained away.

Russell in many of his writings tries to remove Hume's acknowledged exception to his principle. He says: "Hume made himself an unnecessary difficulty in regard to the theory that images 'copy' im-

pressions." Russell thinks that his master's puzzle could be solved
if we recognize:

... that images are always more or less vague copies of impressions, so that an
image might be regarded as a copy of any one of a number of different impressions of slightly different shades. In order to get a test case for Hume's question,
we shall have to suppose that there was a broad band of the spectrum that the
man had never seen – say the whole of the yellow. He would then, one may
suppose, be able to form images which, owing to vagueness, might be applicable
to orange-yellow, and others applicable to green-yellow, but none applicable to
a yellow midway between orange and green. This is an example of an unreal
puzzle manufactured by forgetting vagueness.[1]

Russell asks:

Could you imagine a shade of color you had never seen, if it was intermediate
between two very similar shades that you have seen? The answer is that you could
not form so precise an image, even of a color that you had seen, but that you
could form a vague image, equally appropriate to the shade that you had not
seen and to the two similar shades that you had seen.[2]

Russell criticizes Hume by saying that:

Berkeley and Hume, in their attack on general ideas, do not allow for the
vagueness of images; they assume that every image has the definiteness that a
physical object would have. This is not the case, and a vague image may well
have a meaning which is general.[3]

It seems to me that Russell is right in concluding that Hume's exception to his principle no longer remains an exception if we grant
that images are as a rule not of one definite prototype, but of a number of similar prototypes. However, to do justice to Hume we should
remember, as we mentioned before, that Hume does not deny that
images may sometimes be vague.

We come now to examine Hume's statement "*that all ideas are
copy'd from impressions.*" (T. 163). I think if it ever makes sense to use
the terminology of "copying" or "exact representation" with reference to images, it is only possible with regard to visual sense-data.
In a loose sense, we may talk about colors that we see in our
mind's eye as copies of colors previously seen by us with our eyes
open. However, the terminology of "copying" or "exact representation" is in no way fitted for describing the ideas of the smells, tastes,
passions, pains, etc.

At this point, I want to assert that despite Hume's statement that

[1] Bertrand Russell, *An Outline of Philosophy*, London, 1949, pp. 199–200.
[2] *Idem, Human Knowledge*, p. 109.
[3] *Idem, The Analysis of Mind*, p. 208.

"all ideas are copy'd from impressions," we find that he does not really care whether ideas in fact are the exact copies of impressions. For example, in the Appendix, Book I, instead of using the terminology of copying he mentions that "all ideas are *borrow'd* from preceding perceptions." (T. 634).

All that Hume cares to establish is the fact of the priority of impressions to ideas, and the derivability of the latter from the former, and not the thesis that ideas are copies of impressions. It is the principle of the priority of impressions to ideas which was explictly declared by Hume to be his most important discovery. It is this principle used again and again by him as a criterion which determines the significance of philosophical concepts. Hume not only states that all ideas are derived from impressions, but also that "we have no idea, that is not deriv'd from an impression." (T. 155); that "where we cannot find any impression, we may be certain that there is no idea." (E. 78).

Now T. H. Green, instead of taking the thesis of derivability of ideas from impressions as a fundamental maxim, takes the copyterminology of Hume seriously and objects that:

> It should follow that space is either a colour or feeling of touch. In the terms which Hume himself uses with reference to "substance," "if it be perceived by the eyes, it must be colour; if by the ears, a sound; and so on, of the other senses." As he expressly tells us that it is "perceived by the eyes," the conclusion is inevitable.[1]

Yet what Hume wants to establish is not that all of our ideas are copies of impressions, but only that they are causally dependent on impressions. He argues that the idea of time and space are causally dependent on impressions but none of them are copies of any set of impressions.

The idea of space arises from the *manner* or order of *arrangement* of visual and tactual impressions. Thus unlike Green's assumption, space is not "either a colour or feeling of touch," but rather, as Hume says, "The idea of space is convey'd to the mind by two senses, the sight and touch." (T. 38). Likewise, "the idea of time," as Hume says, "is not deriv'd from a particular impression mix'd up with others, and plainly distinguishable from them; but arises altogether from the manner, in which impressions appear to the mind, without making one of the number." (T. 36).

The same objection could also be brought against R. W. Church,

---

[1] T. H. Green, *op. cit.*, p. 195.

when, in reference to Hume's statement that "there are bodies vastly more minute than those which appear to the senses,"he says that here, "Hume grants us ideas which cannot be images, but are the result of 'sound reason' thus contradicting his first principle."[1]

3. ON THE RELATION OF WORDS AND IMPRESSIONS

As we have already observed, the main criterion of meaning which Hume employs in his work is the criterion of the priority of impressions to ideas.

For Hume, since words are generally used to convey ideas, most expressions should ultimately designate sensible entities or the impressions which are the origin or causes of the ideas. For this reason, the inquiry into the origin of our ideas, according to him, is an indispensable prerequisite *for the perfect understanding of our ideas.*

The negative consequence of this theory is the belief that since the legitimate (that is to say, the sensible) ancestry of many philosophical or ordinary concepts cannot be established by means of the old Lockean historical method, such concepts are to be regarded as pseudo-ideas or *vain concepts.* Thus, Hume is fully aware of Lord Bacon's contention that, "Words are the counters of wise men, but money of fools," – that to use linguistic expressions is not necessarily to have thought or ideas. Hume's primary message is that mere verbal dispute is useless; we should rather turn our attention to the denotation of symbols.

It might reasonably be expected in questions which have been canvassed and disputed with great eagerness, since the first origin of science and philosophy, *that the meaning of all the terms, at least,* should have been agreed upon among the disputants; and our enquiries, in the course of two thousand years, been able to pass from words to the true and real subject of the controversy. (E. 80).[2]

---

[1] R. W. Church, *Hume's Theory of Understanding*, London, G. Allen and Unwin, 1935, p. 59.
Likewise A. H. Basson, in his recent book on Hume writes: "According to Hume's theory, for a word to have a meaning it is not sufficient that it should have a use: it must also stand for an idea which determines the use. And this idea is a kind of image or picture of something which the word represents or means. Moreover, every idea is a copy of some possible impression. It follows that a word can have meaning only if it stands for an idea, which is in turn a copy of some possible impressions." *David Hume,* Pelican Philosophy Series, 1958, p. 31 and 123.

[2] Here, it seems that Hume supposes that 'Thinking,' being a transitive verb, should be supplied with accusatives such as 'Ideas' or 'Meaning,' which denote objects of thought, and these objects not only are prior to and independent of linguistic symbols which they are expressed, but also they are "the true and real subject of controversy." In this way ideas are the meaning of linguistic symbol, as Propositions are supposed, by some modern logicians, to stand for the meaning of sentences.

With the intention of ending the prolonged, verbal arguments of ancient and modern philosophers, Hume established the principle of meaning, asserting that any expression which is not ultimately cashable by means of impressions is to be regarded as devoid of cognitive significance.

However, Hume's theory concerning the relation of expressions and impressions, despite its originality and its effectiveness, is open to the following major difficulties:

The difficulty with the recurrence of impressions.

The difficulty with the privacy of impressions.

The difficulty of establishing meaning by finding the origin of our ideas.

4. THE DIFFICULTY WITH THE RECURRENCE OF IMPRESSIONS

We observed that Hume, in his attempt to solve philosophical puzzles, constantly asks his readers to "produce the original impression," to "trace the orginal sentiment," "to point out the impression that produces the idea"; yet all the while he describes the original impression in such a way that to carry out his demand is to achieve an impossible task. "All impressions," according to Hume, "are internal and perishing existences, and appear as such," (T. 194), so that "there is no impression constant and invariable." (T. 251). It follows that the test for establishing the meaning of expressions is possible only if we are able to recall, *per impossibile*, those perishing impressions which caused our ideas.

Hume himself was aware of such a difficulty, though the question before him was how to account for the difference between true and false beliefs. Hume defines "truth" by saying that "truth or falsehood consists in an agreement or disagreement either to the *real* relations of ideas, or to *real* existence and matter of fact." (T. 458).

Hume realizes that no correspondence theory of truth could be stated in his system, "it being impossible to recal the past impressions, in order to compare them with our present ideas, and see whether their arrangement be exactly similar." (T. 85).

But he did not realize that the same difficulty would also arise in his, so to speak, Correspondence Theory of Meaning (the theory which asserts that meaning is a form of correspondence between symbols and things). Passmore, with regard to the above quotation, rightly observes that Hume "never realizes the full implications of this admission. Taken seriously, it would destroy his positivist method. There is now no way of discovering whether a supposed idea in fact derives from an impression."[1]

Russell also points out the very same difficulty, though with reference to the subject of knowing the resemblance (not knowing the origin of ideas) between impression and idea. He says:

> Why do we believe that images are, sometimes or always, approximately or exactly, copies of sensation? The difficulty of this question arises through the fact that the sensation which an image is supposed to copy is past when the image exists and can therefore only be known by memory, while on the other hand, memory of past sensations seems only possible by means of present images. How then, are we to find any way of comparing the present image and the past sensation? The problem is just as acute if we say that images differ from their prototypes as if we say that they resemble them; it is the very possibility of comparison that is hard to understand.[2]

Thus, it seems that Hume's request for producing the original impression of an idea is, by hypothesis, an impossibility, unless we take his often used conjunction of "impression" and "object" to mean that these expressions are intended to be used interchangeably. But now if Hume includes public perceptual objects in the class of objects, then it seems that the use of the Lockean historical method for the discovery of the original impression is not suited for the occasion. Instead of employing this method, Hume could simply use the ostensive method, and by pointing out the object, end the dispute. Yet, even though we can define some, we cannot ostensively define all impressions; of some impressions there can be given no spatial description. And to point out what defies spatial description is an absurdity. Let us also remember that when Hume asks for the impression of an idea, he never asks, "Point out the impression to me"; rather, he asks, "Point out" or "produce" the impression (for yourself). And in fact, he readily admits that someone might be able to get hold of an impression, which, despite his utmost endeavor, escapes his net.

Thus we conclude that, since Hume's historical method can not be identified with the processes of ostensive definition, and since "impression" and "object" can not always be interchangeably used in Hume's text, our initial objection to Hume's principle remains.

---

[1] Passmore, *op. cit.*, p. 94.
[2] Russell, *The Analysis of Mind*, p. 159.

5. THE DIFFICULTY WITH THE PRIVACY OF IMPRESSIONS

Laying aside the problem of the recurrences of the impression, we are still faced with the question: If the data of our experience are inaccessible to others, how then can we communicate our ideas in language? Now suppose we begin with remembrance of things past, and by so doing, bring to our attention traces left by the impression (and not the impressions themselves as Hume demands), can we agree with Hume that terms which do not signify these entities are altogether nonsignificant?

The assignment of names for all the occasions of one's perception (if this could be possible) does not substantiate belief in a private language. We do not want to discuss here the possibility of inventing a private language, but it suffices to mention that the inventor of a private language could not properly make use of his own invention, since in the absence of an external check, the only check that he could have of the correctness of his use of names is his own memory. But this fairy tale has no direct bearing on our problem.

Hume's question – from what impressions, for example, the idea of substance, necessary connection, etc., are derived – makes sense, if and only if there is a public language, and a public language is possible, if there is a community of entities which are amenable to public observation. Thus, to comply with Hume's demands, we must be able to point to something besides our private data, and hence to public objects.

Once again epistemological considerations wreck Hume's semantic theory. Unless Hume intended to use "impression" and "object" interchangeably and unless he includes among his objects the public perceptual object, his methodological device is incapable of producing results.[1]

In a passage in the *Enquiry* we find that Hume grants the public nature of data. He argues that one reason for the undecidability of philosophical arguments is ambiguity of expression, i.e. the disputants assign different denotations for the same expression. "From this circumstance alone, that a controversy has been long kept on foot, and remains still undecided, we may presume that there is some ambiguity in the expression, and that the disputants *affix dif-*

---

[1] Perhaps Urmson refers to such difficulties when he says that "thus to know the meaning of a word is to know with what type of impression it is linked by ostensive definition. This seems to be the kernel of Hume's doctrine on this point *after the psychological husk has been stripped from it.*" J. O. Urmson, *Philosophical Analysis*, 1956, p. 108.

ferent ideas to the terms employed in the controversy." (E. 80).

He rules out the possibility that the absence of communication might be due to the fact that each man perceives different objects, since, if this were the case, no communication would be possible.

For as the faculties of the mind are supposed to be naturally alike in every individual; otherwise nothing could be more fruitless than to reason or dispute together; it were impossible, if men affix *the same ideas to their terms*, that they could so long form different opinions of the same subject. (E. 80).

The lack of communication is neither due to dissimilarity of our faculties, nor due to privacy of the objects given to our faculties; it is only due to the fact that the "meaning of all the terms" is not "agreed upon among the disputants." (E. 80).

6. THE DIFFICULTY OF ESTABLISHING MEANING BY LOOKING FOR THE ORIGIN OF IDEAS

We have established that the usefulness of Hume's criterion rests upon the assumption of the public nature of data. Let us then neglect epistemological considerations and interpret Hume's maxim, "no idea without a corresponding impression," to mean "no meaning without a corresponding denotation."

The latter statement means that the denotation of an expression and its meaning are closely connected. That is, unless the expression stands for some object, that expression can have no meaning. Given this interpretation, we may ask two questions:

First, how far is this theory plausible?

Second, granted that the theory has some plausibility, how useful is it as a criterion of meaning?

The principle of the priority of impressions to ideas or of denotation to meaning, for Hume, is a safe generalization based upon much evidence. To give a child an idea of scarlet, we should provide him with scarlet impressions; to form for ourselves a just idea of the taste of pineapple we should actually taste this fruit; and to produce an idea of color in a man born blind, we have to restore his sight-organ. By giving these examples, Hume, in effect, wants to establish the generalization that meaningful expressions are those that are either ostensively definable, or those that are verbally definable in terms of other expressions, which are themselves ostensively definable.

With regard to Hume's evidence, we may say that no doubt we

learn as children perceptual words, by being acquainted with the public-perceptual objects and by being taught linguistic conventions which are used in talking about these objects. We cannot, in general, make use of perceptual-expressions properly without learning perceptual lessons, and we cannot learn perceptual lessons without having the proper perceptions.

However, it is possible that we use perceptual expressions sometimes properly without ever having been acquainted with the proper perception. Hume himself wondered when he found out that the blind poet Blacklock used proper color expressions in his poetry. But the explanation was simple. Blacklock confessed that he knew how to use color-expressions; he learned that certain expressions appear usually in a certain context, but he did not know the meaning of these expressions. He was using parrot-like symbols without ever knowing what the symbol stood for.[1]

It follows that the proper usage of perceptual-expressions either by chance or by association with other expressions is not incompatible with the rule that these expressions must be ostensively definable if they are to be used significantly.

However, it is a mistake to assume that simply by pointing to an entity, i.e., a scarlet specimen, a child can understand the meaning of "scarlet." The process of ostensive definition is not so simple. A child may learn the meaning of an ostensively defined object, provided that he already has passed the stage in which words are meaningless noises, and provided that he already understands the meaning of other words, etc. Wittgenstein points out the difficulties involved in the process of ostensive definition. "The ostensive definition explains the use – the meaning of the word when the overall role of the word in language is clear. Thus, if I know that someone means to explain a colour-word to me, the ostensive definition 'That is called "sepia"' will help me to understand the word."[2]

Now it is important to realize that, although Hume's actual evidence in support of his generalization is all about perceptions,

---

[1] E. C. Mossner writes: "The case of Blacklock ... was immediately recognized by the mid-eighteenth century as a variant of the Lockean problem. 'I think he is the greatest Curiosity in the World,' observed Hume, and all the world concurred."

Mossner also quotes Hume's saying, "I once said to my friend, Mr Blacklock, that I was sure he did not treat love as he did colours; he did not speak of it without feeling it. There appeared too much reality in all his expressions to allow that to be suspected. He said: 'The sweetness of the voice has a mighty effect upon me: the symptoms of youth too, which the touch discovers...' E. C. Mossner, *Le Bon David*, 1942, pp. 14–28.

[2] Ludwig Wittgenstein, *Philosophical Investigations*, Oxford, 1953, p. 30.

i.e., having the idea of scarlet, orange, or the taste of a pineapple, of the relish of wine, of the feeling of generosity, etc., his conclusion is, "We have no idea, that is not deriv'd from an impression." (T. 155). "All the materials of thinking are derived either from our outward or inward sentiment." (E. 19).

However, we do, as a matter of fact, use significantly non-descriptive symbols as well as descriptive signs in our discourse. We all use non-descriptive expressions, and hence expressions which do not stand for any of our internal or external feelings, quite properly in accordance with the conventions and rules governing their correct usage. In describing our perceptions, we cannot avoid using syncategorematic expressions, i.e., expressions which are meaningful only in context but which name nothing.

But even if one discovers corresponding perceptions for some of these expressions, such as an "if-feeling" or a "but-feeling," that does not prove that these supposed feelings are the causes of such concepts, for the reasons that in the absence of these feelings we are able to use these expressions meaningfully; and these feelings might occur, but not the meaning of these terms.

We shall see later in detail, when we deal with Hume's logic, that his attempt to explain formal relations, such as contrariety or identity, and logical constants, such as negation and affirmation, in terms of psychological links, led to overwhelming difficulties.

Quite apart from the syncategorematic terms, there are meaningful expressions which do not require reference to perceptions, in a sense that the absence of perception does not deprive them of significance. Frege observes that the words "the celestial body most distant from the Earth" have a sense, but it is very doubtful that they have also a reference. The expression "the least rapidly convergent series" has a sense; but it is known to have no reference, since for every given convergent series, another convergent, but less rapidly convergent, series can be found.[1] But if it will be objected that such expressions for Hume signify complex ideas and hence do not necessarily constitute counter examples to Hume's generalization, perhaps the Euclidean concept of points and arithmetical expression, such as zero, not to mention imaginary numbers, are enough to prove our point. If further objection is raised that these concepts are also class concepts, and thus are to be regarded as com-

---

[1] Gottlob Frege, *On Sense and Reference*, in translations from *The Philosophical Writings of Gottlob Frege*, edited by Geach and Black, 1952, p. 58.

plex ideas, we shall take care to point out that for Hume all complex ideas are ultimately reducible to simple ideas, and it seems that no simple idea could be a candidate for the membership of classes of points and zeros.

How then does Hume account for the meaning of such concepts in a way that is consistent with his principle of the priority of impressions to ideas? This question will be answered later.

So far the only statement which could be made in favor of Hume's principle is that the principle seems plausible provided that we make an important emendation. That is, if by "idea" Hume means not *whatever* we think about, but only those ideas which are about our perceptions and feeling, then it seems that thinking about perceptions and feelings (which amounts to talking to one's self or to others about these things) presupposes having had some experience. And it seems quite impossible for a person to talk properly on all appropriate occasions about perceptions without ever having had one.

Here Ryle's comment on Hume's "causal theory" would be of interest to us.

The only thing that is true in this account is that what I see in my mind's eye and what I hear in 'my head' is tied in certain ways to what I have previously seen and heard. But the nature of this tie is not at all what Hume supposed. All that is required is to see that learning perceptual lessons entails some perceiving, that applying those lessons entails having learned them.[1]

Granted that the causal dependency between knowing the meaning of perceptual expressions and having certain perceptions is true, we are still far removed from arguing that having a proper perception and knowing the origin of our ideas is a necessary condition for knowing the meaning of all sorts of concepts. The question which is before us is whether having certain perceptions is a necessary condition for understanding all expressions, or rather, whether it

---

[1] G. Ryle, *op. cit.*, pp. 271–72.

I think Ryle is somehow belittling Hume's theory. For aren't "perceptual lessons" the very lessons that we ought to learn if we want to know anything about the world! If it is true that the language of science is essentially descriptive, then it is also true that such a language has a referential character and the meaning of descriptive expressions is in some way bound up with this character.

Russell in his recent work criticizes a purely syntactic approach to the problem of meaning. He takes essentially a Humian approach when he writes: "Sentences are composed of words, and, if they are to be able to assert facts, some, at least, of the words must have that kind of relation to something else which is called 'meaning'" *My Philosophical Development, loc. cit.*, p. 235.

is often an irrelevancy which may even distract our attention in understanding linguistic expressions.

We grant to Hume that we cannot understand the meaning of perceptual expressions without having some perception. Let us grant to him also, for the sake of argument, that all meaningful expressions, even mathematical terms and logical constants, are in some sense connected with some experience. Does it follow that knowing the original impression, to use Hume's expression, is to understand the idea?

We hold that Frege's advice, "Never take a description of the origin of an idea for a definition,"[1] should be taken seriously not only in defining mathematical concepts, but also in defining almost all abstract ideas.

Frege, with regard to arithmetical concepts, observed that an inquiry into the origin of such concepts does not give us any clue into the meaning of such concepts.

Do the concepts, as we approach their supposed sources, reveal themselves in peculiar purity? Not at all; we see everything as through a fog, blurred and undifferentiated. It is as though everyone who wished to know about America were to try to put himself back in the position of Columbus, at the time when he caught the first dubious glimpse of his supposed India.[2]

Indeed Hume, in trying to find the original data of all meaningful expressions, faces inextricable difficulty in explaining all abstract expressions. The problem of the abstract idea arises as a consequence of a prejudice that every expression ultimately denotes a simple entity – that all words are names of entities. Berkeley and Hume, accepting this premise, had to deal with general words. For they observed rightly that general words neither denote all the members belonging to a class, nor denote a vague image which represents all the members of a class. We do not want, on this occasion, to examine Hume's theory of abstract ideas. Let it suffice to state here that we cannot eliminate general words merely by substituting for them the names of perceptions. We may substitute in some contexts two expressions provided that they are synonymous. Or we may say that if two expressions can do exactly the same job in our language, we may eliminate one in favor of the other. But the fact is that expressions such as "time," "space," "entity," "relation," and "numbers" play different roles in language than the expressions of perceptions.

[1] Frege, *The Foundations*, *op. cit.*, p. VI.
[2] *Ibid.*, p. VIII.

Of course, from the fact that certain concepts are not reducible, let us say, to some naturalistic quality, it does not follow that these concepts denote a non-natural quality – that besides John and Mary, etc., there is such a *thing* as a class of man which the expression "man" denotes. John Wisdom in reference to Moore's discussion of time mentions that:

True, Moore did not *find* a definition [of time], but he showed how it was a mere accident of language that we could not provide a definition and thus remove an uneasy feeling about Time, just as we did when we had the uneasy feeling that, though the class of all men is not to be identified with its members, yet there were not in addition to the facts about men, e.g., that men exist, that all are mortal, facts about the class of men, e.g., that it exists, has members, has members which are mortal.[1]

Let us now turn our attention to some issues concerning the denotation theory. Quine mentions that the term-by-term theory of Hume is an unnecessarily restrictive and even "impossible" criterion of meaning. He writes that: "The idea of defining a symbol in use was, as remarked, an advance over the impossible term-by-term empiricism of Locke and Hume. The statement, rather than the term, came with Frege to be recognized as the unit accountable to an empiricist critique."[2]

Now Frege advises us "never to ask for the meaning of a word in isolation, but only in the context of a proposition."[3]

Frege's advice could be linked up with his discovery that the denotation theory of meaning is deficient even with regard to names. Two names may denote the same object; but it is easy to find a context in which these two names are not replaceable without damaging the meaning of the whole context.

Quine, referring to Frege's recognition that the meaning of words should be looked for in the context of the statement, says that "this emendation would unquestionably have been welcome to Locke and Hume... but historically it had to await an important reorientation in semantics – the reorientation whereby the primary vehicle of meaning came to be seen no longer in the terms but in the statement."[4]

We observed that Hume is not altogether oblivious to contextual considerations. In dealing with complex ideas, Hume reveals his awareness by hinting that to know the meaning of a statement ex-

[1] John Wisdom, *Metaphysics and Verification*, appears in *Philosophy and Psychoanalysis*, p. 72.
[2] W. V. O. Quine, *From a Logical Point of View*, p. 42.
[3] Frege, *The Foundations*, p. X.
[4] Quine, *From a Logical Point of View*, p. 39.

pressing a complex idea, we should know, besides the meaning of its component terms, whether or not these terms are properly used in a specific context. One obvious criterion of misuse is the use of a self-contradictory expression. Hume implies that nonsense may be produced, not only by using words which do not stand for ideas, but also by violating "the custom, which we have acquir'd of attributing certain relations to ideas [which] still follows the words." (T. 23). We find that Hume, in dealing with the expression "I promise" and finding that it is not a name for a "distinct sentiment," does not say that such an expression is meaningless. On the contrary, as we observed, Hume tries hard to discover the proper context in which such expressions are significantly used.

The case of promises, I think, is analogous to the problem of causation. In the analysis of causation Hume provides us with some "rules by which to judge of causes and effects." (T. 173). Concerning these Canons of Induction or rules, he says, they "are form'd on the nature of our understanding, and on our experience of its operations in the judgments we form concerning objects." (T. 149).

In the case of promise, I think the rules which govern the significant use of this expression boil down to the conventions governing its correct use. But in what sense is the canon of induction, or we may ask, the rules for correct usage of promises, a generalization from experience? Hume is not very explicit about this.

We know, nonetheless, one thing about Hume's fundamental rule of the principle of the priority of impressions to ideas; that is, it is neither a pragmatic device nor an *article of inquisition*, as alleged by Reid. The criterion, with all its defects and merits, is a generalization from experience; and I think Quine is quite right in assuming that Hume unquestionably would have welcomed the emendation of his criterion. My judgment rests upon the empirical spirit of Hume which shows itself throughout his works and especially in the final paragraph of Book One of the *Treatise*.

'Tis easier to forbear all examination and enquiry, than to check ourselves in so natural a propensity, and guard against that assurance, which always arises from an exact and full survey of an object. On such an occasion we are apt not only to forget our scepticism, but even our modesty too; and make use of such terms as these, *'tis evident, 'tis certain, 'tis undeniable;* which a due deference to the public ought, perhaps, to prevent. I may have fallen into this fault after the example of others; but I here enter a *caveat* against any objections, which may be offer'd on that head; and declare that such expressions were extorted from me by the present view of the object, and imply no dogmatical spirit, nor conceited idea of my own judgment.... (T. 274).

CHAPTER THREE

The Principle of Analyticity

1. INTRODUCTION

The belief of modern empiricism in some fundamental cleavage between truths which are analytic or grounded in meaning independently of matters of fact, and truths which are synthetic or grounded in fact, was foreshadowed in Hume's distinction drawn in the *Treatise* between relations which are *invariable, depending solely upon ideas,* and relations which *may be changed without any change in ideas ;* and a simpler distinction made in the *Enquiries* between Relations of Ideas and Matters of Fact. Thus, Hume, by offering criteria for analytic truths as well as for meaning, made himself a true precursor of modern empiricism.

To be sure, Hume's criteria for analyticity, as we shall see, are in no way definitive; and I think Hume, by omitting the cumbersome discussion of Philosophical Relation (*Treatise* 14, 60, 69) from the *Enquiries,* and by substituting a new distinction between analytic and synthetic judgments, was aware, at least, of the defect of his former criterion.

Nonetheless, it cannot be denied that Hume's theory on the different kinds of truth, as MacNabb announces, "has become the corner-stone of modern empiricism, and its chief weapon against rationalistic metaphysics."[1]

Quite apart from the issue of the historical importance of Hume's contention, the analytic-synthetic dichotomy itself, for the following reasons, plays a fundamental role in Hume's system:

First: Hume's important distinction between the deductive and inductive sciences, or what he calls Knowledge or "Science strictly so-called," and Probability or "Moral Reasoning," rests upon the contrast between analytic and synthetic judgments, since for him, Knowledge is exclusively conversant with Relations of Ideas, and Probability only with Matters of Fact.

[1] D. G. C. MacNabb, *David Hume: His Theory of Knowledge and Morality,* p. 46.

Second: Hume, while maintaining the principle of phenomenal-ism, endeavors to explain the nature of the deductive sciences with reference to his principle of analyticity. (How successful his endeav-ors are we shall soon see.)

Third: Hume's famous arguments with regard to the denial of necessary connection in the causal axiom or in the bundles of data which constitute, according to him, our personal identity, and also his denial of the logical impossibility of our knowledge of the ex-istence of the external world rest upon the analytic-synthetic dis-tinction.

The analytic judgment, in short, constitutes for Hume the para-digm, against which all other judgments, such as factual, moral, and aesthetic, are examined and declared to be undemonstrable. That is, if we can never know (in the strict sense) that the sun will rise tomorrow, that pleasure is good, or the circle is beautiful, it is because, Hume holds, that the objects of knowledge are only certain specific relations of ideas, and that expressions of such relations are the only propositions subject to demonstration.

The main part of this chapter will be devoted to a full exposition of Hume's criteria of analyticity, as stated in the *Treatise* and in the *Enquiries*. We will then provide an analysis of the criteria. Finally, we shall state and criticize Hume's treatment of logical concepts and his view of logic in general. The positive use of the principle of ana-lyticity in Hume's system will be discussed in detail in the following chapter (The Domain of Deductive Reason).

2. STATEMENT OF THE PRINCIPLE

Hume first classifies all perceptions (impressions and ideas) into simple and complex. "Simple perceptions," he says, "are such as admit of no distinction nor separation. The complex are the con-trary to these, and may be distinguished into parts." (T. 2).

Then he divides complex ideas into relations, modes and sub-stances.

By saying that relations are complex ideas, I think he means that the use of relation-terms presupposes the use of relata and hence ex-pressions of relations are *ipso facto* expressions of complex ideas, and not that relations are themselves ideas with the same ontological status as their components.

After this classification Hume takes note that the term "relation" s used in two different senses. He says that "in common language" the term "relation" is used "for that quality, by which two ideas are connected together in the imagination, and the one naturally introduces the other." (T. 13). The name which Hume gives for such a relation is "natural relation."

Natural relations are habitual, unreflective, associative links between ideas; and "these associations," he says, "are the only links that bind the parts of the universe together or connect us with any person or object exterior to ourselves... these are the only ties of our thoughts, they are really *to us* the cement of the universe and all operations of the mind must, in a great measure, depend upon them."[1] He also says that "wherever the mind constantly and uniformly makes a transition without any reason, it is influenc'd by these relations." (T. 92).

The term "relation," according to Hume, is also used in philosophy "for that particular circumstance, in which, even upon the arbitrary union of two ideas in the fancy, we may think proper to compare them... 'tis only in philosophy, that we extend it to mean any particular subject of comparison, without a connecting principle." (T. 13). Hume calls relation when used in such a broad sense "philosophical relation."

The description of natural relation reminds us of Russell's description of animal inference. Russell writes that "we must bear in mind the distinction between inference as understood in logic, and what may be called 'animal inference.' By 'animal inference' I mean what happens when an occurrence A causes a belief B without any conscious intermediary."[2]

Hume wholly agrees with Russell that there are two kinds of inference, and hence two kinds of reason, though, as we shall see, he sometimes overlooks this distinction in favor of animal inference.

Hume divides philosophical relations into two important classes which we shall call (A) *Relations* and (B) *Relations*.

(A) *Relations* are described as those which "depend entirely on ideas," are "invariable, as long as our ideas remain the same," are "unalterable so long as the ideas continue the same," are "discoverable from mere ideas," (T. 69, 74, 89). He is referring to this class of relations when he uses expressions such as "real relations," "real

[1] Hume, *An Abstract*, p. 32.
[2] Bertrand Russell, *Human Knowledge*, p. 182.

connection," "constant relations," "necessary relation," and "inseparable and inviolable connexion."

The members of the class of (A) *Relations* are the relations of
resemblance, contrariety, degrees of quality, and proportions in
quantity or number. These four relations are "the foundation of
science." (T. 73).

However, of these relations, only proportion of quantity or number is the relation of which we can have demonstrative knowledge.
The others, since they "are discoverable at first sight,... fall more
properly under the province of intuition than demonstration."(T.
70).

(B) *Relations* are described as those which "may be chang'd without any change of ideas," depend "on a hundred different accidents,
which cannot be foreseen by the mind," are "never discoverable
merely from their ideas." Further, he says, "We receive information from experience, and not from any abstract reasoning or reflexion." (T. 69).

The members of the class of (B) *Relations* are identity, relations
of time and place, and causation.

Here, as in his discourse on (A) *Relations*, Hume reasserts that we
only reason about relations which are not discoverable at first sight.
"We ought not to receive as reasoning any of the observations we
may make concerning *identity*, and the *relations* of *time* and *place* ; since
in none of them the mind can go beyond what is immediately present to the senses." (T. 73).

The only member of the class of (B) *Relations* which is the subject
of reasoning is causation; "the only one, that can be trac'd beyond
our senses, and informs us of existences and objects, which we do
not see or feel, is *causation*." (T. 74).

At this point we should mention that Hume's main interest lies
in (B) *Relations* which, according to him, are the foundation of the
empirical sciences, and not in (A) *Relations* which are the subjects of
demonstration and "the objects of knowledge and certainty." Thus
in Part III of Book I which is titled *Of Knowledge And Probability*,
Hume only briefly discusses the important problem of knowledge
strictly so called, leaving the remainder of the chapter to deal with
the main issue of probability and causation. Indeed, Hume's concern with knowledge and with relations embodied in the demonstrative sciences is only negative, as we shall see.

The distinction between the classses of (A) and (B) *Relations* is

urther supplemented by a principle known as Hume's principle
of atomism. Though Hume does not relate this principle to the clas-
ification of relations, he employs it as another means for indentify-
ng ideas associated with (B) *Relations*.
The principle of atomism, like Hume's principle of meaning, is
tated and employed on many occasions in the *Treatise*. The state-
nent of the principle is as follows:

> We have observ'd, that whatever objects are different are distinguishable, and
> that whatever objects are distinguishable are separable by the thought and im-
> gination. And we may here add, that these propositions are equally true in the
> nverse, and that whatever objects are separable are also distinguishable, and that
> vhatever objects are distinguishable are also different. (T. 18).

The principle of atomism is often conjoined with another complementary principle, viz., the principle of conceivability: "*That
whatever the mind clearly conceives includes the idea of possible existence*, or
n other words, *that nothing we imagine is absolutely impossible*." (T. 32).
In the *Enquiries*, Hume drops altogether the discussion of philo-
ophical relations, and with that, the troublesome distinction be-
ween the classes of (A) and (B) *Relations*.
In this book for (A) *Relations* he substitutes simply relations of
deas, and for (B) *Relations* he substitutes a new expression, mat-
ers of fact, and real existence. These new expressions were also
used previously in the *Treatise*.

> Reason is the discovery of truth or falsehood. Truth or falsehood consists in
> n agreement or disagreement either to the *real* relations of ideas, or to *real* ex-
> stence and matter of fact. (T. 458).

> .. the operations of human understanding divide themselves into two kinds, the
> omparing of ideas, and the inferring of matter of fact.... (T. 463).

In the *Enquiries*, Hume begins by dividing "all objects of human
eason or enquiry" into two classes of "relations of ideas, and matters
of fact."
Propositions of the sciences of geometry, algebra, and arithme-
ic, and in short, "every affirmation which is either intuitively or
demonstratively certain" belong to the class of relations of ideas.
Hume gives some examples of such propositions which are demon-
tratively certain.
"*That the square of the hypothenuse is equal to the square of the two sides*,
s a proposition which expresses a relation between these figures.
That three times five is equal to the half of thirty, expresses a relation be-
ween these numbers." (E. 25).

Hume implies that the method of verifying such propositions and "our evidence of their truth" is entirely different from the method of verifying statements expressing matters of fact.

We discover "propositions" expressing relations of ideas

... by the mere operation of thought, without dependence on what is anywhere existent in the universe. Though there never were a circle or triangle in nature, the truths demonstrated by Euclid would for ever retain their certainty and evidence. (E. 25).

Matters of fact propositions, on the other hand,

... are not ascertained in the same manner; nor is our evidence of their truth, however great, of a like nature with the foregoing. The contrary of every matter of fact is still possible; because it can never imply a contradiction, and is conceived by the mind with the same facility and distinctness, as if ever so conformable to reality. *That the sun will not rise to morrow* is no less intelligible a proposition, and implies no more contradiction than the affirmation, *that it will rise*. (E. 26).

After stating the logical characteristics of statements expressing matters of fact, Hume seeks to explain "the nature of that evidence which assures us of any real existence and matter of fact, beyond the present testimony of our senses, on the record of our memory." As a result of this inquiry he finds that "all reasonings concerning matter of fact seem to be founded on the relation of *Cause and Effect*... and that, the knowledge of this relation is not, in any instance, attained by reasoning *a Priori*; but arises entirely from experience." (E. 26-27).

3. AN ANALYSIS OF HUME'S PRINCIPLE

To formulate and systematize Hume's various assertions on the nature of analyticity is indeed a hard task. The main difficulty, I maintain, lies in Hume's attempt to explain logical relations in terms of psychological and thus factual links – and also in his endeavor to describe the different kinds of propositions, without availing himself of the tools of linguistic analysis like proposition, syncategorematical terms and syntactical rules, such as the law of contradiction, which is indispensable to his theory of analyticity.

In the *Treatise*, our difficulty in apprehending the nature of what he calls "invariable relations," which are "discoverable from mere ideas," reaches its highest peak.

In the *Enquiries*, though the distinction between what we call analytic and synthetic statements is expressed in much clearer terms, yet, as Laird maintains, "this tamer view is difficult to reconcile with Hume's phenomenalism."[1]

Let us begin with the *Treatise*. Roughly speaking, we may say that Hume regards as analytic any statement of complex ideas, if the terms expressive of ideas are conjoined by invariable relations, i.e., (*A*) *Relations*.

We may also say that Hume considers as synthetic any statement of complex ideas if the terms expressive of ideas are conjoined by separable relations, i.e., (*B*) *Relations*.

After describing the different nature of analytic and synthetic judgments, it seems that Hume wants to consider a different issue, namely the different methods of verification which we employ when we claim that certain statements are analytic and certain statements are synthetic. This epistemological issue should be sharply separated from the ontological issue concerning the nature of different propositions, though this distinction is blurred in Hume's system.

Hume seems to imply that we can discover two different kinds of analytic as well as two different kinds of synthetic statements. The differentia which marks these classifications is the different methods of verification.

The first kind of analytic statements comprises those whose truth is "discoverable at the first sight" by "mere passive admission of the impressions through the organs of sensation." The specimens which Hume provides of such statements are expressions of complex ideas which are conjoined by relations such as resemblance, contrariety, and degrees of quality.

When any objects *resemble* each other, the resemblance will at first strike the eye, or rather the mind; and seldom requires a second examination.... And tho' it be impossible to judge exactly of the degrees of any quality, such as colour, taste, heat, cold, when the difference betwixt them is very small; yet 'tis easy to decide, that any of them is superior or inferior to another, when their difference is considerable. And this decision we always pronounce at first sight, without any inquiry or reasoning. (T. 70).

Let us suppose that the following statements were uttered by someone:

"My left hand resembles my right hand."

"This shade of green is lighter than that shade of green."

Let us also assume that, for Hume, both of these assertions are analytic of the first type. The question is: Why does Hume consider that the above statements are analytic?

---

[1] John Laird, *Hume's Philosophy of Human Nature*, p. 53.

First, I think he would say that both statements are analytic be-cause any changes in relata may produce changes in relation. That is, if my hands (or even if one of them) undergo a detectable change in respect to their resembling qualities, the statement that "my hands resemble each other in some specific respect" no longer remains true. Likewise, if one of those green shades turns to yellow, it may be no more true to say, "that specific shade of green is lighter than the other shade."

Second, Hume would say that these statements are analytic be-cause they are epistemologically indubitable. He says that "when both the objects are present to the senses along with the relation, we call *this* perception rather than reasoning." (T. 73). Perception, or rather, sense-data statements, being indubitable, are the bases of all empirical sciences. "The only existences, of which we are certain, are perceptions, which being immediately present to us by con-sciousness, command our strongest assent, and are the first foundation of all our conclusions." (T. 212).

This conviction of Hume's is similar to the belief held by some mod-ern epistemologists on the indubitability of sense-data statements. The belief is based on the argument that, when all the facts are pres-ent, there can be no factual mistakes, but only linguistic ones.

The second kind of analytic statements are those whose truth is discoverable by abstract reasoning and demonstration when the "mind can go beyond what is immediately present to the senses, either to discover the real existence or the relations of objects." (T. 73). Hume maintains that only proportions of quantity and number fall into this category.

The second type of analytic judgments is considered by Hume to be the most important, since, according to him, demonstrative rea-soning is possible only when we deal with analytic statements of the second type.

There are also for Hume two distinct types of synthetic judgments. The mark of distinction for these two classes is exactly the same dif-ferentia which separates the two types of analytic judgments.

The first type of synthetic statements are those which contain separable relations, such as identity, the relations of time and place, etc., which are intuitively discoverable without "any exercise of thought."

The second type of synthetic judgments are those which contain separable relations which are not given immediately, and are discoverable by *thought*. "'Tis only *causation*, which produces such a connexion." (T. 73).

Thus Hume holds, in effect, that reason is conversant only with the second type of analytic statements, i.e., proportion in quantity and number, and with the second type of synthetic statements, i.e., statements of cause and effect.

If, in our reasoning, we employ the second type of analytic statements, we may have demonstrative reason (deductive), and if we employ the second type of synthetic statements, we shall have probable reason (inductive).

The classification of relation into classes of (*A*) and (*B*) and the subdivision of these classes into relations which are given to us perceptually and relations which are the subjects of reason are the foundations for Hume's later distinction between the two distinct kinds of reason.

For example, he says that, "All kinds of reasoning consist in nothing but a *comparison*, and a discovery *of those relations, either constant or unconstant*, which two or more objects bear to each other." (T. 73 - i.m.). And then he immediately excludes, from the domain of reasoning, statements expressing relations which are intuitively discoverable.

The same opinion is expressed in the *Enquiry*: "All reasoning may be divided into two kinds, namely, demonstrative reasoning, or that concerning relations of ideas, and moral reasoning, or that concerning matters of fact and existence." (E. 35).

Though in the opening of the *Treatise* Hume makes the fundamental distinction between (*A*) *Relations* and (*B*) *Relations*, only in a few instances does he directly refer to them again. In the *Treatise* he asserts that "if we have really no idea of a power or efficacy in any object, or of any *real connexion* betwixt causes and effects, it will be to little purpose to prove, that an efficacy is necessary in all operations." (T. 168).

Likewise in the *Enquiries* he says:

When we reason *a priori*, and consider merely any object or cause, as it appears to the mind, independent of all observation, it never could suggest to us the notion of any distinct object, such as its effect; much less, show us the *inseparable* and *inviolable connexion* between them. (E. 31 – i.m.).

In the *Treatise* he argues that beasts, though capable of some sort of reasoning, i.e., animal inference, are certainly not capable of discovering (*A*) *Relations* and reasoning deductively.

"Beasts are endow'd with thought and reason as well as men." (T. 176). But, he goes on to say, they "certainly never perceive any *real connexion* among objects. 'Tis therefore by experience they infer one from another." (T. 178 - i.m.).

Not only beasts are incapable of finding real connection, but no man (to be sure, Hume himself) is able to find such connection a-mong distinct perceptions of the mind. "*That the mind never perceives any real connexion among distinct existences...*, did the mind perceive some *real connexion* among them, there wou'd be no difficulty in the case." (T. 636 - i.m.).

We observe that Hume, on many occasions, employs his principle of atomism in order to distinguish analytic from synthetic judgments.

To repeat, the principle of atomism is: "Whatever objects are different are distinguishable, and.... whatever objects are distinguishable are separable by thought and the imagination."

He distinguishes between two kinds of *difference*. "Difference is of two kinds as oppos'd either to identity or resemblance. The first is called a difference of *number;* the other of kind." With this distinction in mind, I interpret Hume's principle to mean that whatever objects are different in kind, are also distinguishable and separable.

Hume does not say that the converse of his principle holds, that whatever objects are not different in kind, are not distinguishable and separable.

In the *Enquiries*, as I shall point out in detail in the subsequent chapter, we find statements which seem to indicate that there are some data which are perfectly similar in kind and thus, perhaps, are not separable from each other.

As the component parts of quantity and number are *entirely similar*, their relations become intricate and involved; and nothing can be more curious, as well as useful, than to trace, by a variety of mediums, their equality or inequality, through their different appearances. *But as all other ideas are clearly distinct and different* from each other, we can never advance farther, by our utmost scrutiny, than to observe this diversity, and, by an obvious reflection, pronounce one thing not to be another. (E. 163 - i.m.).

It is not possible to explicate the meaning of the above polemical statement without understanding at the same time Hume's assertions about the possibility of separating distinct ideas out of the associations or bundles of ideas.

Now Hume provides us with abundant examples of ideas which are different in kind and thus separable from each other. Perhaps, by examining these specimens, we may find out whether there are ideas which constitute an inseparable chain for Hume.

Hume employs his principle of atomism in order to prove that the statement *"whatever begins to exist, must have a cause of existence"* is not analytic and hence is incapable of demonstrative proof. He is convinced that only analytic truths are the objects of demonstration.

Hume argues that in order to show that the above maxim is necessarily true, one should also show that it is logically impossible "that anything can ever begin to exist without some productive principle." (T. 79). Then he states:

... that the latter proposition is utterly incapable of a demonstrative proof, we may satisfy ourselves by considering, that as *all distinct ideas are separable from each other*, and as the ideas of cause and effect are evidently distinct, 'twill be easy for us to conceive any object to be non-existent this moment, and existent the next, without conjoining to it the distinct idea of a cause or productive principle. The *separation*, therefore, of the idea of a cause from that of a beginning of existence, is plainly possible for the imagination; and consequently the *actual separation of these objects is so far possible, that it implies no contradiction nor absurdity; and is therefore incapable of being refuted by any reasoning from mere ideas; without which 'tis impossible to demonstrate the necessity of a cause.* (T. 79–80 – i.m.).

The same conviction is expressed in the *Enquiries*. "The mind can never possibly find *the effect in the supposed cause*, by the most accurate scrutiny and examination. For *the effect is totally different from the cause, and consequently can never be discovered in it.*" (E. 29).

In considering the problem of mental substance, we see that Hume again employs the same principle.

... what we call a *mind*, is nothing but a heap or collection of different perceptions, united together by certain relations.... Now as every perception is distinguishable from another, and may be consider'd as separately existent; it evidently follows, that there is no absurdity in separating any particular perception from the mind. (T. 207).

A very important result follows from the above assertions. If the mind is composed of distinct perceptions, and if there is no logical tie among the bundle of perceptions which we called "self," then there is no absurdity in conceiving that some of these perceptions may continue to exist in the absence of other perceptions.

Thus Hume concludes that "the supposition of the continu'd existence of sensible objects or perceptions involves no contradiction." (T. 208).

In so employing the principle of atomism, Hume rescues himself from the solipsistic predicament, without calling God or any mysterious entity to his aid. He is quite aware that his ingenious argument escaped the attention of his predecessors. Perhaps with an eye to Berkeley's God he makes the following statement:

> ... since all our perceptions are different from each other, and from everything else in the universe, they are also distinct and separable, and may be consider'd as separately existent, and may exist separably, and have no need of anything else to support their existence. (T. 233).

The question what kinds of ideas can be separated by the imagination and what kinds of ideas are incapable of separation leads us to Hume's notion of conceivability.

The principle of atomism is used by Hume to prove that certain complex ideas are separable from each other because they are not connected by any inseparable tie, i.e., (A) Relations.[1] Hume, however, seldom proves his point by showing merely that such relations are absent among certain complex ideas. Instead, he uses the argument that separation of ideas from the bundle is possible, if it is conceivable for these ideas to appear without the others. Thus the principle of atomism, logically is based upon the principle of conceivability.

He maintains in the opening of the Treatise that all simple ideas may be separated by the imagination, and may be united again. We may conjoin the idea of flame with the idea of warmth, as well as with the idea of coolness. But Hume soon modifies this assertion. Though nothing is freer than one's imagination, we cannot conjoin logically incompatible ideas together, nor can we separate logically complementary ideas. In the Treatise he writes: "All objects, which are not contrary, are susceptible of a constant conjunction," (T. 147), and, "Where objects are not contrary, nothing hinders them from having that constant conjunction." (T. 173).

---

[1] The same Principle is used by Hume to show both that all complex ideas which are distinct are separable into parts, and also to prove that we cannot separate ideas of inseparable impressions except by distinction of reason which could be drawn only concerning simple perceptions. Hume employs his principle against Platonism in arguing that "'tis utterly impossible to conceive any quantity or quality, without forming a precise notion of its degree," and "precise length of a line is not different nor distinguishable from the line itself; nor the precise degree of any quantity from the quality."

But, as it is pointed out by commentators, this line of argument breaks down since by distinctions of reason we can separate what is inseparable in reality. Thus Kemp Smith writes: "Now quite evidently he is allowing, *under a new title*, what he has seemed to deny in the earlier parts of the section. By *the direction of attention*, the mind distinguishes what is not actually separable." N. Kemp Smith, *The Philosophy of David Hume*. London, 1941, p. 266.

And in the *Enquiries* he writes: "What never was seen, or heard of, may yet be conceived; nor is any thing beyond the power of thought, except what implies an absolute contradiction." (E. 18).

In the *Abstract* the same idea is expressed. "What implies a contradiction cannot be conceived."

Now Hume, in effect, maintains that it is logically possible for any statement of complex ideas to be true, provided that there is no self-contradiction in such statements. "*That whatever the mind clearly conceives includes the idea of possible existence, or in other words, that nothing we imagine is absolutely impossible.*"[1]

The example which Hume provides for the above assertion is illuminating: "We can form the idea of a golden mountain, and from thence conclude that such a mountain may actually exist. We can form no idea of a mountain without a valley, and therefore regard it as impossible." (T. 32).

Of complex ideas which can never be conceived separately we find other examples. "Every effect necessarily presupposes a cause since effect is a relative term, of which cause is the correlative." The same is true with "every husband must have a wife." And in the *Dialogues*, "We lie under a necessity of always conceiving twice two to be four."

These cases are all examples of analytic statements; though Hume would say that only in the latter case we are confronted with an expression which is really subject to proof and demonstration.

All analytic statements, however, have this peculiar characteristic – that one who believes them to be true is bound under pain of violating the law of contradiction to conceive them in certain inviolable order.

... with regard to propositions, that are prov'd by intuition or demonstration..., the person, who assents, not only conceives the ideas according to the proposition, but is necessarily determin'd to conceive them in that particular manner, either immediately or by the interposition of other ideas. Whatever is absurd is unintelligible; nor is it possible for the imagination to conceive any thing contrary to a demonstration. But as in reasoning from causation, and concerning matters of fact, this absolute necessity cannot take place, and the imagination is free to conceive both sides of the question. (T. 95).

In the *Enquiries*, also, the principle of conceivability in alliance with the notion of contradiction is employed as a criterion for distinction between analytic and synthetic judgments.

---

[1] As we pointed out in Chapter Two, the above maxim is only applicable to complex ideas. Of course each component should be caused by its corresponding impression.

"The contrary of every matter of fact is still possible; because it can never imply a contradiction." (E. 25).

"There is no matter of fact which we believe so firmly that we cannot conceive the contrary." (E. 48).

No negation of a fact can involve a contradiction. The non-existence of any being, without exception, is as clear and distinct an idea as its existence. The proposition, which affirms it not to be, however false, is no less conceivable and intelligible, than that which affirms it to be. The case is different with the sciences, properly so called. Every proposition, which is not true, is there confused and unintelligible. (E. 164).

Hume's general view on analytic-synthetic judgments can be summarized as follows:

The first distinction between analytic-synthetic judgments is made with reference to the different kinds of relations. Any statement expressive of a complex idea is analytic if the components of the complex idea are conjoined by one of the invariable relations, i.e., *(A) Relations*. On the other hand, any statement expressive of a complex idea is synthetic if the components of the complex idea are conjoined by one of the separable relations, i.e., *(B) Relations*.

All relations which hold between ideas are discoverable either intuitively or by demonstration or by causal reasoning.

If we intuitively discover certain relations it is not really our reason but perceptions that we employ in finding them. It is only proportions in quantity and number which are discoverable by demonstration. It is only causal relations which are discoverable by probable reasoning.

The second criterion which Hume employs for distinguishing between analytic-synthetic judgments is the principle of atomism founded on the principle of conceivability, the latter principle, in the final analysis, being explained in terms of the concept of contradiction.

Analytic statements are those which express certain arrangements of ideas which are necessarily linked together. In other words, Hume might say that these ideas, not being different in kind, are not separable from each other. The reason why we are "necessarily determin'd to conceive them in that particular manner" is that to give any different arrangement to such ideas is to commit a contradiction. Thus, analytic statements, if negated, Hume is convinced, are absurd or unintelligible.

Synthetic statements, on the other hand, are those which express certain contingent arrangements of ideas. If we are able to conceive any kind of arrangement of ideas then the statements about these ideas are synthetic. Synthetic statements are perfectly intelligible even though they may be incredible.

Finally, the third distinction between analytic-synthetic judgments is made in the *Enquiries* with a direct reference to the notion of proposition.

All propositions stating matters of fact are synthetic; because the negation of such propositions is conceivable. All propositions of relations of ideas are analytic, because the denial of such statements is inconceivable and the denial is inconceivable because it is self-contradictory.

4. HUME'S EXPLANATION OF LOGICAL CONCEPTS

As we have observed, Hume's explanation of the nature of analytic and synthetic judgments is ultimately based upon the distinction in the *Treatise* between factual and logical relations, and in the *Enquiries* upon the notion of self-contradiction.

Many critics have attacked Hume's general theory of relation on the ground that a statement of complex ideas can not be exhaustively analyzed into its components alone. Obviously, any statement of complex ideas does contain, besides terms which denote ideas, relation terms; and it is contested that Hume did not account for the denotation of such terms. T. H. Green, for example, writes:

"What, then, is the one impression from which the idea of relation is derived? He [Hume] does not attempt to meet this difficulty in its generality...."[1]

Huxley, in considering Hume's difficulty with relations, suggests that he should regard relations as impressions generated by other impressions.

These feelings (succession, similarity, co-existence) are the foundation for everything that we call a relation. They are no more capable of being described than sensations are – they are as little susceptible of analysis into simpler elements – they are ultimate – they must be called *impressions of relation....* They differ from the other impressions, in requiring the pre-existence of at least two of the latter. Though devoid of the slightest resemblance to the other impressions, they are, in a manner, generated by them.[2]

[1] T. H. Green and T. H. Grose (eds.). *The Philosophical Works of David Hume*, Vol. I, p. 174.
[2] Thomas H. Huxley, *Hume, with Helps to the Study of Berkeley*, New York, 1896, pp. 81–82.

To me, however, the greatest problem in Hume's theory of relation lies not in his inability to account for the "impression of relations," but in his attempt to explain logical relations in terms of psychological links of association.

Hume himself, in the *Appendix*, points out his difficulty when explaining the nature of non-formal relations. His explanation indeed makes Huxley's emendation superfluous, but at the same time puts Hume in an embarrassing position with regard to his theory of the nature of the mind. The question which Hume asks himself is:

> But having thus loosen'd all our particular perceptions, when I proceed to explain the principle of connexion, which binds them together,... I am sensible, that my account is very defective.... If perceptions are distinct existences, they form a whole only by being connected together. But no connexions among distinct existences are ever discoverable by human understanding (T. 635).

The connections are not discoverable because there are no observable impressions of relation, i.e., impressions of sensation. However, "we only *feel* a connexion or determination of the thought, to pass from one object to another." (T. 635).

He has already discovered the locus of a non-formal relation, i.e., necessity "in the mind" of the observer and not "in the objects." He maintains that:

> Necessity, then, is the effect of this observation, and is nothing but an internal *impression of the mind*, or a determination to carry our thoughts from one object to another.... Necessity is nothing but that determination of the thought to pass from causes to effects and from effects to causes, according to their experienc'd union. (T. 165–6 – i.m.).

In the face of this analysis there arises a question neglected by Hume and rarely touched upon by his critics. The question is not about the denotation of expressions of non-formal relations, but about the nature of logical connections whose appearance between our loose ideas, according to Hume, makes our mind "necessarily determin'd to conceive in a certain manner." In other words, we may ask: "Having loosen'd all our particular perceptions," how does Hume explain the denotation of those logical connections whose appearance among our perceptions produces necessary connection?

That there are logical relations, such as "inference," "necessity," "equality," apart and distinct from non-formal relations, such as animal "inference," "necessity or determination to pass from causes to effect," etc., Hume is quite confident. But that the status and nature of logical relation is quite dubious in Hume's system is a point that may be asserted without hesitation.

Hume, in the *Enquiries*, questions the nature of inference from past regularities to future regularities. He asks, "What logic, what process of argument secures you against this supposition?" and declares, "I want to learn the foundation of this inference." (E. 38).

We are raising the very same question, not with regard to the nature of inductive reasoning (the main issue for Hume) but with regard to the nature of deductive reasoning, which was never fully explained by him. We are asking ourselves simply, what could Hume mean by such expressions as: "reasoning from *mere ideas;* without which 'tis impossible to demonstrate the necessity of a cause. (T. 80 – i.m.). Such a *connexion* wou'd amount to a demonstration, and wou'd imply the absolute impossibility for the one object not to follow, or to be conceiv'd not to follow upon the other." (T. 162, i.m.).

"Such *an inference wou'd amount to knowledge, and wou'd imply the absolute contradiction and impossibility of conceiving any thing different.* But as all distinct ideas are separable, 'tis evident there can be no impossibility of that kind." (T. 87 – i.m.).

We observe that not only the nature of logical relations is in need of explanation, but also the very nature of the ideas (relata) which are the objects of deductive reasoning. If ideas are considered by Hume to be merely the perceptions of the mind, we may ask, how is it possible to reason deductively from "mere ideas"? For the present we shall postpone our inquiry into the latter issue until we discuss in detail the nature of mathematical objects in the next chapter.

Returning to the problem of relations, we find that Hume, having no recourse to what is called "syntactics"[1] or the theory of the syntactical relations of signs to one another in abstraction from the relations of signs to objects or to interpreters, was forced to give a psychological account of formal relations.

If, as Hume maintains, "All events seem entirely loose and separate. One event follows another; but we never can observe any *tie* between them. They seem *conjoined*, but never *connected*," (E.74), then logical connection, like non-formal connection, cannot be *in*

---

[1] W. Morris, "Foundation of the Theory of Sign," *International Encyclopedia of Unified Science*, Vol. 1, No. 2, p. 13.

the object. Where then can such relations be? The conclusion is inevitable: they too are in the mind of the observer.[1]

Again we find that Hume actually finds the locus of logical necessity, like that of factual necessity, in the mind of the observer

> Thus as the necessity, which makes two times two equal to four, or three angle of a triangle equal to two right ones, lies only in the act of the understanding, by which we consider and compare these ideas; in like manner necessity or power, which unites causes and effects, lies in the determination of the mind to pass from the one to the other. (T. 166).

In the *Dialogues* the same train of thought is expressed:

> It will still be possible for us, at any time, to conceive the non-existence of what we formerly conceived to exist; nor can the mind ever lie under a necessity of supposing any object to remain always in being; in the same manner as we lie under a necessity of always conceiving twice two to be four. The words, therefore *necessary existence*, have no meaning; or, which is the same thing, none that is consistent.[2]

We have already observed that in the *Treatise* he stated that "with regard to propositions, that are prov'd by intuition or demonstration ... the person, who assents, not only conceives the ideas according to the proposition, but is necessarily determin'd to conceive them in that particular manner," since it is not possible for the imagination to conceive anything to the contrary.

But what does Hume mean by the terms "contradiction," "negation," and "the relation of equality between numbers,"[3] which he employs in describing the nature of analytic judgments, or in giving examples of such judgments?

Let us begin with an explanation of "contradiction," in which Hume reaches the height of absurdity. To begin with, Hume maintains that:

> Wherever ideas are adequate representations of objects, the relations, contradictions and agreements of the ideas are all applicable to the objects... that whatever *appears* impossible and contradictory upon the comparison of these ideas, must be *really* impossible and contradictory, without any farther excuse or evasion. (T. 29).

---

[1] Hume indeed populated the mind with entities which for him could not be discovered among his *outward sentiments*. As MacNabb puts it, "... beauty is in the mind of the beholder as virtue in the mind of an approver and necessity in the mind of the inferer." Yet Hume need not do this. From the fact that some terms do not denote an impression of sensation, it does not follow that they denote an impression of reflection. But why should every term denote objects?

[2] David Hume, *Hume's Dialogues*, N. K. Smith, ed., p. 233.

[3] The analysis of the relation of equality will be given in the next chapter in explaining Hume's view on Geometry.

Taking the above assertion as it stands, it seems that all relations, including that of contradiction, could appear among impressions as well as among ideas. The relation of contrariety is one of the philosophical relations which entirely depends on the ideas which are being compared, and is discoverable at first sight. In giving an example of such a relation, Hume writes:

That no two ideas are in themselves contrary, except those of existence and non-existence, which are plainly resembling, as implying both of them an idea of the object; tho' the latter excludes the object from all times and places, in which it is supposed not to exist. (T. 15).

Again,

No one can once doubt but existence and non-existence destroy each other, and are perfectly incompatible and contrary. (T. 70).

He maintains that it is

.. the flattest of all contradictions... for the same thing both to be and not to be. (T. 19).

Hence, we should seek to understand what Hume means by "existence" and "non-existence," "to be and not to be," these being basic notions used by him in explaining the relation of contradiction.

That there is no specific impression of existence, in this Hume is emphatic. "The idea of existence is not deriv'd from any particular impression." (T. 66).

The conclusion, however, is not that "existence" is a meaningless term. Since "existence," though not the name of a particular impression, designates, in a manner of speaking, a property which all our data have in common. "The idea of existence is nothing different from the idea of any object, and that when after the simple conception of any thing we wou'd conceive it as existent, we in reality make no addition to or alteration on our first idea." (T. 94).[1]

Now if "existence" is a family name for all data, what could the

---

[1] In Hume's analysis of existence lies the germ of Kant's distinction between formal and material concepts, and even Russell's theory of description. Kant following Hume, observes clearly that judgment of the form: "something exists" contains only the single concept of that thing (whatever it may be), not two concepts of a *Thing* and *Existence*. This analysis makes us see that existence is a purely formal concept and it should not be treated as if it were a material concept. Russell provides a method for the analysis of descriptive phrases which have no descripta, such as "the most perfect being," or "The golden mountain." Though such phrases may contribute to the meaning of a sentence, neither existence nor subsistance of anything is implied by them.

term "non-existence" refer to? As we observed, Hume previously stated that the idea of non-existence excludes the object from all times and places in which it is supposed not to exist.

We may translate Hume's statements in the following way: To say that "a particular datum does not exist" means "a particular datum never occurred in any time and any place." But then to say that "a particular datum exists" means "a particular datum did occur in some place and time," and does not mean as Hume implies merely "a datum."

This analysis is compatible with Hume's statement in the *Enquiries* that "the non-existence of any being without exception, is as clear and distinct an idea as its existence." (E. 164). In so reading Hume the statement that "no two ideas are in themselves contrary, except of existence and non-existence" is translatable into the following:

To say: "A particular datum P, did occur in such a place and such a time," and to say that "P never occurred in any time and any place" is to say a pair of contradictory statements.

It follows that "contradiction" in the last analysis is defined in terms of "negation." But no account is given of the logical constant negation, which is used in the *Treatise* with reference to the concept of contradiction and in the *Enquiries* with reference to matter of fact statements. Instead, Hume in discussing the subject of relation, gives an explanation of the nature of difference. He says that:

> It might naturally be expected, that I should join *difference* to the other relations. But that I consider rather as a negation of relation, than as any thing real or positive. Difference is of two kinds as oppos'd either to identity or resemblance. The first is called a difference of *number*; the other of *kind*. (T. 15).

But now it seems clear that negation (and hence non-existence) cannot be defined in terms of non-resemblance or the absence of relation; nor may affirmation (and hence existence) be defined in terms of resemblance or the presence of relation. For example, to say that "Socrates is mortal" does not mean that "Socrates resembles mortals" or even "Socrates is related to mortals" and to say that "Socrates is not mortal" is not to say that "Socrates is not related to mortals"; and even if for the sake of argument we take the two latter statements as identical in meaning, we clearly perceive that the negation constant is employed rather than eliminated from our discourse.

I conclude that Hume, despite his ingenuity, failed to explain the relation of contrariety or the relation of contradiction in such terms as incompatibility of existence and non-existence. This defect, in itself, is sufficient to undermine the foundation of his principle of analyticity.

Now, if we neglect the logical difficulty which underlies Hume's principle and take into account the psychological criterion of conceivability which is often used by Hume for the distinction between analytic and synthetic judgments, we will face a new difficulty.

Hume's often repeated assertion that the contrary of matters of fact is conceivable, but the contrary of an analytic statement or a chain of analytic statements (called by him "demonstration") is inconceivable, *prima facie* looks like an empirical statement. It is as if Hume is saying that we cannot in our mind's eye picture an idea of the cube root of sixty-four, which is equal to the half of ten, but we can picture that the sun will not rise tomorrow (his own example in the *Enquiries*).

But we may ask why we are unable to conceive certain arrangements of complex ideas. On this issue Wittgenstein makes an important statement:

He asks, "What does it mean when we say: 'I can't imagine the opposite of this or' 'What would it be like, if it were otherwise?'" He observes that:

...Of course, here "I can't imagine the opposite" doesn't mean: my powers of imagination are unequal to the task. These words are a defence against something whose form makes it look like an empirical proposition, but which is really a grammatical one. But why do we say: "I can't imagine the opposite"? Why not: "I can't imagine the thing itself"?
Example: "Every rod has a length." That means something like: we call something (or *this*) "the length of a rod" – but nothing "the length of a sphere".[1]

Here, in like manner, I maintain that Hume's statements on inconceivability of the opposite or conceivability of certain arrangements of ideas, though they seem like empirical propositions, in fact, are statements concerning syntactical rules which govern natural or conventional languages.

Nonetheless, we should mention that in so far as Hume did not have any theory of propositions (as we shall see in the following section), he could not escape from explaining syntactical rules in psychological terms.

---

[1] Ludwig Wittgenstein, *Philosophical Investigations*, paragraph 251.

5. HUME'S VIEW OF LOGIC

An examination of Hume's maturer notion of analytic-synthetic judgments leads us into an investigation of his view on the nature of judgment and proposition, and this inquiry raises the question: what is Hume's opinion of logic in general?

As we observed, in the *Treatise* the distinction between analytic and synthetic judgment is based upon the nature of certain relations which connect our ideas. But, though Hume sometimes employs the term "proposition," he does not use this term with reference to his theory of relation.

In the *Enquiries*, on the other hand, the distinction between analytic and synthetic judgment is made primarily with reference to propositions and not with reference to the relation which holds between ideas. Here Hume explicitly refers to analytic statements as "*propositions* which are discovered by the mere operation of thought," and to synthetic statements, as "propositions," the negation of which implies no more contradiction than their affirmation. Despite these assertions, the very notion of proposition which is fundamental for syllogistic logic was criticized in the *Treatise*, as we shall see.

There is no doubt that Hume felt a deep-rooted antagonism toward Aristotelian logic which he associates with the philosophy of the Schoolmen; and I think that in this he shares the view of other notable empiricists, such as Bacon and Locke.[1] Hume's criticism of syllogistic logic is a counterpart of his view on what the subject-matter of logic ought to be.

It seems to me that Hume considers logic to be a science analogous to what is called "pragmatics" or the science of "the relation of signs to their interpreters, dealing with all the psychological, biological, and sociological phenomena which occur in the functioning of signs."[2]

For Hume, logic is in part an inquiry into the causal operation of "our reasoning faculty" (philosophical psychology), in part consists of rules which an experimental scientist ought to observe in his search for causal connection (canons of induction), and in part consists of principles which a philosopher ought to accept if he wants to talk sense and not nonsense (principle of meaning). The

[1] Chapter One
[2] C. W. Morris, *op. cit.*

inquiry into the formal relation of terms and propositions (syntactics) is regarded by Hume as trivial and pretended reasoning.

In the introduction to the *Treatise*, Hume writes that "the sole end of logic is to explain the principles and operations of our reasoning faculty, and the nature of our ideas." (T. xix).

In section fifteen of this book, under the heading *Rules by which to judge of causes and effects*, Hume introduces what are called canons of induction. After stating seven rules for judging causes and effects, he goes on to say:

> Here is all the Logic I think proper to employ in my reasoning; and perhaps even this was not very necessary, but might have been supply'd by the natural principles of our understanding. Our scholastic headpieces and logicians shew no such superiority above the mere vulgar in their reason and ability, as to give us any inclination to imitate them in delivering a long system of rules and precepts to direct our judgment, in philosophy. (T. 175).

That logicians have to consider "the principles and operations of our reasoning faculty" or "provide rules by which to judge of causes and effects" or "treat of probabilities" is a belief which Hume repeats throughout his writings.

In *An Abstract*, he writes:

> The celebrated *Monsieur Leibnitz* has observed it to be a defect in the common systems of logic, that they are very copious when they explain the operations of the understanding in the forming of demonstrations, but are too concise when they treat of probabilities, and those other measures of evidence on which life and action entirely depend, and which are our guides even in most of our philosophical speculations. In this censure, he comprehends *the essay on human understanding, La recherche de la vérité and l'art de penser*. The author of the *treatise of human nature* seems to have been sensible of this defect in these philosophers, and has endeavoured, as much as he can, to supply it.[1]

One may add that Hume was indeed too sensible of the defects in the logic of his forerunners, so much so, that he refuses to recognize any place in the domain of reason for demonstrative logic. The first criticism of syllogistic reasoning appears in a footnote in Part III of the *Treatise*. He writes that:

> We may here take occasion to observe a very remarkable error, which being frequently inculcated in the schools, has become a kind of establish'd maxim, and is universally received by all logicians. This error consists in the vulgar division of the acts of understanding, into *conception, judgment* and *reasoning*, and in the definitions we give of them. Conception is defin'd to be the simple survey of one or more ideas: Judgment to be the separating or uniting of different ideas: Reasoning to be the separating or uniting of different ideas by the interposition of others, which show the relation they bear to each other. (T. 96).

[1] An Abstract, *op. cit.*, p. 8.

Hume proceeds to reject this classification on the following grounds:

> ... For *first*, 'tis far from being true, that in every judgment, which we form, we unite two different ideas; since in that proposition, *God is*, or indeed any other, which regards existence, the idea of existence is no distinct idea, which we unite with that of the object, and which is capable of forming a compound idea by the union.
>
> *Secondly*, as we can thus form a proposition, which contains only one idea, so we may exert our reason without employing more than two ideas, and without having recourse to a third to serve as a medium betwixt them. We infer a cause immediately from its effect; and this inference is not only a true species of reasoning, but the strongest of all others. (T. 96–97).

Hume's insight that "existence" is not a logical predicate, though it is used as a grammatical predicate, is no doubt illuminating. But his conclusion that "we can thus form a proposition, which contains only one idea" seems to be a non-sequitur. The expression, "God is," does not mean God. "God" is a proper name and not a proposition. Rather the proposition "God is" is translatable, according to Hume's own analysis of existence, to "there occurs such and such an event, in such and such place and time, and the name of that event is "God." Hume wants to substitute for judgment ("the separating or uniting of different ideas") only "a strong and steady conception of any idea." He maintains that "whether we consider a single object, or several...; the act of the mind exceeds not a simple conception; and the only remarkable difference, which occurs on this occasion, is, when we join belief to the conception, and are perswaded of the truth of which we conceive." (T. 97).

He is telling us, at the same time, that *belief* is not a different idea added to another, but rather "the manner" in which an idea is conceived or "the vivacity of those perceptions."

This substitution will not do. We cannot have a judgment either true or false by merely having a lively idea or ideas. In order to make a judgment, besides expression of ideas, we need logical connections. An idea or ideas believed or disbelieved are neither true nor false; rather what is true or false is the expression of belief, viz., judgment.

Thus Hume was not able to eliminate proposition or judgment in favor of the mere expression of an idea – believed or disbelieved.

Neither did Hume prove that animal inference "is the strongest of all others, and more convincing than when we interpose another idea to connect the two extremes." He only showed that besides deductive inference, there is also such a thing as animal inference and such reasoning is seldom considered by logicians.

The above statement of Hume's is not a casual expression of opinion. Hume's preference for animal inference to logical inference appears everywhere.

In the *Enquiries* he writes:

... that, as this operation of the mind, by which we infer like effects from like causes, and *vice versa*, is so essential to the subsistence of all human creatures, it is not probable, that it could be trusted to *the fallacious deductions* of *our reason*, which is slow in its operations; appears not, in any degree, during the first years of infancy; and at best is, in every age and period of human life, extremely liable to error and mistake. (E. 55 – i.m.).

To do justice to Hume's assertion, it should be noted that if we recognize Hume's criterion of conceivability as a mark for distinction between analytic and synthetic judgment, and also as a criterion for distinguishing demonstrative from non-demonstrative arguments, then we should also admit that inferences without the middle term are more conceivable (in our mind's eye) than inferences which involve logical connections. Since conceivability is taken by Hume often as the ultimate court of appeal which may pass a verdict on what is a demonstrable argument and what is not, it is quite easy to see why he prefers an animal inference to the *fallacious deduction of our reason*, and maintains that "the principal difficulty in the mathematics is the length of inferences and compass of thought, requisite to the forming of any conclusion." (E. 61). (The unhappy consequence of appeal to conceivability will be discussed soon in an investigation of Hume's scepticism with regard to reason.)

The second criticism of demonstrative logic is based on Hume's erroneous assumption that logical demonstration is possible only when the premises of an argument are analytic.

According to Hume, only mathematical statements are really analytic. Therefore, only mathematical statements could be the subject of demonstration.

Now Hume, in finding valid (but non-mathematical) demonstrations, saves his theory by saying that the premises of the argument are not self-evident, and by arguing that if they are self-evident, they are tautologies and hence the whole argument is nothing but a chain of tautologies.

In the *Enquiries*, he refers to Descartes' method which is considered to be "a sovereign preservative against error and precipitate judgment." The Cartesians say, "We must assure ourselves, by a chain of reasoning, deduced from some original principle, which cannot possibly be fallacious or deceitful." But Hume says, "Neither is there any such original principle, which has a prerogative above others, that are self-evident and convincing: or if there were, could we advance a step beyond it?" (E. 150).

The difference between valid arguments which are based on analytic and informative premises, and valid arguments which are grounded on analytic and non-informative premises, could be discovered in a paragraph stated in the *Enquiry*.

> It seems to me, that the only objects of the abstract science or of demonstration are quantity and number, and that all attempts to extend this more perfect species of knowledge beyond these bounds are mere sophistry and illusion.... That *the square of the hypothenuse is equal to the squares of the other two sides*, cannot be known, let the terms be ever so exactly defined, without a train of reasoning and enquiry. But to convince us of this proposition, *that where there is no property, there can be no injustice*, it is only necessary to define the terms, and explain injustice to be a violation of property. This proposition is, indeed, nothing but a more imperfect definition. It is the same case with all those pretended syllogistical reasonings, which may be found in every other branch of learning, except the sciences of quantity and number; and these may safely, I think, be pronounced the only proper objects of knowledge and demonstration. All other enquires of men regard only matter of fact and existence; and these are evidently incapable of demonstration. (E. 163).

Throughout his writings Hume analyzes (in a manner similar to his examination of Locke's argument on property, stated, in part, above) other valid arguments and condemns them as tautologies. The technical term "tautology" is used by Hume in the *Enquiry* (p. 37) where he denies that the conclusion of any inductive argument is either a tautology or a proposition identical with the premises. In the *Treatise* he maintains that the *principium individuationis* is actually boiled down to the proposition that "*an object is the same with itself*," and in making that proposition, "if the idea express'd by the word, *object*, were no ways distinguish'd from that meant by *itself*, we really shou'd mean nothing...." (T.200).

Likewise, he observes that:

> ... in saying, that the idea of an infinitely powerful being is connected with that of every effect, which he wills, we really do no more than assert, that a being, whose volition is connnected with every effect, is connected with every effect; which is an identical proposition, and gives us no insight into the nature of this power of connection." (T. 248).

On the other hand, we find that he argues that geometrical definitions are, in fact, descriptive propositions and not verbal definitions. For if they were merely verbal definition, he reasons, they would be tautologies and non-informative.

'Tis true, mathematicians pretend they give an exact definition of a right line, when they say, *it is the shortest way betwixt two points*. But in the first place, I observe, that this is more properly the discovery of one of the properties of a right line, than a just definition of it. For I ask any one, if upon mention of a right line he thinks not immediately on such a particular appearance, and if 'tis not by accident only that he considers this property?... In common life 'tis establish'd as a maxim, that the straightest way is always the shortest; which wou'd be as absurd as to say, the shortest way is always the shortest, if our idea of a right line was not different from that of the shortest way betwixt two points. (T. 49–50).

In this part we do not want to take issue with Hume concerning his theory of geometrical proofs and axioms. We consider, however, that from Hume's premises that syllogistical reasoning is tautological, and hence non-informative, it does not follow at all that demonstration is only possible in mathematics. It seems that Hume is also wrong in supposing that the validity of an argument has anything to do with the nature of propositions. It is possible to produce valid arguments with analytic propositions as well as with synthetic, categorical, hypothetical and ethical premises.

Finally, the argument that geometrical truths cannot be known "without a train of reasoning and enquiry," whereas syllogistical conclusions can be discovered simply by analysis of terms, does not prove that "reasoning and enquiry" is not essential in logic.

6. SUMMARY OF THE CHAPTER

We may state the conclusions at which we have arrived in this chapter as follows:

First. Hume's distinction between analytic and synthetic judgments, which in the *Treatise* is expressed in terms of the different kinds of relations, i.e., *(A) Relations* and *(B) Relations*, and in the *Enquiries* more effectively in terms of relations of ideas and matters of fact – his recognition that there are two different kinds of judgments and hence that there are two different methods of verification for establishing truth and falsehood of judgments, seems to me, without doubt, an important insight.

Second. Hume's explicit belief that mathematical statements, though they are analytic, are informative, and in this differ from analytic statements, which he implicitly recognizes as tautologies, is a significant belief, even if such opinion is incompatible with most of his other tenets. (See the next chapter.)

Third. What is questionable is not the distinction which he makes between two sorts of judgment, but rather the reasons which he offers for such a distinction.

Fourth. The difficulty with Hume's criteria, in general, I think, is due to his phenomenalism or one may say to his principle of meaning. Of course, a phenomenalist, as such, might maintain that all the terms which constitute a given sentence denote sense-data, and at the same time might argue that the sentence itself is analytic in the sense of requiring no empirical verification in order to be assertable as true. But what makes such a proposition true is a problem which a pure phenomenalist could not easily solve unless he provides, besides semantical rules which explain the relation of terms and data, syntactical rules which govern the relation of linguistic entities to one another. But neither Hume's criterion of conceivability nor his theory of relation is an adequate substitute for syntactical rules and formal relations.

Fifth. The criterion of conceivability itself was explained in terms of the law of contradiction, and the notion of contradiction was explained in terms of psychology and not syntax. In Hume's system, the substitution of psychology for logic is inescapable since there is no place for formal relations in the world of contingent facts, viz., in the world consisting only of loose and separable sense-data connected together in our mind by psychological links of association.

Sixth. Hume was not successful in reducing formal relations such as implication and logical inference, to natural relations. Neither was he able to reduce the logical constants such as affirmation and negation, to resemblance and difference, nor was he successful in substituting steady or loose ideas for true or false judgments.

Seventh. Nonetheless, Hume's mistakes are instructive. Where there are only perceptions, whether "steady or loose," and no propositions, there is as yet no distinction between analytic and synthetic truths. It is indeed futile to attempt to explain the distinction between two kinds of truths without referring directly to the statements which express these truths; and there will be no statements, unless, besides the terms expressive of data, we have logical constants and relation-terms, and rules and procedures which govern the behavior of such terms.

CHAPTER FOUR

Statement of the Problem

1. HISTORICAL SETTING

The polemic of classical empiricists against scholastic and rationalistic metaphysics was an endeavor to prove that the only avenue to the kingdom of knowledge is sensory experience. This general conviction has been expressed in a variety of ways up to the present time.

John Locke tells us that in experience, "*All* our knowledge is founded; and from that it ultimately derives itself."[1] George Berkeley reveals that "language and knowledge are *all* about ideas, words stand for nothing else,"[2] that there is "no reasoning about things whereof we have no idea"[3] (ideas are of "sensible qualities"), and David Hume informs us "*that all our ideas are cop'yd from our impressions,*" (T. 72), that "*all the materials of thinking* are derived either from our outward or inward sentiment." (E. 19 - i.m.).

The contemporary philosopher Quine calls the belief that all knowledge is based on experience, "The dogma of reductionism." According to Quine, this is a belief "that each meaningful statement is equivalent to some logical construction upon terms which refer to immediate experience."[4] Quine declares that both classical and modern empiricists have been conditioned by the same conviction. He says,

---

[1] John Locke, *Essay Concerning Human Understanding*, Bk. II, Chap. I, Sec. 1. A. C. Fraser's edition, Oxford Press (italics mine).

[2] George Berkeley, *The Works of George Berkeley, Philosophical Commentaries*, edited by A. A. Luce and T. E. Jessop, p. 39 (italics mine).

[3] *Ibid.*, p. 42.

[4] W. V. Quine, *From a Logical Point of View*, Harvard University Press, 1953. Article, "Two Dogmas of Empiricism," p. 38.

Radical reductionism in one form or another well antedates the verification
theory of meaning explicitly so called. Thus Locke and Hume held that every
idea must either originate directly in sense experience or else be compounded of
ideas thus originating... we might rephrase this doctrine in semantical jargon by
saying that a term, to be significant at all, must be either a name of a sense datum
or a compound of such names or an abbreviation of such a compound.[1]

To establish the general conviction that all knowledge is derived
from experience, the classical empiricists used the retrospective
method of inquiry. Locke describes the retrospective method of
inquiry as the *"historical, plain* method."[2]

The historical, plain method is simply a procedure that one may
adopt in order to establish the evidence for one's own belief. It is
assumed that the safest way to establish the evidence for one's own
belief, or we may say, the significance for one's own assertion, is to
look back to the source of one's own idea.

The retrospective method used by the classical empiricists is private
and backward, rather than public and predictive. In recommending
this private method of inquiry, the classical empiricists had taken for
granted the Cartesian belief that one's own mind and its furniture
are indubitable, whereas the rest of our beliefs were subject to doubt
and uncertainty.

Locke claims that by using this historical method we can know
the scope and the limit of human knowledge. He says that, "by this
inquiry into the nature of the understanding, I can discover the
powers thereof; how far they reach; to what things they are in any
degree proportionate; and where they fail us."[3]

Hume tells us that this kind of investigation may lead us to discover "the extent and force of human understanding" and "the
proper province of human reason." (E. 12).

The empiricists' main purpose in using the retrospective method
was to free mankind from fruitless metaphysical speculation. Locke
says that his historical method "may be of use to prevail with the busy
mind of man to be more cautious in meddling with things exceeding
its comprehension; to stop when it is at the utmost extent of its tether;
and to sit down in a quiet ignorance of those things, which, upon
examination, are found to be beyond the reach of our capacities."[4]

More emphatically, Hume claims that, "The *only method* of freeing
learning, at once, from these abstruse questions, is to enquire seri-

---

[1] *Ibid.*
[2] John Locke, *op. cit.*, Bk. I, Chap. 1, Par. 2, 4.
[3] Locke, *op. cit.*, Bk. I, Chap. 1, par. 2, 4.
[4] *Ibid.*

ously into the nature of human understanding and show, from an exact analysis of its powers and capacity, that it is by no means fitted for such remote and abstruse subjects." (E. 12 – i.m.)

Historically, the attempt to destroy the schoolmen's false pretensions of knowledge and the endeavor to question the truth of the basic assumptions of the rationalists' synoptic systems via the Baconian method of purification of the mind from the idols (via negativa), or the Lockian *historical plain method*, were conditioned by advances made in the field of the experimental sciences. The rise of the experimental sciences went hand in hand with the empiricists' emphasis upon experience, rather than on speculation, and upon the use of inductive method rather than on the employment of deduction from seemingly self-evident principles.

However, the classical empiricists, while charmed by the new method of the experimental sciences, in their attempt to combat the speculative philosophies failed to give a complete account of the nature of Knowledge traditionally so-called. While the empirical sciences were justly exalted, the demonstrative sciences were unwisely linked with sensory perception, and thereby were deprived of their ideal exactitude.

In their admirable endeavor to establish an empirical basis for knowledge, classical empiricists displayed an undue hostility toward the demonstrative sciences. This attitude was taken by the forefather of the empiricists, Francis Bacon, and was echoed throughout by Locke, Berkeley, Hume and Mill. Bacon, according to Russell,[1] not only despised the syllogism, but undervalued mathematics, presumably as being insufficiently experimental.

In *The New Organon*, Bacon, after complaining that "in ordinary logic all work is spent upon the syllogism," goes on to say, "I on the contrary reject demonstration by syllogism, as acting too confusedly and letting nature slip out of its hands.... The syllogism consists of propositions, propositions of words; and words are the tokens and signs of notions. Now if the very notions of the mind (which are the soul of words and the basis of the whole structure) be improperly and overhastily abstracted from facts, vague, not sufficiently definite, faulty in short in many ways, the whole edifice tumbles. I therefore reject the syllogism."[2]

---

[1] Bertrand Russell, *A History of Western Philosophy*, New York, 1945, p. 543.
[2] Francis Bacon, *The Philosophical Work of Francis Bacon*, ed. John M. Robertson, London, 1905, p. 249.

Locke declares that the principles of logic are *not sacrosanct, innate* and *eternal* truths. He ponders whether the syllogism is *the proper instrument of reason* and the most useful way of reasoning, and he answers that it is neither. He further says no one "makes syllogisms in reasoning within himself. God has not been so sparing to men to make them barely two-legged creatures, and left it to Aristotle to make them rational."[1]

Berkeley's hostility toward pure mathematics is reflected in his famous statements: "Folly of the mathematicians to despise the senses." "The Mathematicians think there are insensible lines, ... We Irishmen can conceive no such lines." "I'll not admire the Mathematicians ... I am but one of common sense." ...[2]

Hume in the *Enquiries* refers to syllogistic reasoning as "pretended and useless," and in the *Treatise* deprecates the activities of logicians where he says, "Our scholastic headpieces and logicians shew no ... superiority above the mere vulgar in their reason and ability, as to give us any inclination to imitate them in delivering a long system of rules and precepts to direct our judgment, in philosophy." (T. 175).

Mill believes that deduction is merely *apparent inference*, and that syllogistic reasoning is "not really entitled to be called reasoning at all."[3]

This general attitude of hostility toward the demonstrative sciences could be explained partly by observing that the rationalists often attempted to construct synoptic systems on the basis of some self-evident principles and in doing so, often neglected and even sacrificed matters of experience for the mere sake of consistency; and partly by observing that many philosophers, on the basis that mathematical concepts are independent of experience, argued that their metaphysical notions are likewise of such "refin'd and spiritual nature." Indeed, this explanation was offered by Hume himself. He says, "'Tis usual with mathematicians, to pretend that, those ideas, which are their objects, are of so refin'd and spiritual a nature...."

Hume goes on to explain why this is an appealing theory. "'Tis easy to see, why philosophers are so fond of this notion of some spiritual and refin'd perceptions; since by that means they cover many of their absurdities, and may refuse to submit to the decisions of clear ideas, by appealing to such as are obscure and uncertain." (T. 72).

---

[1] Locke, *op. cit.*, Book IV, Chap. 17, p. 4.
[2] Berkeley, *op. cit.*, *Philosophical Commentaries*, Par. 393 and 368.
[3] R. Jackson, *An Examination of Deductive Logic of John Stuart Mill*, Oxford University Press, 1941, p. 192.

It is noteworthy that Kant, in contradistinction to Hume, thought
(as we shall see later) that metaphysics could be saved by being in
"the good company of mathematics."[1] He criticizes Hume on the
ground that had Hume fully realized the bearing of his general
conviction, he would have recognized that "the blows intended for
metaphysics would certainly have also fallen on mathematics," but
this, he goes on to say, "was not and could not be his [Hume's] intention."[2]

The important point is that both Hume and Kant thought that
the *a priori* nature of mathematics might provide a support to the
a priori notions of metaphysics. On this assumption some empiricists
sought to establish that mathematics is not *a priori* (or if it is *a priori*,
only because it is tautology) and thus it could not be an ally to metaphysics, while some non- empiricists, like Kant, tried hard to defend
metaphysics.

Finally, this general attitude of hostility toward the demonstrative
sciences may also be explained by recalling that most empiricists
did not have a thorough knowledge of mathematics, whereas their
opponents had a better understanding of the demonstrative sciences.

2. THE EMPIRICISTS' DILEMMA

Having expounded the general principle that all knowledge is derived from experience, or in the vernacular of the semanticists, that all
meaningful words either refer to immediate experience or are definable in terms of other words which themselves refer to immediate experience, the empiricists were faced, at the outset, with the problem
of accounting for the derivation of non-sensory concepts.

The theory that all ideas are of "sensible qualities," such as Berkeley's, or the belief that it is impossible to understand any idea without tracing it to its primary impression, such as Hume's, inevi-
tably seemed to make a puzzle out of sentences like those about numbers and relations which are not used to ascribe qualities. Either
mathematical and logical concepts enjoy a status other than that en-
joyed by the data of the senses, or we have to force all non-sensory
concepts into the pigeon-hole of sense-data. Either mathematical
and logical statements are of a different nature than the statements

---

[1] Immanuel Kant, *Prolegomena to Any Future Metaphysics*, translated by P. G. Lucas,
Manchester University Press, 1953, p. 22.
[2] *Ibid.*

which express matters of fact and there is a fundamental cleavage between analytic and synthetic statements, or all statements are the reports of experience.

Granted that the principles of logic, as Locke insists, *are not sacrosanct, innate and eternal truths,* and conceding to Hume that the rules and precepts devised by "our scholastic headpieces and logicians" are by themselves useless in discovery of matters of fact, we ask: how could our Friends of the Senses (to alter Plato's parable) give a true account of the meaning of the non-sensory concepts and the status of demonstrative sciences?

3. A BRIEF COMPARISON

A brief comparison between the theories of some of the rationalist and empiricist philosophers perhaps can make the nature of the problem more explicit. There are at least three different positions concerning the meaning and the status of the mathematical sciences which have been taken by philosophers. We call the position taken by Plato, Leibniz and Frege (in *The Foundations of Arithmetic*) *The Platonic Position.*[1] We take Berkeley's stand on this issue to represent roughly *The Formalist Position*; and we let Mill's theory stand for *The Phenomenalist Position.*

Plato

Without pretending to provide a detailed account of Plato's position, I shall try to present in an outline form Plato's view, as developed in the *Phaedo* and the *Republic.*

Phaedo and the Republic

The passage in the *Phaedo*[2] which is relevant to our inquiry begins by Socrates' suggestion that recollection "may be derived from things either like or unlike." That is, either we may recollect by resemblance, like seeing a picture of Simmias leads us to remember

---

[1] This view is also attributed to Gödel. Nagel writes: "Platonic realism takes the view that mathematics does not create or invent its "objects," but discovers them as Columbus discovered America ... Gödel appears to hold a similar view when he says, 'classes and concepts may ... be conceived as real objects ... existing independently of our definitions and constructions. It seems to me that the assumption of such objects is quite as legitimate as the assumption of physical bodies and there is quite as much reason to believe in their existence.'" Ernest Nagel and James Newman, *Gödel's Proof,* New York University Press, 1958, p. 99.

[2] Plato, *The Dialogues of Plato,* translated by B. Jowett, Volume One, *Phaedo,* pp. 73–74.

Simmias, or we may recollect by contiguity, as seeing a lyre leads us to remember its owner. When we recollect by resemblance, we may want to note whether the thing perceived falls short of that of which it reminds us. Now by observing equal pieces of wood, stones, etc., we recollect the idea of equality itself. Hence, Socrates maintains that there is such a thing as equality itself which is not given to us by observing objects, since the observed equals sometimes appear equal to one person and not to another; but equals themselves can never be unequal.

In this way, Plato suggests that there is a difference between the applied notion of equality and the pure definition of equality which is hypostatised by him and called "Absolute equality." He also wants to show that we are aware of Absolute equality by pure intellectual insight, and not by counting heads and measuring lots.

According to David Ross, "Perfect particular instances of an idea are here (in the *Phaedo*) distinguished both from imperfect sensible particulars and from the idea itself; this is important as the earliest hint of belief in mathematical entities, as something intermediate between ideas and sensible particulars."[1]

In the *Republic*, through the *Simile of the Divided Line*, Plato locates the mathematical objects in the realm of the intelligible world. Though mathematical objects are distinct from sensible objects and we can discover them, not by observation, but by *Thought*, in Plato's hierarchy they are not as perfect as pure ideas.

Aristotle attributes the very same view to Plato. He reports that between sensible objects and the ideas Plato placed "things mathematical," which differed from sensibles in being eternal and unmoved, but differed again from the ideas in that there can be many mathematical objects of the same kind, while the idea is one only; e.g. the idea of triangle is one, but there may be any number of mathematical triangles as of visible triangles, namely the perfect triangles of which the visible triangles are imperfect copies.[2]

In the *Republic* Plato again makes a sharp distinction between what we call pure and applied geometry. Socrates says:

... you know that they [those who occupy themselves with geometries and calculations and the like] make use of visible figures and argue about them, but in doing so they are not thinking of these figures but of the things which they represent; thus it is the absolute square and the absolute diameter which is the object of their argument, not the diameter which they draw; and similarly, the things

[1] David Ross, *Plato's Theory of Ideas*, Oxford, 1951, p. 23.
[2] T. L. Heath, *A History of Greek Mathematics*, p. 288.

which they actually model or draw, and which may also have their images in shadows or in water, are themselves in turn used as images, the object of the inquirer being to see their absolute counterparts which cannot be seen otherwise than by thought.[1]

Thus we conclude that Plato first makes a full distinction between pure and applied mathematical concepts, and secondly maintains that we can have knowledge strictly so-called about mathematical objects; that is, the statements exhibiting mathematical relations are necessary and universal. Thirdly, he assumes that this sort of knowledge is not derived from experience, but rather is gained by reason. How this kind of knowledge is attained by reason he does not say, except that in the *Phaedo* and the *Meno* there is a hint that this kind of knowledge is gained by the soul recollecting ideas intuited in the Realm of Being.

Leibniz

For Leibniz, the *plain, historical method* of Locke can not lead us to understand the meaning of mathematical entities. He says that "the question here does not concern the history of our discoveries, which is different in different men, but the connection and natural order of truths, which is always the same."[2] Concerning the question: how the proposition made upon a subject can have real truth, if this subject, i.e., the Euclidian triangle, does not exist, he says, "The fact is that the truth is only conditional, that in case the subject ever exists, it will be found such."[3]

He holds that the necessary truths, such as are found in arithmetic, must have principles whose proof does not depend on examples, and therefore not on the evidence of the senses; though doubtless without the senses it would have occurred to no one to think of them. For him "the whole of arithmetic is innate and is in virtual fashion in us."[4]

The question of what Leibniz really meant by "innate" is controversial. For our purpose, it is enough to give his own definition. He

[1] Plato, *Republic*, VI (S1OC–E), in Jowett (ed.), *op. cit.*
"Indeed Plato distinguishes sharply between, e.g., one physical apple and the Form of Oneness. He did not regard a physical thing as an instance of the Form of Oneness nor did he regard the network of logical relations involving the inexact concept 'physical unite' as isomorphous with the network of logical relations involving the exact Form 'Oneness.' (His term μέθεξις) excludes both instaniation and isomorphism." S. Körner, "On the Nature of Pure And Applied Mathematics," *Ratio*, Vol. II, No. 1.
[2] Leibniz, *New Essays, Concerning Human Understanding*, Langley edition, Open Court, 1916, p. 470.
[3] Leibniz, *op. cit.*, p. 516.
[4] Leibniz, *op. cit.*, Erdmann Edition, pp. 208–212.

says, "It is not true that everything a man learns is not innate. The truths of number are in us and still they are learned."[1] Again he asserts that "... it is incontestible that the senses do not suffice to show their necessity, and that thus the mind has a disposition (active as well as passive) to draw them itself from its own depths; the senses are necessary to give it the occasion and attention for this, and to carry on to some rather than to others."[2] He goes on to say that, "We can then make for ourselves these sciences (arithmetic and geometry) in our study, and even with closed eyes, without learning through sight or even through touch the truths which we need, although it is true that we would not consider the ideas in question if we had never seen or touched anything."[3]

However, the problem of the ontological status of mathematical concepts (mathematical concepts are "essences" and "possibilities" distinct from physical entities) was a bothersome problem for Leibniz. Leibniz himself faces the question, and then attempts to provide an answer. It is questioned, he says, "if no mind existed, what then would become of the real ground of this certainty of the eternal truths?" This leads us, he says, "finally to the ultimate ground of truths, viz: to that Supreme and Universal Mind, which cannot fail to exist, whose understanding, to speak truly, is the region of eternal truths, ..."[4]

As a sequel to Leibniz, a word about Frege may not be out of place. In the book, *The Foundations of Arithmetic*, in line with Leibniz, Frege distinguishes between the historical origin of mathematical concepts, the psychological origin, and the ultimate ground upon which mathematical reasoning is built.

First, he argues that a history of such concepts does not provide us with their meaning. "Do the concepts, as we approach their supposed sources, reveal themselves in peculiar purity? Not at all; we see everything as through a fog, blurred and undifferentiated. It is as though everyone who wished to know about America were to try to put himself back in the position of Columbus, at the time when he caught the first dubious glimpse of his supposed India."[5]

Then, he argues that the meaning of mathematical concepts could not be exhausted by reference to our mental images. We associate

---

[1] Leibniz, *op. cit.*, Erdmann Edition, pp. 208–212.
[2] Leibniz, *op. cit.*, Langley Edition, p. 78.
[3] *Ibid.*
[4] Leibniz, *op. cit.*, Langley edition, p. 516.
[5] Frege, *The Foundation of Arithmetic*, Austin Translation, Oxford, 1950, VII, VIII.

different mental pictures with numerals, such as "hundred." These various mental pictures are accidental to the meaning of "hundred." When we speak of "the number one" we indicate by means of the definite article a definite and unique object. There are no diverse numbers one, but only one.[1]

Therefore, according to Frege, the description of the historical and psychological origin of our ideas does not exhaust the meaning of numbers.

On the constructive side Frege defines numbers in terms of the logical notion of classes which are assigned to concepts. Classes, for him, are not fictitious, but are objective without being sensible.

Berkeley

Berkeley, being in some way a more consistent empiricist than his predecessor Locke (who, though claiming that all knowledge is founded in experience and ultimately derives from it, still unequivocally admitted self-evident propositions "instructive" as distinguished from "trifling") tried hard to account for the meaning of mathematical concepts without violating his principle that language and knowledge are all about ideas and ideas are of "sensible qualities."

He admits that numbers are not qualities of objects. "It ought to be considered that number... is nothing fixed and settled, really existing in things themselves ... we call a window one, a chimney one, and yet a house in which there are many windows and many chimneys, hath an equal right to be called one, and many houses go to the making of one city."[2]

From this observation Berkeley concludes that since numbers are not properties of things, they are "entirely the creature of the mind considering either an idea by itself, or any combination of ideas to which it gives one name and so makes it pass for a unit. According as the mind variously combines its ideas, the unit varies; and as the unit, so the number, which is only a collection of units, doth also vary."[3]

Berkeley rejects vehemently the Platonic Position. He insists that there are no ideas of number *in abstract* denoted by the numeral names and figures.[4] "Number" he says, "is visibly relative, and depen-

---

[1] Frege, *op. cit.*, pp. 48–49.
[2] Berkeley, *A Theory of Vision*, Par. 109.
[3] Berkeley, *op. cit.*, Par. 109.
[4] Berkeley, *Principles of Human Knowledge*, Par. (E. 120).

dent on men's understanding that it is a strange thing how any one
should give it an absolute existence without the mind."[1] For him the
theory which regards numerals as names of elusive abstract things is
both superfluous and dangerous. The danger lies in that some mathematicians, excited with the idea that they are exploring the secrets
of some high non-empirical realm, may "dream of *mighty mysteries*
involved in numbers, and may even attempt the explication of natural things by them."[2]

The positive part of Berkeley's theory is as follows:

First, apart from sensible objects, there are signs "made to signify
... some one thing or whatever kind they had occasion to reckon."
That "theorems concerning numbers are, in reality, conversant a-
bout no object distinct from particular numerable things; except
only names and characters, which originally came to be considered
on no other account but their being *signs*, or capable to represent
aptly whatever particular things men had need to compute."[3]

Second, the system of signs then becomes elaborated into a conventional notion, and rules are found for "computing in signs."

Third, Berkeley was aware of the difference between pure and applied mathematics. In pure mathematics we "regard not the things
but the signs."[4] The exactness of mathematical demonstration is due
to the fact that we deal with pure signs and arbitrary rules." The
reason why we can demonstrate so well about signs is that they are
perfectly arbitrary and in our power, made at pleasure."[5]

Fourth, algebra being doubly removed from things is more trifling. "Algebraic Species or letters are denominations of Denomination"[6] letters representing numerals and numerals representing
things. He insists that mathematical reasoning becomes "jejune and
trifling" if we have in mind no practical problem.

John Stuart Mill

Mill's views concerning mathematics, which were much ridiculed
by Frege as "gingerbread arithmetic," are the logical consequences
of his strict adherence to the empiricists' criterion of meaning.

He rejects both Platonic and Formalist positions. To him there are

[1] *Ibid.*, Par. (E. 12), Par. (E. 119).
[2] *Ibid.*
[3] Berkeley, *op. cit.*, Par. 122.
[4] Berkeley, *op. cit.*, Par. 12, Par. 119.
[5] Berkeley, *Philosophical Commentaries*, Luce and Jessop, Par. 732.
[6] *Ibid.*

no numbers in the abstract. "All numbers," he says, "must be numbers of something. There are no such things as numbers in the abstract. Ten must mean ten bodies, or ten sounds...."[1] He also rejects formalism by declaring that it seems to him impossible to regard such statements as "2 + 1 = 3" as merely "a statement that mankind has agreed to use the name *three* as a sign exactly equivalent to two and one."[2] According to him the formalists' theory does not explain the applications of arithmetic and algebra. He says, "The doctrine that we can discover facts, detect the hidden processes of nature, by an artful manipulation of language, is so contrary to common sense, that a person must have made some advances in philosophy to believe it."[3]

Mill's positive theory is as follows:

First: The axioms of arithmetic and geometry are laws of nature known to us by experience. Though it is possible to reduce arithmetic to some axioms (in fact he tried to prove the formula $5 + 2 = 7$ on the principle that "whatever is made up of parts, is made up of parts of those parts") he also informs us that the axioms and definitions of arithmetic are not definitions in the logical sense; not only do they fix the meaning of a term, but they also assert along with it an observed matter of fact. The only observed matter of fact which Mill refers to is the so-called fact which is supposed to be relevant to the definition of the number 3. This fact consists in this, that collections of objects exist which, while they impress the senses thus, $^o_o{}^o$, may be separated into two parts, thus, oo o.[4]

Second: In order to justify himself in calling arithmetical truths "laws of nature," Mill attributes to them a sense which they do not bear. For example, he holds that the identity $1 = 1$ could be false, on the ground that a one-pound weight does not always weigh precisely the same as another.[5] (Let us recall that from the very same observation Plato deduced a different conclusion.)

Third: Mill concludes that "the science of number is thus no exception to the conclusion we previously arrived at, that the processes even of the deductive sciences, are altogether inductive, and that their first principles are generalizations from experience."[6]

---

[1] John Stuart Mill, *A System of Logic*, Eighth Edition, 1872, Vol. I, p. 293.
[2] *Ibid.*
[3] *Ibid.*, p. 292.
[4] Frege, *op. cit.*, pp. 9–13.
[5] *Ibid.*
[6] Mill, *op. cit.*, p. 298.

Fourth: Concerning geometry, Mill holds that the truths of geometry are never precise, certain and necessary, because the definitions of geometry can not be taken literally. The axioms of geometry, like those of arithmetic, are generalizations from observation. Mill is quite aware that this theory is controversial. He says, "This opinion runs counter to a scientific prejudice of long standing and great strength, and there is probably no proposition enunciated in this book for which a more unfavourable reception is to be expected."[1]

Fifth: Concerning syllogistic logic, Mill maintains that it is "not really entitled to be called reasoning at all."[2] For him "deductive reasoning is merely apparent inference, because the assertion of the conclusion is the assertion of premises, but the premises and the axioms of deductive reasoning are real propositions, that is, they are inductive generalizations."[3]

4. THE MAIN ISSUE

In view of such conflicting opinions with regard to the nature of non-sensory concepts and the status of the fundamental principles of the deductive sciences, an analysis of Hume's theory of demonstrative reasoning is of the utmost importance.

The significance of Hume's position lies in the fact that he, in Russell's words, "shrank from nothing in the pursuit of theoretical consistency" and unlike many of his predecessors did not "accept comfortable inconsistencies."[4]

Where Locke admits self-evident instructive propositions, for Hume "neither is there any such original principle, which has a prerogative above others, that are self evident and convincing: or if there were, could we advance a step beyond it." (E. 150).

Where Berkeley, seeing that numbers and relations are not qualities of objects, concludes that they are arbitrary creatures of his "dubious" Mind; Hume denies the arbitrariness of "the science of quantity and numbers." For him "all pretended syllogistical reasonings" are mere verbal definitions, "except the sciences of quantity and number." (E. 163).

But though, for Hume, the objects of the science of quantity and number, are not empty definitions, they are neither Platonic objects of

---

[1] *Ibid.*, pp. 209, 266.
[2] *Ibid.*
[3] Jackson, *op. cit.*, pp. 191–192.
[4] Russell, *op. cit.*, p. 672.

pure reason. "'Tis usual with mathematicians," Hume says, "to pretend, that those ideas, which are their objects, are of so refin'd and spiritual a nature, that they fall not under the conception of the fancy, but must be comprehended by a pure and intellectual view, of which the superior faculties of the soul are alone capable.... But to destroy this artifice, we need but reflect on that principle so oft insisted on, *that all our ideas are cop'yd from our impressions.*" (T. 72).

At this point we may ask: Having no recourse to Plato's intelligible realm or Leibniz's *supreme being* and *universal mind* to furnish them with the *eternal truths* of reason, how then does Hume, the consistent empiricist, give an account of the nature of the demonstrative sciences, i.e., logic, arithmetic and geometry?

Hume's account of what traditionally is called Knowledge, is in no way clear and explicit. Indeed, the vagueness of Hume's position in this domain gave occasion to Kant's critical remarks, that had Hume fully realized the bearing of his main teaching upon his theory of mathematical science, he would have hesitated to carry through his principle. According to Kant, Hume's problem was to question the nature of the causal axiom (everything which happens has its cause). Hume realized that the statement of the principle is neither *a priori* nor synthetic. But Hume did not sufficiently universalize his problem. Had he done so, he would have recognized that not only the inductive sciences could not be justified but also the pure mathematical sciences whose *a priori* nature he had rightly admitted.

In the *Critique of Pure Reason*, Kant writes:

> David Hume, who among all philosophers approached nearest to that problem (how are synthetical judgments *a priori* possible? and the problem of distinction between analytic and synthetical judgments), though he was far from conceiving it with sufficient definiteness and universality, confining his attention only to the synthetical proposition of the connection of an effect with its causes (*principium causalitatis*), arrived at the conclusion that such a proposition *a priori* is entirely impossible. According to his conclusions, everything which we call metaphysic would turn out to be a mere delusion of reason, fancying that it knows by itself what in reality is only borrowed from experience, and has assumed by mere habit the appearance of necessity. *If he had grasped our problem in all its universality, he would never have thought of an assertion which destroys all pure philosophy, because he would have perceived that, according to his argument, no pure mathematical science was possible either, on account of its certainly containing synthetical propositions a priori; and from such an assertion his good sense would probably have saved him.*[1]

Kant, in the *Critique*, concludes that the empirical position of

[1] Kant, *Critique of Pure Reason*, translated by Max Muller, London, 1949, p. 723–724 (italics mine).

Hume is incompatible with the necessity and universality of the mathematical sciences. "This empirical deduction, which was adopted by both philosophers (Locke and Hume) cannot be reconciled with the reality of our scientific knowledge a priori, namely pure mathematics ...."[1]

In the *Prolegomena* Kant asserts that Hume considers seriously the field of *a priori* knowledge, as a good philosopher ought to do. But he mistakenly separates the whole field of pure mathematics from the rest of the domain of *a priori* knowledge, on the ground that pure mathematics merely contains analytic propositions and rests upon the principle of contradiction alone. According to Kant, Hume's mistake lies in his lack of realization that statements of mathematics, like the principle of causality, are both *a priori* and synthetic.

Now in this he [Hume] made a very great mistake, which clearly had injurious consequences for his comprehension as a whole. For if he had not done this he would have enlarged his question about the origin of our synthetic judgments far beyond his metaphysical concept of causality, and would have extended it to include the possibility of mathematics *a priori; for he would have had to take mathematics as also being synthetic.* But he would then never have been able to ground his metaphysical proposition on mere experience, because *otherwise he would also have submitted the axioms of pure mathematics to experience; and he had too much insight to do this.* The good company into which metaphysics would then have been introduced would have saved it from the danger of vile maltreatment, for the blows intended for metaphysics would certainly have also fallen on mathematics which was not and could not be his intention; and so the sagacious man would have been drawn into considerations which must have been similar to those that now occupy us, but which would have gained immeasurably from his inimitably fine style.[2]

Edward E. Caird in *A Critical Account of the Philosophy of Kant* argues that what Kant attributes to Hume does not, however, correspond to Hume's position. "Did Hume consider mathematical truth to be analytical? Kant thinks that he must have done so; but from the well-known contrast of 'relations of ideas' and 'matters of fact,' we should rather conclude that, in the *Essays*, he had fallen back on the opinion of Locke, that such truth is merely ideal. In the *Treatise* he more consistently treats mathematical truth as derived from the analysis of sensible experience, and he is therefore forced to deny its exactness. Kant indeed says that Hume would have hesitated to carry out his principle (that necessity is merely subjective) if he had

---

[1] *Ibid.*, p. 742.
[2] Kant, *Prolegomena to Any Future Metaphysics*, P. G. Lucas, trans., *op. cit.*, p. 21 (italics mine).

seen its application to mathematics. But why not? In the earlier treatise which Kant does not seem to have studied, Hume had actually attempted to reduce mathematical truth within the limits of sensational experience."[1]

It is not difficult to cite some of the conflicting opinions of Hume's critics concerning his theory of analytic-synthetic, and his view on the nature of arithmetic and geometry. Perchance the vagueness and vacillating position of Hume's account of the nature of the mathematical sciences (as we shall see) is responsible for the difference of opinion of Hume's critics.

As we observed, Kant assumed that for Hume mathematical science is *a priori* and analytic while Windelband in *A History of Philosophy* goes further. He provides a reason for some of Hume's unaccountable assertions by assuming that Hume postulated, apart from the world of contingent experience, a possible world of necessary truths, in which mathematical statements retain their necessity and universality. He says:

> But mathematics is also the sole demonstrative science; and is that just because it relates to nothing else than the possible relations between contents of ideas, and asserts nothing whatever as to any relation of these to a real world. In this way the terministic principle of Hobbes is in complete control with Hume, but the latter proceeds still more consistently with his limitation of this theory of pure mathematics.[2]

On the other hand, J. J. Baumann in his book *Die Lehren von Raum, Zeit und Mathematik*, endeavors to reconcile Hume's position with his general principle of empiricism:

> Wenn wir einmal, ist Hume's Meinung, durch voraufgehende Eindrücke und Empfindungen die Ideen der Mathematik erhalten haben, so sind die Relationen dieser Ideen in der Macht unseres Geistes, wir können aus ihnen die ganze Mathematik entwerfen, vorausgesetzt, dass wir die Grundlagen nicht durch den Aufbau selbst zerstören, dass die Beweise nicht gegen die Definitionen streiten. Die Relationen der Ideen hängen nicht von Eindrücken weiter ab, sondern bloss von dem die Relationen wahrnehmenden Geist, die Ideen selbst aber hingen immerhin ursprünglich gleich allen Ideen von Eindrücken und Empfindungen ab. Die Worte: gäbe es keinen Kreis und kein Dreieck in der Natur u.s.w., bekommen dadurch einen sehr beschränkten Sinn; entweder meint Hume, wie Hobbes, die Mathematik würde ewige Wahrheit bleiben, auch wenn alle Dreiecke aus der Welt verschwänden, nachdem sie erst uns durch den sinnlichen Eindruck die Idee gegeben hätten, oder er meint nur, dass, wenn die Idee als nach Empfindung copiert einmal vorausgesetzt sei, wir uns um die Empfindung oder den Eindruck

---

[1] Edward Caird, *A Critical Account of the Philosophy of Kant*, London, 1877, pp. 215 and 219.

[2] W. Windelband, *A History of Philosophy*, Tufts trans., London, 1901, p. 473.

nicht mehr zu kümmern brauchten. Eine reine Anschauung des Geistes, eine Idee ohne Eindruck oder Empfindung, kann er nicht meinen, denn die ist durch seinen obersten Grundsatz und durch die Erklärungen im 9. Abschnitt, schlechterdings ausgeschlossen.[1]

Rudolfph Metz in *David Hume: Leben und Philosophie* disagrees with Baumann's foregoing interpretation. In reference to this interpretation Metz writes:

Die besonders von Hedvall und Baumann unternommenen Erklärungsversuche, auch diesen Satz in Einklang mit Humes Empirismus zu setzen, um keine Standpunktsverschiebung vom früheren zum späteren Werk annehmen zu müssen, scheinen mir doch zu gekünstelt und zu wenig in Humes Text fundiert zu sein.[2]

However, both Baumann and Metz agree that Hume's account of the nature of arithmetic and geometry is defective. Baumann writes:

Vergeblich hat Hume die Mathematik sensualistisch zu erklären gesucht, damit nichts rein Geistiges und ganz Gewisses bleibe, oder, was noch bleibt, zu einer Reihe von Ideenassoziationen wird mit Beliebigkeit der Entscheidung für irgend eine Hypothese.[3]

Metz's remarks on Hume's theory of mathematics are as follows:

Hier ist also in der Tat an einer bedeutsamen Stelle des Systems der sensualistische Impressionismus durchbrochen und aufgegeben, und Hume macht keinen Versuch, diesen Teil seiner Lehre auch nur äusserlich an das Ganze zu binden.[4]

On the other hand, for an interpreter like V. Kruse, there is no difficulty with regard to Hume's position. In his book *Hume's Philosophy* Kruse writes, "Mathematics is not an *a priori* science but empirical, because its first principles are sensible."[5]

I believe these conflicting opinions of Hume's critics call for a thorough investigation of Hume's position. I furthermore claim that the settling of these issues is germane to a clear understanding of Hume's entire theory of knowledge.

Here I should mention that though Kant's assertion that "he [Hume] worthy of a philosopher, cast his eyes over the whole field of pure knowledge a priori...."[6] "though he was far from conceiving it with sufficient definiteness and universality, confining his attention only to the synthetical proposition,"[7] seems to be justified; it is

---

[1] J. J. Baumann, *Die Lehren von Raum, Zeit und Mathematik in der neueren Philosophie*, Berlin, 1869, Band II, p. 569.
[2] R. Metz, *David Hume, Leben und Philosophie*, Stuttgart, 1929, pp. 153–154.
[3] Baumann, *op. cit.*, p. 673.
[4] Metz, *op. cit.*, pp. 153–154.
[5] V. Kruse, *Hume's Philosophy*, p. 127.
[6] Kant, *op. cit.*, p. 21.
[7] Kant, *Critique, op. cit.*, p. 723.

unwarranted to assume that for this reason our problem has no significant bearing upon Hume's theory of knowledge. Not only does Hume recognize that in some domain, i.e., mathematics, our claim to knowledge is justifiable, but also many of his fundamental arguments, with regard to the denial of demonstrability of causal axioms, of matters of fact, of personal identity, of belief in the external world, and of ethical judgments, rest on the very recognition of the possibility of knowledge in the realm of mathematics, which for him is the paradigm of all sciences.

The importance of mathematics for Hume's theory of knowledge is recognized by T. H. Green. He writes: "In thus leaving mathematics. .... out of the reach of his skepticism, and in *making them his basis of attack upon what he conceived to be the more pretentious claims of knowledge*, Hume was again following the course marked out for him by Locke."[1]

Indeed the often repeated comparison and contrast between relations which can provide us with *knowledge*, and relations which yield to *probabilities*, in the *Treatise*, between relations of Ideas and *matters of fact* in the *Enquiries*, between *demonstrative reasoning* and *moral reasoning*, in both works, is one of the main issues of Humian analytical philosophy.

---

[1] T. H. Green and T. H. Grose, *The Philosophical Works of David Hume*, London, 1874, Vol. I, p. 187 (italics mine).

CHAPTER FIVE

The Domain of Deductive Reason

1. INTRODUCTION

The primary aim of this chapter is to present a true description of Hume's theory of deductive sciences, viz., arithmetic and geometry, which appears scattered throughout his work; and to settle once and for all the divergent and often contradictory assertions of Hume's critics, e.g., Kant, Baumann, Metz, Windelband, etc., on this issue. Secondarily, the aim is to show the inadequacy of Hume's two principles, i.e., the principle of meaning and the principle of analyticity, as these principles are applied in the domain of mathematics. The chapter is divided into six sections. Following the Introduction, there is a discussion in the second section of (A) Hume's view on the nature of knowledge (strictly so called); (B) his criticism of the Platonic view of mathematics; (C) his own constructive theory of general ideas; and (D) some criticism of his theory. The third section describes (A) Hume's view on the nature of arithmetical relations; (B) the nature of arithmetical data – Malezieu's argument on the relation of number to unit – Locke's theory of the epistemological basis of the idea of number; and (C) my own criticism of Hume's idea of number. Section four is concerned with (A) Hume's conception of geometry; and (B) an interpretation of Hume's view on geometry. Section five describes (A) Hume's scepticism with regard to deductive reason; and (B) criticism of his scepticism. Finally, section six provides our concluding answers to questions we posed in the first chapter concerning the relation of Hume's principles to his explanations of the nature of arithmetic and geometry.

2. KNOWLEDGE AND ITS OBJECTS

A. Nature of Knowledge

Hume, in his discussion *Of Knowledge and Probability* (T. Part III), and also in other parts throughout the *Treatise* and *Enquiries*, assumes the traditional view held by many other philosophers (Plato, Descartes, Locke, etc.) that "knowledge" is the name of a two-term relation – on the one hand, there is a knower and on the other hand there are relations among objects which can be known; that only in some specific domains is our claim to knowledge justifiable. For example, under some specific conditions we may properly say, "If *A knows* that P is Q, then necessarily P is Q," whereas under other conditions it is proper to say, "*A* only *believes* that P is Q," which is compatible with the assertion "P might not be Q."

Once Hume adopted this traditional view of the nature of knowledge he was forced to admit that the only objects of knowledge are certain specific relations of ideas, viz., relations which "depend entirely on the ideas." There are four kinds of such relations, namely resemblance, contrariety, degrees in quality, and proportions in quantity or number; however, of these relations only proportions in quantity or number are objects of knowledge. The others, since they "are discoverable at first sight," "by a mere passive admission of the impressions," "fall more properly under the province of intuition than demonstration." (T. 70). Thus, for Hume, knowledge in the strict sense is attainable only in the domain of mathematics, where "the mind can go beyond what is immediately present to the senses to discover ... the relations of objects" (T. 73), and where "we can carry on a chain of reasoning" about certain "invariable relations," (T. 69), or relations of ideas (E. 25), viz., proportion in quantity or number "to any degree of intricacy, and yet preserve a perfect exactness and certainty" (T. 71). The expressions of such relations are the only propositions subject to demonstrative reasoning. We called such propositions, in contrast to propositions expressing intuitively discernible relations, "analytic statements of the second type."[1]

Quite apart and distinct from the domain of knowledge, which is limited to mathematical reasoning, there is, for Hume, a domain which is called probability, and in this domain fall causal relations, or what we have called "synthetic statements of the second type." This is the domain with which Hume is primarily concerned, to such an extent that his discussion of the other domain is significantly brief.

Despite Hume's lack of real concern about knowledge, the dichotomy between knowledge and probability, demonstrative and

[1] Chapter Four.

causal reason, deductive and animal inference is fundamental in his system. Throughout his work Hume on many occasions indicates the distinct nature of knowledge and probability (though, as we shall see, in his sceptical mood he obliterates his earlier distinctions). We note the following statements in the *Treatise*:

Knowledge and probability are of such contrary and disagreeing natures, that they cannot well run insensibly into each other. (T. 181).

The understanding exerts itself after two different ways, as it judges from demonstration or probability; as it regards the abstract relations of our ideas, or those relations of objects, of which experience only gives us information. (T. 413).

All kinds of reasoning consist in nothing but a *comparison*, and a discovery of those relations, either constant or inconstant, which two or more objects bear to each other. (T. 73).

There is no probability so great as not to allow of a contrary possibility; because otherwise 'twou'd cease to be a probability, and wou'd become a certainty. (T. 135).

And finally, an explicit assertion in the *Enquiries*:

All reasonings may be divided into two kinds, namely, demonstrative reasoning, or that concerning relations of ideas, and moral reasoning, or that concerning matter of fact and existence. (E. 35).

From all these assertions we can safely conclude that Hume intended to make a sharp distinction between two species of reason – deductive and inductive reason; and this distinction is fundamental in his system.

Since in this part we are concerned mainly with deductive reason and with the sciences which fall within this domain, we shall not discuss the other side of the coin, namely Hume's theory of probability and inductive reason, which have been discussed in detail by others.

What Hume says on the nature of the mathematical sciences and the status of objects and relations susceptible to deductive reasoning may be separated into two parts. Many of Hume's statements on the nature of mathematics, especially geometry, consist of assertions directed against a view which we have called Platonism.[1] These

---

[1] I use the term "Platonism" in the broadest sense to stand for a belief that general words, as distinct from proper names, denote non-perceptual entities, whether these entities populate the intelligible realm of Plato, or "the Universal Mind" of Leibniz, or even the "Human Mind" of Locke. In this sense Platonism also includes Conceptualism.

assertions are generally expressed in a simple and direct manner. On the other hand, Hume's positive explanation of the nature of mathematical concepts and the peculiar relations holding among such entities is expressed in an oblique and complicated way, to such an extent that various interpretations of his theory have resulted (as we observed in the first chapter).

I shall begin my inquiry by examining Hume's criticism of Platonism in mathematics, which is an integral part of his positive theory.

B. Criticism of Platonism in Mathematics

Hume, faithful to his main principle of meaning, argues that there are no such *things* as properties, besides perceptions, that could be described as red or black, sweet or bitter, pleasure or pain, etc., that there are no such *things* as numbers, points, or extensions, over and above numbered things, perceived (but indivisible) points, and configurations of such points which make extended lines or surfaces.

Now, though Hume accepts without much ado "a principle generally receiv'd in philosophy, that every thing in nature is individual" (T. 19), and hence there are no such *things* as properties, numbers and triangles as such, which are abstracted from particulars, he clearly sees that we do nonetheless use significantly such concepts in ordinary discourse as well as in the technical language of the exact sciences. Recognizing this fact, Hume produces a nominalistic theory of how we come to know abstract ideas, including mathematical concepts, despite the fact that expressions of these ideas, as he believes, neither designate a *particular* entity existing in our external or internal worlds, or in the realm of Platonic ideas, nor denote all the members of certain classes.

Before we deal with Hume's nominalistic theory of generalized ideas, we shall see what he has to say against Platonism.

Hume, in an early section of the *Treatise* titled *Of Abstract Ideas*, argues that any theory which holds that general terms designate "abstract ideas" which have "no particular degree of either quantity or quality" is erroneous. For it is psychologically impossible, he argues, "to conceive any quantity or quality, without forming a precise notion of its degrees." Moreover, he reasons that as a matter of fact it is not possible to separate certain kinds of simple ideas from each other, such as "the precise length of a line from the

line itself" or "figure from body figur'd and motion from body
mov'd" and hence, one cannot conceive the idea of a line, for example, in abstraction from perceived lines. He admits that by
distinction of reason we may observe different resemblances and
relations among certain simple ideas and "may still view them in
different aspects." However, though by distinction of reason the
mind can distinguish what is not actually separable, Hume believes
that we are not able to form separate *images* of things which are
inseparable in reality. There is, therefore, no such thing as a general
idea of a line, or a general idea of a triangle distinct and separate
from the idea of a particular line or a particular triangle – "the
general idea of a line, notwithstanding all our abstractions and
refinements, has in its appearance in the mind a precise degree of
quantity and quality." (T. 19). He says again in the *Enquiries*: "Let
any man try to conceive a triangle in general, which is neither
Isosceles nor Scalenum, nor has any particular length or proportion of sides; and he will soon perceive the absurdity of all the
scholastic notions with regard to abstraction and general ideas."
(E. 155).

Hume also attacks a theory of geometry according to which "the
objects of geometry, ... not only never did, but never can exist in
nature." This theory is akin to a theory now called "pure geometry"
in holding that geometrical concepts assert nothing about physical
space.

Hume first states this theory, and then rejects, for various reasons,
this view of geometry. He says that according to some mathematicians,
"A surface is *defin'd* to be length and breadth without depth: A
line to be length without breath or depth: A point to be what has
neither length, breadth nor depth." (T. 42). He objects that such
definitions are perfectly meaningless unless we define extension in
terms of configuration of perceived but at the same time, indivisible
points (his own theory). "'Tis evident that all this is perfectly unintelligible upon any other supposition than that of the composition
of extension by indivisible points or atoms." (T. 42). He argues that
unless we assume that line, surface, etc. is composed of indivisible
points, geometry would be wholly unintelligible. "How else cou'd
any thing exist," he asks, "without length, without breadth, or
without depth?" Now Hume observes that such Euclidean definitions of geometrical concepts (T. 42) still could be retained if one
assumes that:

... the objects of geometry, those surfaces, lines and points, whose proportions and positions it examines, *are mere ideas in the mind; and not only never did, but never can exist in nature.* They never did exist; for no one will pretend to draw a line or make a surface entirely conformable to the definition: They never can exist; for we may produce demonstrations from these very ideas to prove that they are impossible. (T. 42 – i.m.).

Hume rejects this Platonic theory by rejecting two arguments which support the theory: namely the argument that primitive concepts of geometry "never can exist: for we may produce demonstrations from these very ideas to prove that they are impossible" and the argument that they "are mere ideas in the mind," for they could never be observed as such in nature.

Hume's argument is this, that if such concepts are conceived by clear and distinct ideas, then it is logically possible for them to exist, since according to him, the only complex ideas which cannot be conceived are self-contradictory ideas, and the Euclidean definitions of line, points, etc., are not self-contradictory.

The main argument against the other assumption that the concepts of geometry "are mere ideas in the mind" and thus their meaning "must be comprehended by a pure and intellectual view" is based on his main principle of meaning. He writes:

I shall here take occasion to propose a second observation concerning our demonstrative reasonings, which is suggested by the same subject of the mathematics. *'Tis usual with mathematicians, to pretend, that those ideas, which are their objects, are of so refin'd and spiritual a nature, that they fall not under the conception of the fancy,* but must be comprehended by a pure and intellectual view, of which the superior faculties of the soul are alone capable. The same notion runs thro' most parts of philosophy, and is principally made use of to explain our abstract ideas, and to shew how we can form an idea of a triangle, for instance, which shall neither be an isosceles nor scalenum, nor be confin'd to any particular length and proportion of sides. *'Tis easy to see, why philosophers are so fond of this notion of some spiritual and refin'd perceptions; since by that means they cover many of their absurdities,* and may refuse to submit to the decisions of clear ideas, by appealing to such as are obscure and uncertain. *But to destroy this artifice, we need but reflect on that principle so oft insisted on, that all our ideas are copy'd from our impressions.* (T. 72 – i.m.).

That all our ideas, including mathematical ideas, are derived from the senses is a conviction which Hume holds in all his writings. In the *Enquiries* he asserts again:

It seems to me not impossible to avoid these absurdities and contradictions, if it be admitted, that there is no such thing as abstract or general ideas, properly speaking; but that all general ideas are, in reality, particular ones.
... If this be admitted (as seems reasonable) it follows *that all the ideas of quantity, upon which mathematicians reason, are nothing but particular, and such as are suggested by the senses and imagination.* (E. 158 – i.m.).

Hume observes that there is a close alliance between mathematics and metaphysics. He sees that metaphysicians welcome the theory that mathematical concepts belong to the Platonic realm and not the sensible world – that they "are of so refin'd and spiritual a nature" which "must be comprehended by a pure and intellectual view, of which the superior faculties of the soul are alone capable"; since metaphysicians by such assumption, may "cover many of their absurdities, and may refuse to submit to the decisions of clear ideas, by appealing to such as are obscure and uncertain."

Metaphysicians may argue that in mathematics there are significant concepts which are independent of sense experience, and if the *argument a priori* is convincing in this field, why should we refuse to consider other metaphysical concepts and arguments as significant and convincing? In the *Dialogues* Hume alludes to the same observation which he had already made in the *Treatise* (T. 72) when Philo declares that:

I shall venture to add an observation, that the argument *a priori* has seldom been found very convincing, except to people of a metaphysical head, who have accustomed themselves to abstract reasoning, and who finding from mathematics, that the understanding frequently leads to truth, through obscurity, and contrary to first appearances, have transferred the same habit of thinking to subjects, where it ought not to have place.[1]

From such assertions and from what Hume maintains in his polemic against Platonism in mathematics, we may draw the following conclusions.

First. It seems *prima facie* clear that for Hume mathematical ideas, like other generalized ideas, should be grounded in experience. However, as we shall see later (Section 2, part 4) he believes that though mathematical concepts are grounded in experience, mathematical truths are not guaranteed only by experience in the way that empirical truths are.

Second. It also appears evident that Hume, contrary to Kant's supposition, fully intended to break "the good company of mathematics and metaphysics," and did not hesitate to attack the alleged theory of the *a priori* nature of mathematics, without at the same time "taking mathematics as also synthetic."[2]

How far Hume was successful in preserving the ideal exactness

---

[1] Hume's *Dialogues*, p. 236.
[2] Kant, *The Prolegomena*, *loc. cit.*, p. 21. For the details of Kant's arguments see Chap. One.

and universality of the mathematical sciences, without admitting the Platonic view of Leibniz or the phenomenalistic position of Mill, is another issue which deserves detailed discussion.

Let us now examine Hume's constructive theory on the nature of general ideas, before examining his more specific views concerning mathematical ideas.

C. Hume's Theory of General Ideas

In the preceding discussion I observed that Hume, in his arguments against Platonism, denies that general words designate entities called "universals," and that universals are something above and beyond the particular data furnished by experience. A general word neither designates all the members of a class, "all possible qualities," nor designates an entity which possesses "no particular degree either of quantity or quality." What then are the designata of general words, if (as Hume assumes) significant words usually denote particular entities and general words are significant?

It is in reply to this question that Hume constructs his theory of general ideas. The outline of this theory is as follows: First: We use the same name when we perceive a certain resemblance among several data. The resembling qualities of data are a common quality shared by all; and these common qualities can "strike the eyes or rather the mind" amidst the irrelevant differences. "When we have found a resemblance among several objects, that often occur to us, we apply the same name to all of them, whatever differences we may observe in the degrees of their quantity and quality, and whatever other differences may appear among them." (T. 20).

Second: After this preliminary process of name-giving, we take care always to use the same family name when confronted with any member of that family, and as a result, we acquire a custom or a habit quite analogous to a conditioned reflex.

Third: Because of such a habit, on hearing or reading a family-name, we recall at least a member of that family, and analogously when confronted with a member we recall the family name.

> After we have acquired a custom of this kind, the hearing of that name revives the idea of one of these objects, and makes the imagination conceive it with all its particular circumstances and proportions.... The word raises up an individual idea, along with a certain custom; and that custom produces any other individual one, for which we may have occasion. (T. 20).

Hume maintains that "the words or discourses of others have

an intimate connexion with certain ideas in their mind" and that these ideas also have a connection "with the facts or objects, which they represent." (T. 113). He says also that because "such a particular idea is commonly annex'd to such particular word, nothing is requir'd but the hearing of that word to produce the correspondent idea." (T. 93).

Fourth: In this manner a general word acts as a stimulus by bringing into our mind not all the images of the family, but a particular idea plus a disposition to replace that idea with other similar ideas.

... the word not being able to revive the idea of all these individuals; only touches the soul,... and revives that custom, which we have acquir'd by surveying them. They are not really and in fact present to the mind, but only in power; nor do we draw them all out distinctly in the imagination, but keep ourselves in a readiness to survey any of them, as we may be prompted by a present design or necessity. The word raises up an individual idea, along with a certain custom; and that custom produces any other individual one, for which we may have occasion. (T. 20).

Fifth: Hume maintains that we may use general words quite properly without bringing into our mind their images. But of course, we should be ready to present these stored-ideas, if the credentials of such words are questioned. If we are unable to present ideas which were stored in our mind we might fall into the danger of "talking without thinking" and also the danger of assuming that a mere use of words is enough to bestow on them significance.

...it being usual, after the frequent use of terms, which are really significant and intelligible, to omit the idea, which we wou'd express by them, and to preserve only the custom, by which we recal the idea at pleasure; so it naturally happens, that after the frequent use of terms, which are wholly insignificant and unintelligible, we fancy them to be on the same footing with the precedent, and to have a secret meaning, which we might discover by reflection. (T. 224).

Sixth: Hume realizes, on the basis of his theory, that it is possible, when using a general word, that we may take a singular image which comes before the mind, not only as a representative of this family but as identical with all the members of the family. In that case, of course, the image symbol could not achieve its function and the misuse of a symbol may cause us to utter a false sentence. Suppose for example, in thinking of a triangle, an image of a particular triangle, say an equilateral triangle, comes before my mind. But now if I make the statement "all triangles are equilateral" I am making a false generalization.

Hume finds an ingenious way out of this difficulty. He states that on such occasions the other members of the family of triangles will come before our mind and make us perceive the falsehood of that proposition. These members, unlike the image of an equilateral triangle, which is "present to the mind in fact," are "present in power" (T. 20) ready to appear when they are needed.

... shou'd we mention the word, triangle, and form the idea of a particular equilateral one to correspond to it, and shou'd we afterwards assert, *that the three angles of a triangle are aqual to each other*, the other individuals of a scalenum and isosceles, which we overlook'd at first, immediately crowd in upon us, and make us perceive the falsehood of this proposition, tho' it be true with relation to that idea, which we had form'd. (T. 21).

Hence Hume concludes that:

...the very same idea may be annext to several different words, and may be employ'd in different reasonings, without any danger of mistake. Thus the idea of an equilateral triangle of an inch perpendicular may serve us in talking of a figure, of a rectilineal figure, of a regular figure, of a triangle, and of an equilateral triangle. All these terms, therefore, are in this case attended with the same idea; but as they are wont to be apply'd in a greater or lesser compass, they excite their particular habits, and thereby keep the mind in a readiness to observe, that no conclusion be form'd contrary to any ideas, which are usually compriz'd under them (T. 21).

D. Some Criticism of Hume's Theory of General Ideas

Hume's theory of general ideas is criticized by many of his commentators as being contrary to what in fact happens when we construct class-words and when we use such words in our discourse. It is argued that to have images or to be able to produce images is not only an unnecessary condition for talking to ourselves (thinking) or talking to others, but it may hinder the processes of communication.[1] It is also argued that the meaning of a symbol is not given to us by the presence of an idea. An idea may occur and one may not understand what was intended by that idea and hence meaning can not be identified with having ideas.

Here I wish to examine two main criticisms which have recently been brought against Hume's theory by Stuart Hampshire and John Holloway. The former critic wants to prove that Hume, in spite of his rejection of abstract ideas, "was never a complete nominalist" but perhaps an unaware realist; while the latter wishes to

[1] H. H. Price, *Thinking and Experience*, 1953. "Of course images may sometimes occur in our minds when we are thinking. But, we are told, they are merely irrelevant accompaniments of the thinking process. Indeed, they are worse than irrelevant, because they distract our attention from what we are about...." P. 235.

prove that Hume's nominalism, as it stands, is defective since it neglects to consider the function of a standard or criterion necessary to determine the class of images accompanying a general word. Let us first turn our attention to Hampshire's important criticism of Hume. Hampshire argues that Hume, "In spite of his rejection of abstract ideas, still thought of a perceived relation or relations of resemblances as necessarily involved in all classification and uses of language.... That he was never a *complete* nominalist.... That Hume's mistake was to regard the words 'similarity' or 'resemblance' as names of relations in the sense in which, for instance 'contiguous in time' or 'contiguous in space' or 'to the left of' or 'after' are names of relations." Hampshire points out that "resemblance" looks as if it is a descriptive symbol, but actually it is by itself a vacuous symbol.[1]

In order to verify Hampshire's claim, we should turn our attention to what Hume himself writes about the relation of resemblance. Hume in the early pages of the *Treatise* states that resemblance is a relation "without which no philosophical relation can exist; since no objects will admit of comparison, but what have some degree of resemblance." (T. 14). Hume clearly indicates that not only *natural relations*, defined as "that *quality*, by which two ideas are connected together in the imagination" (T. 13), but also *philosophical relations*, namely "that particular circumstance, in which, even upon the arbitrary union of two ideas in the fancy, we may think proper to compare them" (T. 13) are based on resemblance. This means that even if we artificially put two different entities into a class, the mere fact of classification presupposes reference to some degree of resemblance.

Up to this point, nothing is said concerning the status of resemblance itself. We do not know yet whether resemblance is something that we discover in nature, or whether it is merely the creation of imagination. Now if Hume maintains that resemblance or likeness of objects is to be found in nature, then Hampshire's point is correct, and Hume is not a complete nominalist; but (let us say) a sort of realist who finds universals, not in the mind of the observer (conceptualism), or in the intelligible realm *(universalia ante rem)*, or in names (extreme nominalism), but only in things *(universalia in rebus)*. On the other hand, if Hume maintains that every two or more ideas

[1] S. Hampshire, "Scepticism and Meaning," *Philosophy*, Vol. XXV, No. 94 (July, 1950).

can be compared and classified without having anything in common or that there is nothing universal but names, then Hume's endeavor in constructing his theory of generalized ideas is a succesful attempt to replace conceptualism, without at the same time falling into a kind of realism.

The latter conviction is the view held by R. W. Church:

> In no case of simple ideas (or impressions) compared, is there to be discrim-inated "any common circumstance" of which "resemblance" is the name. This must be so, Hume argues, because the ideas are simple, and hence such that within them there can be nothing over and above what they themselves in-trinsically are. Thus, given two simple ideas (or impressions), P_1 and P_2, to say that P_1 and P_2 are resembling or the same, is not to say anything *about* P^1 and P^2; it is to say nothing *more* than that P_1 is P_1 and P_2 is P_2. Resemblance, or sameness, then, are not proper names of characters or qualities over and above the simple ideas compared. The statement "P_1 and P_2 are similar" means what is meant by the statement "P_1 and P_2 are comparable"; and this statement means what is meant by "P_1 is P_1 and P_2 is P_2.[1]

Church's opinion is based solely on a statement which Hume makes in the Appendix concerning the problem of resemblance and simplicity of ideas. Here Hume writes that particular simple ideas, such as sounds, tastes, and smells, "admit of infinite resemblances upon the general appearance and comparison, *without having any common circumstance the same.*" (T. 637 – i.m.).

The above statement is indeed an important assertion, insofar as it discloses Hume's attempt to escape the difficulty of producing either an external or internal impression for the idea of relation, in this case the idea of resemblance. However, earlier in the body of the *Treatise*, Hume makes some other statements concerning the nature of resemblance which are incompatible both with his asser-tion in the Appendix and with Church's interpretation that for Hume "resemblance" is "not a qualifying predicate" since, by say-ing that two things are similar, he is only asserting a trivial tautol-ogy.

The statements which are contrary to Church's interpretation, and which, on the other hand, support Hampshire's view are as follows:

> As to what may be said; *that the operations of nature are independent of our thought and reasoning, I allow it;* and accordingly have observ'd, that objects bear to each other the relations of *contiguity and succession; that like objects may be observ'd in several instances to have like relations; and that all this is independent of, and antecedent to the operations of the understanding.* (T. 168 – i.m.).

[1] R. W. Church, *op. cit.*, pp. 35–36.

According to this statement, then, the relation of resemblance, as well as the relations of contiguity and succession, are not artificial relations "dependent on our thought and reasoning," but are to be found in nature along with the relata (impressions). Things, then, actually resemble each other, and hence to say that P_1 resembles P_2 is not to assert a mere trivial tautology, that P_1 is P_1 and P_2 is P_2. Hume not only says that "like objects may be observ'd in several instances to have like relations ... independent and antecedent to operations of understanding," but also says that "'tis impossible to found relation but on some common quality," (T. 236), which further indicates that contrary to Church's interpretation, resemblance or sameness stand for common characters or qualities.

I conclude that both Hampshire's and Church's interpretations suffer from reliance on some assertions of Hume to the exclusion of other incompatible assertions by him. The fact is that Hume's account of the nature of resemblance (a relation which plays an essential role in his theory of generalized ideas), and all other relations is quite ambiguous. As we observed, he mentions both that "'tis impossible to found a relation but 'on some common quality," that "no objects will admit of comparison, but what have some degree of resemblance," and also that simple ideas "admit of infinite resemblances ... without having any common circumstance the same," that "since equality is *a relation, it is not, strictly speaking, a property in the figures themselves.*"[1] (T. 46).

The main objection which ought to be brought against Hume's theory of generalized ideas is that Hume mainly concentrates on the psychological view and overlooks the linguistic aspect of the mechanism of generalization. He does not explain fully why, in using general words, we associate only certain images with that word and we drop certain other images as irrelevant accompaniments. To say merely that resembling images are to be accompanied with general words, if these words are to be used properly in language, is to say something which is not instructive. We do not yet know in what respect these images resemble each other; and we do not yet know in what respect images resemble each other unless and until we know how to limit the scope of resemblance by some conventional device. This weak spot in Hume's theory is brought into focus, though incompletely, by John Holloway. Holloway argues that:

---

[1] The relation of equality will be discussed in Section 3 (A).

Hume cannot explain how, although we may frequently call up, or let come into mind, a succession of images which guide us in the use of a word, yet this succession is critically considered; its constituents are accepted or rejected. This process reveals a reference to some pre-existing standard. For Hume this discrimination is inexplicable.[1]

I think Holloway's criticism, though essentially pertinent, is not entirely correct in so far as it neglects to mention some measure which Hume takes in order to account for the fact of selection of images. As we remarked (in the second chapter), Hume observes that in using general words, though any member of a certain family of images may come before our mind and act as a representative of the family, we do not accept the co-presence of any series of ideas. He thus implies that checking of a series of ideas may be done by seeing whether these ideas habitually go together or not. Indeed, in the very paragraph which Holloway quotes incompletely, we see some signs of Hume's awareness of the problem of selection of images in using general words. Holloway, after stating that "both Hume and Berkeley had noticed something which betrays the mistake in their analysis," quotes Hume that:

... we do not annex distinct and compleat ideas to every term we make use of, and that in talking of *government, church, negotiation, conquest*, we seldom spread out in our minds all the simple ideas, of which these complex ones are compos'd.

However, Holloway does not quote the rest of the paragraph:

... 'Tis however observable, that notwithstanding this imperfection we may avoid talking nonsense on these subjects, and may perceive any repugnance among the ideas, as well as if we had a full comprehension of them. Thus if instead of saying, *that in war the weaker have always recourse to negotiation*, we shou'd say, *that they have always recourse to conquest*, the custom, which we have acquir'd of attributing certain relations to ideas, still follows the words, and makes us immediately perceive the absurdity of that proposition; in the same manner as one particular idea may serve us in reasoning concerning other ideas, however different from it in several circumstances. (T. 23).

Not only in this paragraph does Hume recognize the function of custom in accepting or rejecting the co-presence of certain ideas, but in the same section he makes an important distinction between images which are "in fact present to the mind" and those which are present "only in power." The function of the images which are present in the mind only in power, is to "keep the mind in a readiness to observe, that no conclusion be form'd contrary to any ideas which are usually compriz'd under them." Thus Hume says:

---

[1] John Holloway, *Language and Intelligence*, London, 1951, p. 8.

All these terms [a figure, rectilineal figure, a triangle, etc,] therefore, are in this case attended with the same idea; but as they are wont to be apply'd in a greater or lesser compass, they excite their particular habits, and thereby keep the mind in a readiness to observe; that no conclusion be form'd contrary to any ideas, which are usually compriz'd under them. (T. 21).

Hume maintains that in making a false generalization about certain ideas, "other ideas, which we overlook'd at first," that is, those which are present only in power, "immediately crowd in upon us, and make us perceive the falsehood of [that] proposition." (T. 21).

Thus it seems to me that contrary to Holloway's claim, Hume does explain (though inadequately) the discriminative role which the mind plays in choosing the right kind of images for generalized words.

I have mentioned earlier that the real objection to Hume's theory of general ideas is the fact that his criterion, namely, customs or habits, cannot perform its important function, if it is only psychological and not a linguistic criterion. Unless we register the customary association of ideas with words in forms of definition or rules, we cannot properly use general words in language. The problem, no doubt, becomes more acute if these general words stand, not for perceived properties, but for mathematical concepts.

On some occasions, Hume indeed considers the possibility of establishing the meaning of general terms by "fixing a definition," that is, by setting a linguistic habit, and not by reference to images. But he drops this sound suggestion which is indeed irreconcilable with the main tenor of his position that all general terms denote a particular idea. This suggestion appears both in the *Treatise* and in the *Enquiries*.

... we may *fix the meaning of the word, figure*, we may revolve in our mind the ideas of circles, squares, parallelograms, triangles of different sizes and proportions, and may not rest on one image or idea. However this may be, 'tis certain *that* we form the idea of individuals, whenever we use any general term. (T. 22 – i.m.).
If any term be defined in geometry, the mind readily, of itself, substitutes, on all occasions, the definition for the term defined. Or even when no definition is employed, the object itself may be presented to the senses, and by that means be steadily and clearly apprehended. (E. 60).

However, I think it is most essential for Hume's theory of demonstrative reasoning that we do "fix the meaning of the word" and not only rely on mere images. For, otherwise, it is simply impossible, upon his theory, to discover by "a chain of reasoning," for example, "*from the idea* of a triangle ... the relation of equality, which its three angles bear to the right ones" (T. 69) or to know by demonstration, "that the square of the hypothenuse is equal to the square of the two sides or ... That three times five is equal to the half of thirty" (E. 25). Mathematical demonstration, which has its important place in Hume's system, could not be given, if we substitute mere impressions, or even objects, for definitions, or animal inference, in place of rules of inference.

For if a person correctly counts one hundred objects, and then correctly counts one hundred other objects, and correctly counts the total and gets one hundred and ninety-nine objects, we do not question the truth of the formula "$100 + 100 = 200$," which is a demonstrable truth, but rather, we do seek to explain the physical cause of the said mishap. Again, if as a result of measurement we found that the sum of the internal angles of a particular triangle is slightly less than two right angles, we do not question the validity of the Euclidean demonstration which proves that the sum of the internal angles of a triangle is equal to the sum of two right angles, but rather we question either the correctness of our measurement or the straightness of the lines and exactness of the angles of our supposed triangle. In other words, the relation of deducibility, if it holds at all, as Hume thinks it does hold both in geometry and arithmetic, holds between certain expressions and not between series of impressions or objects, as Hume indifferently calls them. We are not able to prove "the falsehood of the demonstration, that the three angles of any triangle are equal to each other," as Hume thinks we can, by merely bringing into our consciousness the images of scalenum and isosceles which are "present in power" in line with the image of equilateral which is "present to the mind in fact," unless, besides images, we have definitions for identification of the geometrical figures, and rules for demonstrating certain geometrical truths. The point becomes even more obvious if we consider the other deductive sciences such as algebra and arithmetic.

3. THE SCIENCE OF ARITHMETIC

A. Hume's View on the Nature of Arithmetical Relations

Now we may begin consideration of our main issue; namely Hume's actual treatment of mathematical sciences.

For Hume, mathematical truths are the paradigm of certainty and exactness in that they are universal and demonstrable, and hence are the only objects of knowledge. The mathematical sciences are classified by him into two distinct subjects, namely: algebra and arithmetic, and the science of geometry. The discussion of the science of algebra and arithmetic is brief, while geometry is discussed in detail.

I should warn the reader from the outset that Hume is concerned only with the philosophical side of mathematics and not with the foundation of mathematics or mathematics as such. He claims indeed that he is examining "the foundation of mathematics." But the inquiry into such a "foundation" in contradistinction, for example, to Frege's findings in *The Foundations of Arithmetic* is not logical but purely epistemological. Hume is mainly concerned with the description of the origin of mathematical ideas such as point, number, equality, etc., and not with reduction of any arithmetical or geometrical system to a set of axioms and definitions. The theme of this epistemological approach was already set in the introduction to the *Treatise* where he says "Even Mathematics ... are in some measure dependent on the science of *Man*, since [they] lie under the cognizance of men, and are judged of by their powers and faculties."

In dealing with Hume's treatment of mathematics, we should consider both the nature of mathematical relations and the nature of mathematical ideas.

I shall begin by first exploring Hume's brief discussion of arithmetic and algebra.

Hume maintains that proportions in quantity and number (both arithmetical and geometrical) are among those philosophical relations which depend entirely on the ideas which we can compare together. We called expressions of such relations "analytic of the second type."

As an example of such relations, we have in the *Treatise*, "'Tis from the idea of a triangle, that we discover the relation of equality, which its three angles bear to two right ones; and this relation is invariable, as long as our idea remains the same." (T. 69). Hume makes certain that such relations are discoverable "not at first sight," but by a chain of demonstrative reasoning. He considers the suggestion that proportions in quantity or number might fall "under the province of intuition." (Analytic of the first type). "We might proceed, after the same manner, in fixing the *proportions* of *quantity* or *number*, and might at one view observe a superiority or inferiority betwixt any numbers, or figures; especially where the difference is very great and remarkable." (T. 70). But he realizes that the method of finding mathematical relations is not so simple, and adds that "In all other cases we must settle the proportions with some liberty, or proceed in a more *artificial manner*." (T. 70).

What he means by "more artificial manner" becomes clear in the subsequent passage where he compares geometry with algebra and arithmetic. He states that algebra and arithmetic are the only exact sciences, since here we have "a *precise standard*, by which we can judge of the equality and proportion of numbers." (T. 71). Thus to use the *artificial manner* of finding mathematical relations, one should erect a standard, such as a standard of equality (actually the proper term is "identity").

Hume himself does establish such a standard or definition. The definition of numerical equality is given in terms of one to one correlation of units in the following manner: "When two numbers are so combin'd, as that the one has always an *unite* answering to every *unite* of the other, we pronounce them equal." (T. 71).

This standard of "equality," I think, should be regarded among those rules which Hume describes to be infallible. "In all demonstrative sciences," he says, "the *rules* are certain and infallible." (T. 180).

Concerning the nature and the status of equality, he says many different things. He seems to be bothered by his own definition of equality; since he sees that such a verbal definition is not a generalization from experience, and therefore its credentials might be questioned. (We shall see later, in our examination of geometry, further symptoms of Hume's anxiety.) On the one hand, equality is among those invariable relations which depend entirely on ideas, and thus constitute part of the description of relata. This fits with the assertion that "'tis impossible to found relation but on some common quality." On the other hand, he maintains that "since equality is a relation, it is not, strictly speaking, a property in the figures themselves, but arises merely from the comparison, which the mind makes betwixt them." (T. 46).

So after all on this account equality, like necessity, is not *in the object*. Does it follow also that like necessity it "lies only in the act of the understanding, by which we consider and compare these ideas"? (T. 166). Hume, at this point, is deliberately ambiguous. In one place he states that equality "arises merely from the comparison, which the mind makes betwixt ideas" (which is of no help). In another place, he implies that the idea of equality is an idealized idea (which, according to his usual account, could be only a figment of the imagination).

> I have already observ'd, in examining the foundation of mathematics, that the imagination, when set into any train of thinking, is apt to continue, even when its object fails it, and like a galley put in motion by the oars, carries on its course without any new impulse. This I have assign'd for the reason, why, after considering several loose standards of equality, and correcting them by each other, we proceed to imagine so correct and exact a standard of that relation, as is not liable to the least error or variation. (T. 198).

Once again we see the difficulty Hume encounters in trying to account for the ontological status of relations, e.g. equality, in conformity with his principle of meaning. He deviates from his principle when he correctly states that since equality is a relation, it is not, strictly speaking, a property in the figures themselves. And he is equally right, I think, when he seeks to provide not a denotation but a standard for equality. But then, seeing that such standard has a dubious status in his system, he modifies his position and adds in the Appendix:

> There are many philosophers, who refuse to assign any standard of *equality* but assert, that 'tis sufficient to present two objects, that are equal, in order to give us a just notion of this proportion. All *definitions*, say they, are fruitless, without the perception of such objects; and where we perceive such objects, we do no longer stand in need of any definition. To this reasoning I entirely agree; and assert, that the only notion of equality, or inequality, *is deriv'd* from the whole united appearance and comparison of particular objects. (T. 637 – i.m.).

But such preoccupation with *derivation* of relations is superfluous. To say that "equality arises merely from the comparison of [figures]" or "is deriv'd from the whole united appearance and comparison of particular objects," even if true, tells us something about the causation and nothing about the meaning of such a concept. And to say "'tis sufficient to present two objects, *that are equal*, in order to give us a just notion of *this proportion* [equality]" is to say nothing at all even about how we come to know such a relation. On the other hand, we cannot know whether things are equal or unequal, unless we know already in what specific respect they have to be considered so. And to know that specific respect is to know a specific standard or definition. Hence Hume should *not* agree with those philosophers who say "we do no longer stand in need of any definition."

By knowing a specific standard or definition for equality or identity, I mean knowing under what conditions a statement of identity is true or false. And this requires reference to a set of rules and stipulations. In this respect, "equality" or "identity" like "resemblance" are incomplete symbols. They have to be completed by definitions if one wants to use them significantly.

I go farther and assert that even if Hume was able to find, in the absence of external impressions, some internal ideas or impressions for such terms as equality or identity or implication, such as "a feeling of determination" which he found for the "necessity which makes two times two equal to four," or such as a feeling of hesitation which Russell finds for the expression "either-or," he could not prove that the appearance or absence of such feelings are necessary conditions for the correct usage of such expressions. From this it follows that the meaning of relation-terms should not be identified with any feeling.

B. The Nature of Arithmetical Ideas

In discussing Hume's polemic against Platonism, we observed that Hume was emphatic that all abstract ideas, including mathematical concepts, are in some sense derived from the data of our experience. Now if we follow Hume's recommendation and search for the impressions of numbers, in order to clarify our ideas, we find, to our regret, only vague assertions and indirect hints made by him concerning such impressions. First, he states that numerical relations may be established among "all those objects, which admit of *quantity*; or *number*." (T. 14). Then in his discussion on abstract ideas he makes some assertions indicating that the ideas of numbers are not always present *in fact* in our mind but only *in power*.

... when we mention any great number, such as a thousand, the mind has generally no adequate idea of it, but only a power of producing such an idea, by its adequate idea of the decimals, under which the number is comprehended. This imperfection, however in our idea, is never felt in our reasonings. (T. 22).

The net result of this statement is that, though numbers are derived from data, we may use numbers without having the correspondent images of these data in our mind. This result is further strengthened by another assertion implying that to think about numbers it is not necessary to have images.

When you tell me of the thousandth and ten thousandth part of a grain of sand, I have a distinct idea of these numbers and of their different proportions; but the images, which I form in my mind to represent the things themselves, are nothing different from each other, nor inferior to that image, by which I represent the grain of sand itself. (T. 27).

Of the idea of number as such, no explanation is given, except in an oblique manner, that it arises from the perception of objects. But the explanation of the derivation of number more aptly fits the description of the idea of plurality than number, and in fact Hume in one place uses the terms multiplicity or number synonymously (T. 201). Here the relation between the idea of number and objects is stated in the following passage when Hume contrasts the idea of unity with the idea of plurality:

> After one object is suppos'd to exist, we must either suppose another also to exist; in which case we have the idea of number: Or we must suppose it not to exist; in which case the first object remains at unity. (T. 200).

Also, he says:

> ... when we consider any two points of this time, we may place them in different lights: We may either survey them at the very same instant; in which case they give us the idea of number. (T. 201).

The latter statements are of no avail in understanding the idea of number. Since, if by such assertions, Hume intends to define number in terms of the plurality of events, then such definitions will not cover the numbers zero and one, much less the other kinds of numbers such as negative numbers; and if he intends to describe the conditions under which we come to understand numbers, then he is only telling us something about our mental history and nothing about the meaning of number. To provide a mental history and to describe how we come to know the meaning of color-words, expression of feelings, etc. is of course Hume's usual procedure. But the point is that this procedure seems to me inadequate when he wants to apply it to such abstract concepts as equality or number.

We see clearly that the above two quotations do not tell us anything about the idea of number. In order to understand what he does mean by number we should look rather into his assertions concerning *units*, which supposedly make up numbers. Hume, in his polemic against the theory of the infinite divisibility of geometrical points (Section 4), supports his views, among other ways, by a reductio argument originated "by a noted author," M. Malezieu. Here we find some statements which may indicate what Hume actually means by "number" and "units." This argument (p. 30,

Treatise) may be summarized in the following way (only the second part of the argument is relevant to our discussion).

To say that "there are numbers" implies that "there are units," since numbers are composed of units. "'Tis evident, that existence in itself belongs only to unity, and is never applicable to number, but on account of the units, of which the number is compos'd. 'There are twenty men' thus implies that 'There are one, two, three, four, etc., men.' 'Tis therefore utterly absurd to suppose any number to exist, and yet deny the existence of units;..."

Now it is supposed by metaphysicians that "extension is always a number, ... and never resolves itself into any unite or indivisible quantity." But this conclusion is false, since from our premises it follows that "extension can never at all exist." If metaphysicians retort that extension is composed of units and the unit "admits of an infinite number of fractions, and is inexhaustible in its subdivision," then it also follows that the "unit" is vacuous.

For by the same rule these twenty men *may be consider'd as an unite*. The whole globe of the earth, nay the whole universe *may be consider'd as an unite*. That term of unity is merely a fictitious denomination, which the mind may apply to any quantity of objects it collects together; nor can such an unity any more exist alone than number can, as being in reality a true number.

The conclusion is that "unit" is not really an arbitrary term, though it may be used as such: "*But the unity, which can exist alone, and whose existence is necessary to that of all number, is of another kind, and must be perfectly indivisible, and incapable of being resolved into any lesser unity.* (T. 31, i.m.).

In order to understand what exactly Hume means by "indivisible unites – whose existence is necessary to all numbers" and by saying in the *Enquiries* that units are entirely similar: "the component parts of quantity and number are entirely similar.... But as all other ideas are clearly distinct and different from each other" (E. 163), I think we should examine a similar though more explicit formulation expressed by Locke.

Locke first speaks of "the simple modes of number."[1] By "modes" he means "complex ideas ... considered as dependences on, or affections of substances." Modes are divided into simple and mixed. Simple modes are "variations, or different combinations of *the same* simple idea, without the mixture of any other," whereas Mixed modes are "compounded of simple ideas of *several kinds*, viz.,

[1] Locke, *op. cit.*, Chapter 16, Book 2.

beauty consisting of certain composition of colour, figure ... etc."
Thus for Locke numbers are a combination of identical simple
ideas. The simple idea which makes number is unity or one.
"Amongst all ideas we have ... there is none more simple, than that
of *unity*, or one," and "by adding one to one, we have the complex
idea of a dozen; and so of a score, or a million, or any number."
If we ask from where do we get the idea of unity or one, which,
when repeated, produces the idea of number, Locke will answer
that the idea of unity or one is suggested to the mind "by all the
ways of sensation and reflection ... every idea in our understanding;
every thought of our minds, brings this idea along with it."
Locke's statements on number throw some light on Hume's vague
assertions on number and unity. It seems that also for Hume numbers are composed of units, and units, unlike numbers which are
Modes (since they cannot exist alone) are substantial entities; they
are not "fictitious denominations." Moreover, units, Hume indicates, like his geometrical points (or *minima visibilia*, described by
him to be the ultimate parts of space), are "perfectly indivisible."
Numbers for Hume then are exactly like Locke's simple modes.
They are modes in the sense that they are complex ideas, whose
existence depends on the existence of units. They are simple in the
sense that they are composed of identical units. Yet both Locke's
and Hume's theory of number for the following reasons seems to be
defective.

C. Criticism of Hume's Idea of Number

1. Though *prima facie* it is possible to give an ostensive definition
of something which approaches the Euclidean definition of geometrical point (in a way which Hume describes), we cannot give
an ostensive definition of number or of units which compose number
by pointing to any entity, since number is not a property of any
object. Whereas a property such as blueness could be properly
applied only to extended bodies, number, as Locke already recognized, "applies itself to men, angels, actions, thoughts – everything that either doth exist or can be imagined."
One speaks properly if one talks of the number of rules and the
number of inferences or of the number of negotiations; and the
sense of the term "number" in such expressions remains the same.
But one cannot in the same sense speak meaningfully of blue rules,
or blue inferences, etc., as one speaks of blue eyes. Hence, a dis-

tinction should be made between property and number. Further-more, in the framework of Humian theory we cannot find "entire similarity" of units among distinct and separate ideas if units are nothing above and beyond ideas. But if units are different from ideas, as Hume seems to indicate, then he is accepting entities which do not have any valid credentials in his system.

2. Aside from these considerations, we shall see, as Frege observes, that expressions such as "identical units" do not help us in understanding anything about number. Frege makes two important points with regard to the theory that numbers are composed of identical units.

(a) If by the term "unit" we mean *the number one*, then number cannot be identified with *units*, since in referring to a specific number by means of the definite article we indicate a unique entity. There are no diverse *numbers one*, but only one, and hence a plural makes no sense.

A distinction must be drawn between one and unit. The word "one," as the proper name of an object of mathematical study, does not admit of a plural. Consequently, it is nonsense to make numbers result from the putting together of ones. The plus symbol in $1 + 1 = 2$ cannot mean such a putting together.[1]

(b) On the other hand if by "units" we mean not *ones*, but similar things to be numbered, then number cannot be defined as units. Moreover, the expression "identical units" or "similar units" does not make any sense.

If we call the things to be numbered units, then the assertion that units are identical is, if made without qualification, false. That they are identical in this respect or that is true enough but of no interest. It is actually necessary that the things to be numbered should be different if number is to get beyond 1. We were thus forced, it seemed, to ascribe to units two contradictory qualities, namely identity and distinguishability.[2]

From these obervations Frege concludes that the concept of unit, employed by Hobbes, Locke, Hume, etc., in the explanation of number, is adopted to conceal a real difficulty.

The word 'unit' is admirably adapted to the task, and this is the real, though no doubt unconscious, reason why we prefer it to the words "object" and "thing." We start by calling the things to be numbered "units", without detracting from their diversity, then subsequently the concept of putting together (or collecting, or uniting, or annexing, or whatever we choose to call it) transforms itself into that of arithmetical addition, while the general term "unit" changes unper-

---

[1] Frege, *op. cit.*, p. 59.
[2] *Ibid.*, p. 58.

ceived into the proper name "one." And there we have an identity. If I annex
to the letter *a* first an *n* and then a *d*, anyone can easily see that that is not number
3. If, however, I bring the letters *a*, *n* and *d* under the concept "unit" and now,
instead of "*a* and *n* and *d*" say "a unit and a unit and a unit" or "1 and 1 and 1"
we are quite prepared to believe that this does give us the number 3. The difficulty is so well hidden under the word "unit," that those who have any suspicion
of its existence must surely be few at most.[1]

Frege's criticism makes clear the real difficulty in defining numbers in terms of units. Neither could the term "unit" be a suitable
substitute for "one" nor could units be identified with numbers.
The challenge is still open to the empiricists to explain the meaning
of number without resorting to such vague concepts.

4. THE SCIENCE OF GEOMETRY

A. On Geometry

We now come to consider Hume's discussion of geometry. Geometry, like arithmetic and algebra, is a demonstrative science:
"...it much excels, both in universality and exactness, the loose
judgments of the senses and imagination." (T. 70). However, Hume
maintains in the *Treatise* (not in his other works) that "geometry
falls short of that perfect precision and certainty, which are peculiar
to arithmetic and algebra" (T. 71), with the result that "When
geometry decides any thing concerning the proportions of quantity,
we ought not to look for the utmost *precision* and exactness." (T. 45).

In order to see for what reason Hume makes the judgment that
geometry is not as exact a science as arithmetic and algebra, we
should see in detail both his empirical theory on the nature of
geometrical concepts and also his polemic against the metaphysical
view of the foundation of geometry, namely, the theory of the
infinite divisibility of extension.

Unlike the vague assertions which Hume makes concerning the
status of arithmetical concepts, he is very explicit that geometrical
expressions such as "points," "lines," "angles," etc., all denote
perceptual entities. Geometrical points are for Hume *minima visibilia*.
A point is an ultimate part of space, and this ultimate part must be
colored in order to be sensed. The *minima visibilia* are the ultimate
limit of perception, and the limit of perception is also the limit of
conception.

---

[1] *Ibid.*, p. 50.

As the ultimate standard of these figures [geometrical] is deriv'd from nothing but the senses and imagination, 'tis absurd to talk of any perfection beyond what these faculties can judge of; since the true perfection of any thing consists in its conformity to its standard. (T. 51).

Hume wages war against the metaphysical theory of infinite divisibility of extensions. He is afraid that once we open the door to such ghostly ideas which do not and cannot have any denotation, the door will be flung wide open to hosts of metaphysical ideas. The first paragraph of the section *Of infinite divisibility of our Ideas of Space and Time* begins with:

Whatever has the air of a paradox, and is contrary to the first and most unprejudic'd notions of mankind is often greedily embrac'd by philosophers, as shewing the superiority of their science, which cou'd discover opinions so remote from vulgar conception. (T. 26).

In the *Enquiries* he maintains that:

No priestly *dogmas*, invented on purpose to tame and subdue the rebellious reason of mankind, ever shocked common sense more than the doctrine of the infinitive divisibility of extension, with its consequences; as they are pompously displayed by all geometricians and metaphysicians, with a kind of triumph and exultation. (E. 156).

Hume provides many arguments against this doctrine. The main argument, however, is simple. We cannot perceive an entity which is infinitely divisible.

'Tis therefore certain, that the imagination reaches a *minimum*, and may raise up to itself an idea, of which it cannot conceive any sub-division, and which cannot be diminished without a total annihilation. (T. 27).

According to Hume, the geometrical point which is the fundamental concept of Euclidean geometry is neither a physical point (an extended point) nor an infinitely divisible extension. Hume thinks that he has found a happy "medium" between "the system of physical points" and the theory "maintain'd in the schools, that extension must be divisible, *in infinitum*." (T. 40). The geometrical point is rather "parts of extension, which cannot be divided or lessened, either by the eye or imagination. These images, then, which are present to the fancy or senses, are absolutely indivisible." (E. 156).

Hume assumes that by defining geometrical point in this way he could easily derive the remaining geometrical concepts. A line, on his assumption, would be a length without breadth or depth, composed of indivisible points; likewise, extensions would be lengths and breadths without depth, composed of colored points. (He does not make clear how such colored but indivisible points can lie alongside one another in such a way as to make up a continuous extension.)

Despite the difficulties inherent in Hume's theory of geometry we can clearly see why Hume describes geometry as a science wanting in the exactness of arithmetic and algebra. The main reason why geometry is not an exact science is that we cannot use the arithmetical standard of equality for the discovery of geometrical relations, for the reason that:

...the points, which enter into the composition of any line or surface, whether perceiv'd by the sight or touch, are so minute and so confounded with each other, that 'tis utterly impossible for the mind to compute their number.... (T.45).

'Tis impossible for the eye to determine the angles of a chiliagon to be equal to 1996 right angles, or make any conjecture, that approaches this proportion.... (T. 72).

If it is "impossible for the mind to compute the number" of the indivisible points constituting a line, and to establish a one to one correspondence among these points (as we can do with numbers by correlations of units) in order to judge that two or more lines have identical length, then Hume argues that for the same reason it is also practically impossible to establish equality of geometrical figures in terms of congruity. In referring to Dr. Barrows' definition, he writes: "There are some, who pretend, that equality is best defined by *congruity*, and that any two figures are equal, when upon the placing of one upon the other, all their parts correspond to and touch each other." (T. 46).

But Hume argues that:

...we must at least have a distinct notion of these parts, and must conceive their contact...; since the contact of large parts wou'd never render the figures equal. But the minutest parts we can conceive are mathematical points; and consequently this standard of equality is the same with that deriv'd from the equality of the number of points; which we have already determin'd to be a just but an useless standard. (T. 46).

Thus it seems practically impossible to use the standard of exact equality (which bestows upon arithmetic and algebra ideal exactness) for discovery of geometrical relations (e.g., equality).

I first ask mathematicians, what they mean when they say one line or surface is Equal to, or Greater, or Less than another? Let any of them give an answer, to whatever sect he belongs, and whether he maintains the composition of extension by indivisible points, or by quantities divisible *in infinitum*. This question will embarrass both of them.... They need only reply, that lines or surfaces are equal, when the numbers of points in each are equal; and that as the proportion of the numbers varies, the proportion of the lines and surfaces is also vary'd. But tho' this answer be *just*, as well as obvious; yet I may affirm, that this standard of equality is entirely *useless*, and that it never is from such a comparison we determine objects to be equal or unequal with respect to each other. (T. 45).

Hume maintains that the ideas which are most essential to geometry are those of equality and inequality, and yet these standards are far from being exact and determinate, and "'tis for want of such a standard of equality in extension, that geometry can scarce be esteem'd a perfect and infallible science." (T. 71).

It is to be noted that though Hume says that the "first principles (of geometry) are still drawn from *the general appearance* of the objects; *and that appearance can never afford us any security*," (T. 71 – i.m.) or that "The reason why I impute any defect to geometry, is, because its original and fundamental principles are derived *merely from appearances*" (T. 71 – i.m.), he does not imply that anything is wrong with appearances of data, but only that the relation between geometrical data could not be established in the way that we establish numerical relation.

The point is, that for Hume actually there are two standards of equality. Both these standards are used in finding some relations among data. But some data, viz., units of number, admit of precise determination; the others, viz., units of space, do not.

The standard of equality which, according to Hume, could be used, and is used in geometrical measurement, is "the inaccurate standard, deriv'd from a comparison of objects, upon their general appearance, corrected by measuring and juxtaposition." (T. 638). This alternative "standard of equality" is not itself, according to Hume, a definition (as in case of numerical equality), but in some sense "deriv'd from the whole united appearance and comparison of particular objects." So he says in the Appendix (T. 637).

In the *Enquiries*, we do not find any assertion expressing the belief that geometry is not as exact a deductive science as arithmetic and algebra. He simply maintains, in this work, that the only objects of abstract science or of demonstration are quantity and number, and numerical, and geometrical relations, if true, are exact and universal.

B. *Interpretation of Hume's View on Geometry*

It seems to me that Hume regards geometry (in both the *Treatise* and *Enquiries*) to be a science which actually is conversant with properties of physical space. Nonetheless, geometry, like arithmetic and algebra, is a deductive science, in the sense that a geometrician may deduce valid conclusions from the axioms of geometry (which for Hume are really descriptions of space) without relying on his senses. That is, I think, Hume wants to say that in establishing a generalized truth concerning a geometrical figure, though it is necessary that we be acquainted with that figure itself, and with the certain perceived relations which hold among parts of that figure, it is neither necessary to be acquainted with every member of the class which that figure represents, nor with every possible relation which may hold among the parts of that figure. (E. 289 and 43). While in holding a generalized truth with regard to causal relation, it is never sufficient to rely on observing once a certain perceived relation, nor is it prudent to claim that we *know* that such relations will hold in the future. What makes geometry a deductive science is the fact that geometrical relations, once they are discovered, can be universalized, and the fact that given certain "known relations" we may deduce certain "unknown relations."

A speculative reasoner concerning triangles or circles considers the several *known and given relations* of the parts of these figures, and thence infers some *unknown relation*, which is dependent on the former. *But in moral deliberations we must be acquainted beforehand with all the objects, and all their relations to each other.* (E. 289 - i.m.).

Once we are acquainted with a circle, and once we discover by measurement or demonstration ("For these conclusions are equally just, when we discover the equality of two bodies by a pair of compasses, as when we learn it by a mathematical demonstration" [T. 449]) certain conclusions about that circle, then we can universalize our conclusion and say that the conclusion is true about all circles.

Reason is incapable of any such variation. *The conclusions which it draws from considering one circle are the same which it would form upon surveying all the circles in the universe. But no man, having seen only one body move after being impelled by another, could infer that every other body will move after a like impulse.* All inferences from experience, therefore, are effects of custom, not of reasoning. (E. 43 - i. m.).

From what Hume says concerning the nature of geometrical concepts, it becomes clear that he does not want to say that geometrical truths can be discovered without *any* observation, that is to say, merely from certain axioms and definitions which are not conversant with real space. He mentions explicitly that:

The great advantage of the mathematical sciences above the moral consists in this, *that the ideas of the former, being sensible,* are always clear and determinate, the smallest distinction between them is immediately perceptible, and the same terms are still expressive of the same ideas, without ambiguity or variation. An oval is never mistaken for a circle, nor an hyperbola for an ellipsis.... If any term be defined in geometry, the mind readily, of itself, substitutes, on all occasions, *the definition* of the term defined: Or even when no definition is employed, the object itself may be presented to the senses, (E. 60 – i.m.).

But these "definitions" are not verbal definitions; they are rather descriptions of physical space.

That *the square of the hypothenuse is equal to the squares of the other two sides,* cannot be known, let the terms be ever so exactly defined, without a train of reasoning and enquiry. But to convince us of this proposition, *that where there is no property, there can be no injustice,* it is only necessary to define the terms.... (E. 163).

This is the same position he holds in the *Treatise,* where he maintains that:

'Tis true, mathematicians pretend they give an *exact definition* of a right line, when they say, *it is the shortest way betwixt two points.* But in the first place, I observe, that *this is more properly the discovery of one of the properties of a right line, than a just definition of it.* (T. 49 – i.m.).

Upon this evidence we may now safely interpret Hume's ambiguous assertions in the *Enquiries* which produced divergent opinions among his critics.[1]

That *the square of the hypothenuse is equal to the square of the two sides,* is a proposition which expresses a relation between these figures. *That three times five is equal to the half of thirty,* expresses a relation between these numbers. Propositions of this kind are discoverable by the mere operation of thought, without dependence on what is anywhere existent in the universe. *Though there never were a circle or triangle in nature, the truths demonstrated by Euclid would for ever retain their certainty and evidence.* (E. 25 – i.m.).

By making this assertion, he does not want to imply that "though there never were a circle or triangle *even for Euclid*" the geometrical truths discovered by him would forever retain their certainty and evidence, but that once Euclid observed a geometrical figure and discovered certain relations, "the conclusions which [he] draws from considering one circle are the same which [he] would form upon surveying all the circles in the universe." (E. 43).

---

[1] See Chapter One.

This is indeed a difficult position to maintain if we refuse, as Hume does, to distinguish between pure and applied geometry. Suppose in observing a circle we discover that a point in the circumference of that circle is not exactly the same distance from the center as the rest of the points in the circumference of the same circle: Is that peculiar relation true about all circles? But if someone objects that this particular circle is not a true circle, he already presupposes a definition of a circle which is not necessarily a description of any observed circle. We may object, for example, that, on the basis of Hume's account, why should we not hold, seeing that a loaf of bread nourishes us, that all bread has this property! If the inference from one statement concerning observed events to another statement concerning future events is not a deductive inference, but always probable and "true" only until further notice, why should Hume hold that in case of mathematical relations this inference is deductive?

In answer to these objections, no doubt Hume would resort to his principle of analyticity. He would say that to assert the antecedent and to deny the consequent of the statement: "If something is a triangle, then the sum total of the internal angles of that thing is equal to two right angles" is to hold to a "demonstrably false" statement. But here we observe that Hume's reason for calling such an assertion "demonstrably false" is not based on measuring the angles of a particular triangle, but is based on accepting certain axioms, definitions and rules of inference. The real reason for Hume's belief in the apodeictic certainty of mathematical truths, viz., that "the truths demonstrated by Euclid for ever retain their certainty and evidence," even if "there never were a circle or triangle in nature," is that he appears to assume we never allow such truths to be controverted by empirical evidence. That is to say, if perchance we find, by measurement, that the sum of the angles of a Euclidean triangle does not equal 180 degrees, either we say that we measured wrongly or we say that the triangle we have been measuring is not Euclidean.

Hume, to be sure, sees clearly that though geometrical concepts are derived from perceptions, the propositions stating geometrical truths do not owe their validity to empirical verification, and hence are not subject to revision upon the discovery of new evidence. But he does not fully explain what makes such truths unassailable.

1 See the Appendix.

A. Of Scepticism with Regard to Deductive Reason

Hume, in line with his tendency to regard logic and mathematics as a part of the science of human nature, in the section under the heading *Of Scepticism with Regard to Reason* (T. 180–187) brings some important objections against the very kind of knowledge which previously he allowed to be certain, exact and universal.

Many of Hume's critics have tried to show that his main argument in this section is a *non-sequitur*,[1] and others, to interpret him in such a way as to save him from inconsistency. However, few have recognized that Hume's arguments are not only compatible with the general tenor of his polemic against rationalism but also follow logically from his premises.

In this part I will first present Hume's argument; second, I will endeavor to show the inconclusiveness of his reasons; and third, I will provide evidence to show that the conclusion of his arguments, though incompatible with his assertions concerning the nature of deductive reason, is a logical consequence of his principles. That is, I will argue that Hume's sceptical arguments against reason do indeed perfectly fit into his system. What has no place in the Humian system is his analysis of the apodeictic nature of deductive sciences.

Let us then consider Hume's arguments in the order in which they appear.

"In all demonstrative sciences," he says, "the rules are certain and infallible." (Let us remember that the only example which Hume gives of such rules is the rule which one may apply in arithmetic and not in geometry, for obtaining numerical equality). Though the mathematical rules are certain, in using them we might make mistakes: "but when we apply them, our fallible and uncertain faculties are very apt to depart from them, and fall into error." The fact that mathematicians may make a mistake in their deduction is further established by observing that:

There is no Algebraist nor Mathematician so expert in his science, as to place entire confidence in any truth immediately upon his discovery of it, or regard it as any thing, but a mere probability. Every time he runs over his proofs, his confidence encreases; but still more by the approbation of his friends; and is rais'd to its utmost perfection by the universal assent and applauses of the learned world. Now 'tis evident, that this gradual encrease of assurance is nothing but the addition of new probabilities. (T. 180).

---

[1] See Passmore, *op. cit.*, Chapter 7.

Besides the external evidence, such as the approbation of friends and the applause of the learned world, Hume points out another method for gaining confidence in holding that certain mathematical calculations are beyond doubt.

For 'tis easily possible, by gradually diminishing the numbers, to reduce the longest series of addition to the most simple question, which can be form'd, to an addition of two single numbers; ... Besides, if any single addition were certain, every one wou'd be so, and consequently the whole or total sum; unless the whole can be different from all its parts. (T. 181).

However, Hume says, "Upon this supposition we shall find it impracticable to shew the precise limits of knowledge and probability." Though "knowledge and probability are of such contrary and disagreeing natures, that they cannot well run insensibly into each other," by using the above method we cannot show in practise the exact limit at which probability ends and knowledge begins. In the final analysis, Hume asserts that since there is no definitive method to show that a certain deduction is valid, "all knowledge resolves itself into probability." He rejects his former assertion about the certainty of mathematics by saying that:

I had almost said, that this was certain; but I reflect, that it must reduce *itself*, as well as every other reasoning, and from knowledge degenerate into probability.
Since therefore all knowledge resolves itself into probability, and becomes at last of the same nature with that evidence, which we employ in common life. (T. 181).

"As demonstration is subject to the controul of probability, so is probability liable to a new correction by a reflex act of the mind." Every judgment concerning "our preceding judgment, being founded only on probability, must weaken still further our first evidence, must itself be weaken'd by a fourth doubt of the same kind, and so on *in infinitum*."

Let our first belief be never so strong, it must infalliby perish by passing thro' so many new examinations, of which each diminishes somewhat of its force and vigour.
When I reflect on the natural fallibility of my judgment, I have less confidence in my opinions, than when I only consider the objects concerning which I reason; and when I proceed still farther, to turn the scrutiny against every successive estimation I make of my faculties, *all the rules of logic require a continual diminution, and at last a total extinction of belief and evidence.* (T. 183).

B. *Criticism of Hume's Scepticism*

In arguing with Hume, first we should state that if we accept his initial position that under certain specific conditions our claim to knowledge is legitimate, then given these conditions, one can maintain, without any hesitation, that one *knows* that "three times five is equal to half of thirty," and to say that, one really does not know that this equation is true, but only *believes* that it is true, is to violate the rules of the Humian game, which tell us that we shall say "I know" under certain conditions, and "I believe" under other conditions. The evidence or ground for the truth of the above equations could be established by using Hume's own standard of equality and finding a one-to-one correspondence between units expressed by the two parts of the equation. The sceptical arguments against the possibility of our ever knowing the validity of certain deductions becomes quite pointless if the sceptic from the outset precludes every condition under which validity of an inference could be ascertained. We can have a guarantee if we allow something to count as a guarantee; but if nothing on earth is going to make us sure that a certain statement is analytic or a certain reasoning is valid, then it is necessarily true that we cannot be sure; the necessity of the sceptical argument is in fact a sure sign of its emptiness.[1]

Hume, in the *Enquiries*, asserts that sceptical arguments can be identified by two marks; that "*they admit of no answer and produce no conviction.*" (E. 155). With reference to Cartesian doubt: "antecedent scepticism" which "recommends an universal doubt, not only of all our former opinions and principles, but also of our very faculties," Hume says, "were it ever possible to be attained by any human creature (as it plainly is not) [it] would be entirely incurable." (E. 150). To be sure, Cartesian scepticism would be indeed "incurable" if we believe *a priori* that none of our faculties could ever be reliable. But the real reason for Hume's assertion that such doubts are "entirely incurable" or "admit of no answer" is simply that the sceptic does not allow any standard to be counted as a guarantee. If, on the other hand, there are established standards for telling us which arguments are to be counted as valid and what kind of answer may be accepted as satisfactory, then, when in doubt, we may rely on that standard. Hence, the argument that we sometimes make a mistake in our deduction can do nothing to disturb our conviction that in that particular case we made no mistake.

---

[1] This is restatement of Wittgenstein's dictum that: "Scepticism is *not* irrefutable, but palpably senseless, if it would doubt where a question cannot be asked. For doubt can only exist where there is a question; a question only where there is an answer, and this only where something *can* be *said.*" Tractatus .6.51.

Hume does not recognize that his own scepticism is entirely incurable or admits of no answer. If he could see the emptiness of his scepticism he would not need to call upon human nature to cure him of such philosophical "melancholy and delirium."[1]

Second: Hume in his argument confuses the rules of demonstration with the activities of the inferrer. But the rules of demonstration, the relation of implication and logical consequence are independent of contingencies of daily life; thence, the fact that a certain statement is a logical consequence of certain premises has no bearing upon what any person may happen to imagine, think, believe, or know at a certain time. One may say with Leibniz that the relation of deducibility is timeless in that it makes no sense to assign time value to such a relation and say that this relation now holds between the two sentences, but did not hold at some other time.[2]

Now since it is the absence of the external contingencies which guarantees the incorrigibility of a deduction, Hume's argument on the fallibility of our faculties does not prove that in the last analysis all arguments are inductive and true only until further notice.

And finally, we should mention that Hume's argument that no process of checking and testing is self-confirmatory but always self-destructive is a *non-sequitur*. Even if we grant that the only way of knowing the validity of certain demonstrations is by gathering empirical evidence, it does not follow that every time we check our evidence the probability of mistakes will increase. On the contrary, in the process of induction, the greater the number of instances of an event observed (provided that no contrary instances have been found or those that have are easily explainable), the less probable it becomes that a new instance of an event will turn out to be negative.

In reviewing Hume's sceptical argument with regard to reason, I would like to make two important points.

---

[1] Richard H. Popkin in his article "David Hume and the Pyrrhonian Controversy," *The Review of Metaphysics*, Vol. VI, No. 1, adequately shows the relation between Hume's scepticism and his theory of natural belief. He writes, "Pyrrhonism may be irrefutable, but nature makes us believers, and hence Pyrrhonism can be ignored. Hume once again surpasses his predecessors, 'Philosophy would render us entirely Pyrrhonian were not nature too strong for it' ... nature does not logically refute Pyrrhonism, it only makes it unbelievable. Hume then develops his theory of natural belief showing all the beliefs of a factual, moral, metaphysical, theological and mathematical variety that nature compels us to believe." I argue, further that Pyrrhonian arguments against possibility of establishing the validity of a demonstration is a logical blunder and hence there is no need for Hume's theory of natural belief in order to account for our belief in the validity of a proof.

[2] Rudolph Carnap, *Logical Foundation of Probability* (The University of Chicago Press, 1950), pp. 37–38.

First, I want to make it clear that this sceptical reasoning, though incompatible with his initial distinction between analytic and synthetic judgment and deductive and inductive sciences, itself is a logical consequence of his psychologism. We find that for Hume the analytic-synthetic distinction is established, in the absence of syntactical rules and propositions, with reference to a psychological phenomenon described as conceivability of thinking of a certain arrangement of complex ideas or the inconceivability of constructing such a series in our mind. Though Hume sometimes makes a distinction between the ontological status of inseparable relations and the psychological fact of our belief concerning such relations, he cannot and does not keep these different issues separate, and ultimately reduces the necessity of reason to the contingencies of matters of fact. He cannot keep his own distinctions separate, since, for him, there cannot be anything besides impressions and ideas. That is why, I think, Hume in one place defines "knowledge" as "the assurance arising from the comparison of ideas" (T. 124), and in another place reduces knowledge to probability, and on another occasion says that the necessity which makes two times two equal to four lies only in the act of the understanding, and yet in another part writes that "according to my system, *all reasonings* are nothing but the effects of custom; and custom has no influence, but by inlivening the imagination, and giving us a strong conception of any object." (T. 149).

Second, I maintain that Hume's stand on the issue of scepticism with regard to reason is compatible with many of Hume's anti-rationalistic assertions. The reduction of all reasoning to factual reasoning, and the justification of causal reasoning in terms of habits of association is quite in line with Hume's initial standpoint. We find, for example, that in *An Abstract* he says that "*almost all reasoning* is there (in the Treatise) reduced to experience; and the belief which attends experience is explain'd to be nothing but a peculiar sentiment." In the *Enquiries*, also, despite his sharper distinction between analytic and synthetic judgments, in a long footnote which appears after the distinction he makes between reason employed in geometrical demonstration and reason as employed in causal inferences, he writes:

Nothing is more useful than for writers, even, on *moral*, *political*, or *physical* subjects, to distinguish between *reason* and *experience*, and to suppose, that these species of argumentation are entirely different from each other. The former are taken for the mere result of our intellectual faculties, which, by considering *a priori* the nature of things, and examining the effects, that must follow from their operation, establish particular principles of science and philosophy....

But notwithstanding that this distinction be thus universally received, both in the active [and the] speculative scenes of life, I shall not scruple to pronounce, that it is, at bottom, erroneous, at least, superficial. (E. 43–44).

Again, in the same book, after he compares the exactness of the mathematical sciences with the obscurity predominant in the moral, he states in a similar manner what he expressed in his sceptical argument with regard to reason in the *Treatise*, that:

One may safely, however, affirm, that, if we consider these sciences in a proper light, their advantages and disadvantages nearly compensate each other, and reduce both of them to a state of equality.... In reality, there is scarcely a proposition in Euclid so simple, as not to consist of more parts, than are to be found in any moral reasoning which runs not into chimera and conceit.... The chief obstacle, therefore, to our improvement in the moral or metaphysical sciences is the obscurity of the ideas, and ambiguity of the terms. The principal difficulty in the mathematics is the length of inferences and compass of thought, requisite to the forming of any conclusion. (E. 60).

6. CONCLUSION OF THE CHAPTER

I think it appropriate to conclude our chapter by answering certain specific questions:

A. Does Hume, in line with his empirical principle, assume that the meaning of arithmetical, logical and geometrical concepts is, exhaustible by reference to the data of the senses?

Does he assert that mathematical concepts are hypothetical entities, abstracted from the world of phenomena, or does he sanction the conviction of the formalist?

We can now reply that Hume, quite consistent with his principle of meaning, believes in general that all mathematical and logical concepts are to be explained by reference to our original data of experience. As we observed, Hume actually tried to explain logical constants, such as affirmation and negation, by reference to *resemblances* and *differences* of the data of our experience. He endeavored to describe the law of contradiction in terms of the occurrence and non-occurrence of a perception, and finds an internal impression for necessary connection which appears in causal as well as mathematical reasoning (Chapter 4).

The geometrical concepts, without exception, such as point, line, and extension, are explained with reference to indivisible points and configuration of such points. Even the relation of equality, according to him, is derived from appearances.

Concerning numbers, there is, no doubt, the desire to establish some empirical basis as a source of their derivation. Numbers, he vaguely implies, are the result of surveying points of time, and are composed of indivisible units; and these units, like units of space, are supposed to be exactly similar, though unlike the units of space, he does not tell us how we can ever perceive such entities. Thus it seems that none of the mathematical concepts could denote an abstract hypothetical entity which is supposed to be of "so refin'd and spiritual a nature," since "it is absurd to talk of any perfection beyond what [our] faculties can judge." It does not seem that he ever considered Berkeley's alternative that mathematical expressions do not stand for any entity and yet could be used significantly – that the units which compose numbers are artificial, and "that the reason why we can demonstrate so well about signs is that they are perfectly arbitrary." Hume might say that this could be said about syllogistic but not mathematical demonstration.

Despite these facts, I believe, if Hume could notice the full implication of his analysis that certain concepts such as "substance" could be used significantly as a class name without assuming that there is such a *thing* as a class besides its members, he would have welcomed Russell's recent statement with regard to the fictitious characteristics of numbers.

"When we say 'there is' or 'there are,' it does not follow from the truth of our statement that what we say there is or there are is part of the furniture of the world.... Mathematical logic admits of the statement 'there are numbers' and metalogic admits the statement 'numbers are logical fictions or symbolic conveniences.' Numbers are classes of classes, and classes are symbolic conveniences."[1]

And in reference to the solution of difficulties which was produced by the definition of number in terms of a set of classes, Russell writes: "But much more important than either of these two advantages is the fact that we get rid of numbers as metaphysical entities. They become, in fact, merely linguistic conveniences with no more substantiality than belongs to 'etc.' or 'i.e.'"[2]

[1] B. Russell, *My Philosophical Development*, p. 234.
[2] *Ibid.*, p. 71.

B. Are the statements exhibited in deductive systems analytic or synthetic for Hume? All mathematical truths are analytic in the sense that once discovered they forever retain their certainty. We cannot change the relation which holds between the terms of the true mathematical expression *without changing the very nature of our ideas* and we cannot deny such a relation without asserting a self-contradictory statement. However, mathematical statements are not analytic in a Kantian sense, i.e., the containment of the predicate in the subject. They are not tautologies like "all bodies are extended" or "for every effect there is a cause," and cannot be discovered "let the term be ever so exactly defined." Geometrical truths are definitely descriptions of reality and not mere verbal definitions. On the other hand, Hume implies that if logical demonstration is valid, its validity is the consequence of certain relations holding between the terms of some verbal definitions. Thus Hume, without using Locke's distinction between trifling propositions and instructive ones, in effect assumes that all mathematical truths are analytic and instructive, but all logically true statements are trifling tautologies.

In so interpreting Hume, it appears that Kant's analysis of Hume's opinion on mathematical truths is mistaken.[1] Kant assumes that Hume would not submit "the axioms of pure mathematics to experience...." But Hume in fact did submit the principles of mathematics to experience without falling subject to Kant's alternative, i.e., "for he would have to take mathematics as also synthetic ... and he had too much insight to do this."

We also see that Windelband's view is mistaken. Though mathematics for Hume "is the sole demonstrative science" (as Windelband rightly states), it is not because "it relates to nothing else than the possible relations between contents of ideas, and asserts nothing whatever as to any relation of these to a real world."[2]

However, we observed that Hume's explanation of the foundations of mathematical concepts and the nature of their relations is quite defective. The more abstract our concepts become, the less successful is Hume's account of the impressions which correspond to such concepts. Neither the exactness nor the universality of mathematical truths has any real place in the Humian world of impressions and ideas. In this we agree with Kant's comments

[1] Kant, *The Prolegomena*, p. 21.
[2] Windelband, *op. cit.*, p. 473.

that: "This empirical deduction, which was adopted by both philosophers [Locke and Hume] cannot be reconciled with the reality of our scientific knowledge *a priori*, namely, pure mathematics."[1]

C. If these statements are analytic, on what ground does Hume construe them to be so?

The full answer to this question is already given in the third chapter. Here we only mention that Hume makes many assertions on what makes a judgment analytic. Analytic judgments are not eternal truths of reason or God-given truths. They are guaranteed by having certain invariable, inseparable relations to relata or by being incorrigible in the sense that we cannot conceive them to be otherwise.

D. If analyticity is explained in terms of certain relations and definitions, what is the nature of these relations and definitions? Are they self-evident truths or mere tautologies?

This question was also previously answered. There are no self-evident truths in Hume's system. Yet mathematical truths are not tautologies. Ultimately the nature of analytical relations is a perceived relation holding between sense-data. But from their known relation we may discover "unknown relations by a chain of reasoning." However, these relations have a dubious status in Hume's system. If relations are not the data of experience the only place which Hume could provide for them is in the mind of the observer. Yet the Humian mind is nothing but a congeries of perceptions.

E. If Hume does make a distinction between analytic and synthetic statements, and between deductive and inductive sciences, how important is this distinction for his theory?

Hume does make such a distinction, and this distinction is fundamental in his system. For it is in virtue of this differentiation that he is able to assume that demonstrative reason has no place in reasoning concerning matters of fact or in moral argument. Moreover, with this distinction in mind, he undermines the very core of rationalistic philosophy, namely that there are innate and eternal truths. That there are certain truths which differ from empirical truth, he agrees, but he denies that they are innate and eternal.

F. Does Hume fully distinguish between the deductive and inductive sciences, or does he obliterate his early distinction in his polemical section "Of Scepticism with Regard to Reason"?

The answer to the latter part of this question is positive. Hume

---

[1] Kant, *Critique*, p. 742.

not only reduces, in that section of the *Treatise*, all knowledge to probability, but in many other places undermines the very foundation of such a distinction, as we have shown in this chapter.

G. And lastly, we want to know: How does Hume give an account of demonstrative reasoning, while he rejects the basic principles of formal logic?

Syllogistic logic, as such, is considered by Hume to be "mere sophistry and illusion" and logical demonstration, if valid, is in reality a chain of tautologies. There are no self-evident logical truths, and if there were, "we cannot go at step beyond them." Demonstrative reason, as such, is limited to the mathematical sciences.

CHAPTER SIX

The Domain of Inductive Reason

1. INTRODUCTION

A considerable part of Hume's philosophy is centered around issues concerning the epistemic foundation of beliefs – ranging from the most rudimentary and unproblematic, such as belief in the existence of unperceived objects or belief in our personal identity to the most sophistical such as belief in the laws of motion or in "Providential Design," and to the most irrational, such as belief in immortality or in miracles and the like.

The search for the foundation of belief is also a search for a method of forming and defending our beliefs. Hume's epistemological inquiries lead him into problems about methodology such as probability, causation, inference and induction.

There is for Hume a domain of inductive or probable reason concerning "matters of fact and existence" which is distinct from the domain of deductive reason, i.e., the domain of Knowledge "strictly so-called." Hume admits the significance of the sciences which fall within the latter domain, namely arithmetic, algebra and geometry (he does not include deductive logic, though it fits the class) but he seems to see no important problem with regard to the epistemic foundation or about the methodology of these sciences.

On the other hand, Hume is deeply interested in the domain of inductive reason, which is also the domain of the empirical sciences, and with their epistemological and methodological problems.

In a passage in the *Abstract* he prides himself on accepting Leibniz's recommendation, i.e. paying due attention to "probabilities, and those measures of evidence on which life and action entirely depend" which was neglected "in the common system of logic." (A. 8)[1]

_____

[1] Perhaps Hume is referring to the following passages in Leibniz's *New Essays*: "O-

Hume is very much concerned with what is now called the "logic of induction," "subjective probabilities" and "the problem of the justification of induction." He is called "the discoverer of the Problem of Induction,"[1] the problem which whose solution engaged the efforts of many distinguished philosophers of 19th and 20th centuries. Since no solution had been found, it is called "the tragic problem of induction."

To get rid of the problem of induction some attempt is made for its dissolution. It is also argued that though there is a problem, induction is not used in science; hence, it is not a problem within the methodology of the empirical sciences.

Despite these attempts few made a close examination of Hume's various statements of the problem. One obviously cannot solve or even dissolve Hume's problem without making a thorough analysis of his text – and this is what I am going to do.

Before we engage in such an inquiry we have to state in detail Hume's doctrine of the foundation of empirical knowledge and the methodology of science, since empirical knowledge falls within the domain of inductive reason.

I will argue then that the problem of induction is not a statable problem and so neither its solution nor its dissolution is efficacious.

Hume's scepticism about induction is applicable *mutatus mutandis*, not only to the issue of future contingencies and prediction, which was his main concern, but also to the issue of our knowledge about the past and retrodiction and our knowledge about what we are immediately acquainted with (the latter assumed to be unproblematic by Hume).

I argue that since there is no such thing as mere knowledge by acquaintance, there cannot be any problem about the justification of our knowledge of the hidden (in the past or the future) which is not also a problem about our knowledge of the given.

Hence if Hume's scepticism about our knowledge of the future is justifiable, it is likewise justifiable with regard to our knowledge

pinion, based on the probable, also deserves perhaps the name knowledge; otherwise nearly all historical knowledge and many other kinds will fall. ... I hold that the *investigation of degrees of probability* would be very important, that we are still, lacking in it, and that this lack is a great defect of our logic." Ch. II.

"I have more than once said that we should have a *new kind* of logic, which would treat degrees of probability." Ch. XVI from Leibniz, edited Philip P. Wiener, New York, N.Y.: Scribner's Sons, 1951.

[1] Hume however does not use the word 'induction' throughout except in the *Appendix* where he writes "I conclude, by an induction which seems to me very evident..." (T. 628)

about the past and the present. Hume's problem starts with the premise that we know something about the immediately given data and that is indubitable (in addition to the suppressed premise that we also know something about the past).

Now if we reject this premise, even without rejecting the suppressed premise, we shall see that the arguments cannot be stated without it. For either we have no *reason* to believe that anything is known or if we have any reason to believe that some given events are known, we have also some reason to believe that some hidden events (past and future) are. And in all these cases we do use same kind of reason.

The insight is Kant's "Intuitions without concepts are blind." There cannot be such things as bare particulars which are known to us without background information. I argue then that since the known particulars are not bare, but are covered by categories of our thoughts, there is no problem about the justification of inference from mere sense-given to unperceived particulars, or in Hume's language, "from instances, of which we have had experience" to "instances of which we had no experience."

To recognize and talk about instances of which we have had experience, is already to transcend them.

Although the subject of the justification of induction deserves our full attention, we shall also deal with other issues. In Hume's system the methodological and epistemological topics are mixed. In this chapter I shall attempt to separate the epistomelogical problem of the reduction of beliefs from methodological issues concerning the nature of causal inference, the logic of belief, and the justification of induction. We shall also study subjects which fall within the domain of inductive reason concerned with matters of fact.

The chapter is divided into Four Parts:

2. The Foundation of Empirical Knowledge
   A. Two kinds of reductions:
      a) Reduction of concepts to sense-data (the issue of innateness)
      b) Reduction of factual belief to experience
   B. The nature of inference
      a) Causal inference (the psychological thesis)
      b) Causal inference (philosophical relation)
      c) The origin of the idea of causation
      d) Definition of causation (first definition – second definition)

2. THE FOUNDATION OF EMPIRICAL KNOWLEDGE

A. Two kinds of reductions

Through his philosophical enterprise, Hume engaged in two kinds of reductions, first, the reduction of some basic concepts to experiential data (roughly to sense-data) and, second, the reduction of some basic beliefs either about *matters of fact and existence* or about the *relation of ideas* or moral, political, religious and aesthetic beliefs to experience.

He was not only concerned with the reduction of what Russell calls "Knowledge by Description" to "Knowledge by Acquaintance," but in a broader sense reduction of all our beliefs to experience.

The purpose behind each type of reduction, to put it in very general terms, is this: If the reduction is successful, we may bestow meaning on our concepts, and truth or probability on our beliefs, and if not, not. Reduction provides us with a demarcation line between *bona fide* concepts and meaningless concepts, and between rational and irrational beliefs.

These two kinds of reductions are distinct and separable though interconnected.

a) *Reduction of concepts to sense-data (the issue of inateness)*

In Chapter One, "The Principle of Meaning," "we already observed how Hume tried to reduce some of our fundamental concepts such as the concepts of material and mental substances, geometrical points, space, time, numbers, God, etc. to some data of experience. We observed that the theory that all of our ideas are copies of impressions did serve him very little.

The theory was then replaced and used (though without any notice and even then, not uniformly) by a sort of causal theory of meaning. Ideas are supposed to be *deriv'd, caused* or even *borrowed* from their corresponding impressions.

This weaker theory is much less testable than the copy-theory. For one may test adopting a realistic language (forgetting various problems concerning the recurrence or privacy of impressions) that certain ideas, primary visual and tactual, stand in relation to impressions, as a picture stands to a pictured object, or a footprint stands to a foot. But we cannot determine in what respect all our ideas are caused by their corresponding impressions.

Now we may resort to Hume's own way out of the dilemma by calling forth the faculty of imagination in order to supply the missing causal link between ideas and impressions. ("I have already observ'd, in examining the foundations of mathematics, that the imagination, when set into any train of thinking, is apt to continue, even when the object fails it, and like a galley put in motion by the oars, carries on its course without any new impulse." (T. 198))

But this *ad hoc* device is not efficacious, as Hume himself observes. In *The Dialogue*, Philo states "That exact similarity of the cases gives us a perfect assurance of a similar event... But where-ever you depart, in the least, from the similarity of the cases, you diminish proportionably the evidence; and may at least bring it to a very weak *analogy*, which is confessedly liable to error and uncertainty." (D. 116)

Unless Hume provides a causal relation among ideas and impressions and not *any* relation among some of them, we should conclude that the theory is unconfirmed or is not testable.

At best Hume showed in some general manner that having sense-experience is somehow connected with the formation of some of our concepts. But he was not able to show that in every case sense-experience is a necessary condition, much less a sufficient condition for concept-formation.

Hume states that his principle about the relation of impressions and ideas is equivalent to Locke's denial of innate ideas. However, he criticizes Locke for classifying all perceptions under the term 'Idea' and so not seeing any difference between impressions and ideas. Hume readily admits that "our stronger perceptions or impressions are innate, and that natural affection, love of virtue, resentment, and all the other passions, arise immediately from nature." (A. 9)

And again: "But admitting these terms, *impressions* and *ideas* in the sense above explained, and understanding by *innate*, what is original or copied from no precedent perception, then may we assert that all our impressions are innate, and our ideas not innate." (E. 22)

What Hume in fact maintains is that our concepts are derivable from "our sensations and passion" but our sensations and passions or even dispositions are not derivable, hence they are original or innate. Not only our passions and sensations are innate, but more importantly our disposition to act and to learn.

In fact, Hume is very much interested with the innate psychological mechanism of habit formation. Man, at the bottom rock, simply is an animal who acts according to his innate disposition without having choice or reason – and 'reason' in one sense "is nothing but a wonderful instinct in our souls, which carries us along a certain train of ideas." What Hume denies is that embodied ideas, or the supposed disembodied ideas, like Descartes' idea of the Ego or God, are in the mind at the start.[1]

b) *Reduction of Factual Belief to Experience*

Given that concepts are reducible ultimately to experiental data, the next question is: what are the grounds for our beliefs when these beliefs are expressed through statements containing those concepts?

[1] Since of late the issue of innateness is revised by some linguists, it is sufficient to show that contrary to some, Hume's empirical stand is not in conflict with the thesis that there are innate dispositions for language-learning. Hume's thesis is refutable if it is shown that there are inborn *concepts*.

We shall now consider Hume's theory with regard to the foundation of empirical knowledge and his attempted reduction of belief in "matters of fact and existence" to experience. We are not concerned here with the reduction of belief in mathematical assertions to assertions about certain basic conceptual relations (see *The Domain of Deductive Reason*, especially Part 5A) or with the reduction of ethical, political, religious, or aesthetical beliefs to experience.

The problem could be stated in this form "Why do we believe that 'x is y'?" To answer this we should raise two questions: 1. What kind of entities are to be substituted for 'x' and 'y', and what kind of a relation exist between them? 2. What is the nature of a belief that something is the case and what are the conditions if fulfilled upon which we can justifiably claim that we *believe* that something is the case, rather than we *know* that something is the case?

The first question falls properly under semantics and logic, and the second under pragmatics. But as we observed for Hume all these inquiries fall within the province of epistemology and psychology.

We shall start with the first question, i.e. the nature of entities and relation among them, and only then with the question about our beliefs about entities and their relations.

We observed that in the *Treatise* a fundamental distinction is made between two kinds of philosophical relations among our ideas, viz., (1) relations which are "ivariable, as long as our ideas remain the same" and "are discoverable from mere ideas" (we call them "(A) Relations") and (2) relations which "may be chang'd without any change of ideas" and are "never discoverable merely from their ideas" but are discoverable "from experience, and not from any abstract reasoning or reflexion." (We call them "(B) Relations").

The only members of (A) Relations which may provide us with *demonstrative knowledge* is proportion of quantity or number (the others, since "they are immediately "given" fall more properly under intuition than demonstration").

The members of the class of (B) Relations are identity, relations of time and place, and causation. Here again Hume dismisses those relations of ideas which are immediately given, such as identity and relations of time and place.

The only relations which "can be trac'd beyond our senses, and inform us of existences and objects, which we do not see or feel, is causation."

In the *Enquiries* a simple distinction replaces (A) and (B) Relations. "All objects of human reason or inquiry" fall within two classes of "relations of ideas" and "matters of fact".

Statements in deductive sciences, "every affirmation which is either intuitively or demonstratively certain," belong to the class of relations of ideas.

But our knowledge is not limited to knowledge of relations of ideas, or, let us say simply "Conceptual Statements." There are also "Matters of fact proposition"... let us call them "factual statement" and our knowledge expressed about matters of fact is derived from a different source.

B. *The Nature of Inference*

Now for Hume our belief, either about facts or concepts, is essentially inferential. Given P we infer Q. P states what is intuitively given and indubitable, and strictly speaking we should say we intuit P. But Q expresses what is not given, and hence not indubitable. If P is true, Q may be false.

In the domain of the deductive sciences, Hume believes there is a fundamental criterion for valid inference. The criterion is this, $(P \rightarrow Q)$ is valid if and only if $(P \wedge \bar{Q})$ is false, or logically incompatable, or is absurd. And if $(P \rightarrow Q)$ is valid, then "necessarily $(P \rightarrow Q)$" and we can claim that we *know* that is the case.

However, in the domain of facts and thus in the empirical sciences, the interence from P to Q is only causal. When we do infer Q from P it is logically possible for P to be the case and Q not the case. Hence causal inference at best and at most represents probabilities and never certainties.

Empirical knowledge consists of assertions about what transcends the given. The move from the given to the hidden is made via the process which may be called inductive inference. Causal inference is a sub-class of inductive inference. Inductive inference is an inference from the given to the hidden *via* appeal to some regularities (laws, or law-like statements). Causal inference is an inference from what is given at the present to what will occur in the future, or in the past. (It requires temporal sequence).

Hume formulated the general problem of inductive inference, though he is mostly concerned with a more limited problem of causal inference. Hence we should begin with representing his view of causal inference, and only then shall we consider more general problems of inductive inference.

a) *Causal inference (the psychological thesis)*

The association of ideas in our mind are by resemblance, contiguity and causation. The train of ideas appear in our mind naturally (not artificially) and habitually (opposed to *rationally* and *philosophically*) in a certain order – and there is a reason for this order.

Seeing a portrait may lead us to think about the model of that portrait, "resemblance," looking at a face may bring about the idea of a body, "contiguity," and hearing a song may induce the idea of the singer, "causation." Causation is the strongest associative link. "There is no relation which produces a stronger connexion in the fancy, and makes one idea readily recall another, than the relation of cause and effect betwixt their objects." (T. 11)

The three principles of associations of ideas, Hume writes in the *Abstract*, "are the only links that bind the parts of the universe together, or connect us with any person or object exterior to ourselves. For as it is by means of thought only that any thing operates upon our passions, and as these are the only ties of our thougths, they are really *to us* the cement of the universe, and all the operations of the mind must, in a great measure, depend on them." (A. 32)

If we move then from one idea to another, it is because of resemblances, or contiguity or causal relations among ideas, and causation is the strongest relation among ideas. It is mainly because of causation that we are able to make inferences. "In so far as it (causation) is a *natural* relation, and produces an union among our ideas, that we are able to reason upon it, or draw any inference from it." (T. 94)

Hume here is obviously stating a psychological thesis akin to later theories of conditioned reflex or stimulus-response. The theory meant to explain the nature of unreflective and natural inference shared by man and animal.

The value of such a theory is limited because it is a species of speculative and purely descriptive psychology. Nonetheless the theory is important in our understanding a major portion of Hume's doctrine about beliefs concerning the external object and belief in our personal identity.

b) *Causal inference (philosophical relation)*

Causation belongs to the class of natural, as well as philosophical relations; it is "a seventh philosophical relation, as well as a natural one." (T. 15)

By "Philosophical Relations" Hume means certain kinds of relations which are discoverable by thinking and reflection "even upon the arbitrary union of two ideas in the fancy, we may think proper to compare them." (T. 13)

Philosophical relations are relations between any two or more sets, "any particular subject of comparison, without a connecting principle" (T. 14)

Some philosophical relations are necessary, (A) relations, such as mathematical relations, and some are contingent relations, (B) relations, such as *causation*. Contingent relations, unlike necessary relations, are discoverable empirically and not conceptually "of which we receive information from experience and not from any abstract reasoning or reflexion." (T. 67)

Now in discovering causal relations, unlike other contingent relations, we use inference and reason by going beyond the given sense-data.

"We ought not to receive as reasoning any of the observations we may make concerning *identity*, and the *relations* of *time* and *place*, since in none of them the mind go beyond what is immediately present to the senses, either to discover the real existence or the relations of objects. 'Tis only *causation*, which produces such a connexion, as to give us assurance from the existence or action of one object, that 'twas follow'd or perceived by any other existance or action. . . . of those three relations, which depend not upon the mere ideas, the only one, that can be trac'd beyond our senses, and informs us of the existences and objects, which we do not see or feel, is *causation*." (T. 73–74)

c) *The origin of the idea of causation*

Reflection upon the idea of causation does not reveal any particular impression which is supposed to be the origins of the idea. But though there is no impression of causation as such, there are certain conditions, which if satisfied explain its origin. Causal relation, in effect, is a second-order relation which stands in need of three other (first-order) relations:

First: Contiguity in time and place.

To say that two sets of events are spatio-temporally contiguous is to say that all points between these two sets is filled by some other chain of events "which are contiguous among themselves and to the distant objects." (T. 75)

Spatio-temporal contiguity vitiate the supposition of *Action at a Distance*. We do say that the sea tides are caused by the moon's gravitational force despite the distance between the earth and its only natural satellite, and this is because every point from the moon to the sea tides is filled by a chain of other contiguous events. We do not believe, however, that praying is the cause of regaining health or that black magic causes death, because there is no causal chain to fill the gap between any members of each pairs of sets. We abstain from believing in telepathy until spatio-temporal contiguity is established between members of sets which are claimed to be causally related.

In a footnote to *Contiguity*, Hume refers to a later discussion in Part IV, Sec. 5. Here he questions "the general opinion" (T. 75); according to it spatial contiguity is supposed to be essential to causation. His argument rests upon the rejection of the materialist's thesis that spatial order is a necessary condition for existence of any events. Taking a Cartesian stand about the so-called secondary qualities, he argues on a purely a prioristic ground that taste, smell, or sound, like passion, do exist "without any place" for if they were in space they should be "figur'd and extended" (T. 238) or they should be "either a circular or a square figure" (T. 236) which he believes they are not.

If this is a case we may establish, or discover, causal relations among those events "which exists without any particular place" (T. 237) and nevertheless are "co-existent" and "co-temporal" with the extended objects such as "the taste and smell of any fruit (which) are inseparable from its other qualities of colour and tangibility." (T. 237)

He then goes further to explain why common sense fabricates spatial order, though there is none.

in the present instance, where from the relations of causation and contiguity in time between two objects, (the smell or taste of a fruit) we feign likewise that of a conjunction in place, in order to strengthen the connexion. (T. 238).[1]

Second: "Priority of time in the cause before the effect."

We observed that temporal order is a necessary condition for the

---

[1] Hume's argument against metaphysical materialism or commonsense is sound. But it does not have any force against modern materialism which is in accord with discoveries in physics and psycho-physics about the location of pleasure or the shape and place of sound waves or brain waves.

ascribing causal relation. Cause, among other things, is that event which is temporary prior to event we call "effect." Hume considered and rejects co-temporarity of cause and effect.[1]

Third: Necessary connection and constant conjunction. Hume states that necessary connection "is of much greater importance than any of the other two above mention'd" (T. 77). He then tries to find the impression of necessary connection. Neither spatio-temporal contiguity nor priority or their conjunction is sufficient for ascription of causal relation. It seems however that

The necessary connexion betwixt causes and effects is the foundation of our inference from one to another. The foundation of our inference is the transition from accustom'd union. (T. 165)

The idea of necessary connection is not derivable from any impression, but it is derivable from the constant conjunction between series of events that we discover through observation.

It's "that propensity, which custom produces, to pass from an object to the idea of its usual attendant... upon the whole, necessity is something that exists in the mind, not in objects.... Either we have no idea of necessity, or necessity is nothing but that determination of thought to pass from causes to effects and from effects to causes, according to their experienc'd union." (T. 165)

As in conceptual necessities, the force of the logical *must* "lie in the act of the understanding by which we consider and compare these ideas," viz. mathematical relations, so contingent or *Post Factum* necessities "which unites causes and effects, lies in the determination of the mind to pass from the one to the other." (T. 166).

Since we move from P to Q, mostly because we had experienced a constant union between P and Q, we say that necessarily (P → Q). Upon observing P we expect Q and upon observing Q we assume that P proceeded Q.

Because we draw such inferences, we assume necessary connection and not vice versa.

the necessary connexion depends on the inference, instead of the inference's depending on the necessary connection. (T. 88)

Thus Hume after his long search for the origin of the idea of necessary connection finally resorts to his psychological thesis and borrows from *Natural Relations* an element, i.e. a habitual "propensity" or "determination" which forces us to move from one

---

[1] We shall state his argument under "General Rules."

event to another, in order to explain the credibility of a philosophical relation. And so he writes,

Thus tho, causation be a *philosophical* relation, as implying contiguity, succession, and constant conjunction, yet 'tis only so far as it is a *natural* relation, and produces an union among our ideas, that we are able to reason upon it, or draw any inference from it. (T. 94)

d) *Definitions of Causation*:

The psychological explanation of the association of causes and effects, the philosophical analysis of conditions under which we attribute causal relations to events and the discovery of the origin of the idea of necessary connection in the mind of the inferer and not in any impression or in any relation among impressions are stepping stones for: (1) Definitions of causation, and the (2) Rejection of various metaphysical concepts of "Cause" in philosophical systems.

Hume provides two different definitions of "Causation." One is objective and realistic, and the other is subjective and phenomenalistic. In the latter case causation is defined not only in terms of some objective relations, among *objects* and *perceptions* but also in terms of these relations and the mind of the observer or the discoverer of these relations.

The First definition: Hume views the world from two different points: (1) as class of "objects" existing in themselves and having certain objective relations with each other, and (2) as a class of "perceptions" which are "the perceptions of human mind" (T. 1).

The shift from one aspect to the other and careless juxtaposition of 'perception' and 'object' is common practice in the *Treatise*. This shift is the main cause of controversy among his commentators on whether he was a phenomenalist or a realist.

What is clear is that Hume definitely realizes that the assumption of existence of either object or perception in themselves, that is without any necessary connection to the mind of the percipient, is a logically possible assumption – an assumption which directly follows from his Principle of Atomism according to which "whatever objects are different are distinguishable, and that whatever objects are distinguishable are separable" (T. 89).

On this ground, he argues that "The supposition of the continu'd existence of sensible objects or perceptions involves no contradiction" (T. 208).

He is quite aware that the juxtaposition of 'perception' and 'object' may be regarded as a categorical mistake. But he argues that since

a *mind*, is nothing but a heap or collection of different perceptions, (and since) every perception is distinguishable from another, and may be consider'd as separately existent; it evidently follows, that there is no absurdity in separating any particular perception from the mind; that is, in breaking off all its relations, with that connected mass of perceptions, which constitute a thinking being. (T. 207)

And so "If the name *perception* renders not this separation from a mind absurd and contradictory, the name of *object*, standing for the very same thing, can never render their conjunction impossible." (T. 207).

The first definition of 'causation' is given on the assumption of the existence of the world, independent of the percepient and Hume states that "As to what may be said, that the operations of nature are independent of our thought and reasoning, I allow it" (T. 168). The definition excludes necessary connection, since, as we observed, this relation exists only in the mind of the inferer and Hume does not presuppose the mind of the inferer in his first definition. Here is then the first definition:

We define a cause to be *an object precedent and contiguous to another, and where all the objects resembling the former are plac'd in a like relation of priority and contiguity to those objects, that resemble the latter.* (T. 172)

In the *Enquiries* a modified version of it appears.

We may define a cause to be *an object, followed by another, and where all the objects similar to first are followed by objects similar to the second. Or in another words where, if the first object had not been, the second never had existed* (E. 76)

Note that the first part of the definition provides a sufficient condition and the second a necessary condition for the true ascription of causal relation between any two or more sets of events. The second definition: In the second definition the idea of necessary connection, in effect, is employed.

We define a cause to be, *An object precedent and contiguous to another, and so united with it in the imagination, that the idea of the one determines the mind to form the idea of the other, and the impression of the one to form a more lively idea of the other* (T. 172)

In each definition reference is made to the existence of some regularities, or what we now call "law or law-like statements" which are assumed to be necessary for causal ascription. To see Hume's point let us depict the structure of causal inference.

We observe certain unions among events:

1. Fa ∧ Ga′	Observed relation
2. Fb ∧ Gb′	Observed relation
3. Fc ∧ Gc′	Observed relation

We conclude then 4. (x) (Fx → (∃y)Gy) Law statement (reading '→' as *de facto* conditional)

Now we observe   5. Fd   Observed event

We then conclude   (∃y)Gy   Expected event

Thus it seems that for Hume causal relation could not hold without appeal to law or to law-like statements. This *seems* to leave singular causal statements unexplained.

Can we say, for example, that the kicking over of a lamp in Mrs. Leary's barn caused the Chicago fire? (Quine's) Now Hume does not claim that we cannot assert any singular causal statement, unless we can state the law which covers that singular statement, but only that the causal ascription to any sets of events, be it unique or singular, such as the Chicago fire or the destruction of Dresden or Hiroshima presupposes existence of certain regularities so that to say that "A caused B" is to believe that (∃x) (x is a causal law and x is instantiated by some true descriptions of A and B).[1]

As we shall see later, Hume states that we may establish a causal relation by a single experiment provided that we tacitly assume that it will hold under similar conditions. However, the puzzling question is not about the ascription of causal relation to unique events, but to human action. Are there any laws, or even any law-like statements, which we have to appeal to in order to explain Churchill's decision to destroy Dresden or Truman's to destroy Hiroshima? Does it follow that if the circumstances were repeated the same kind of action would follow, as it should if Hume is right in saying that, "a cause to be an object, followed by another, and where all the objects similar to the first are followed by objects similar to the second"?

In short, explanation of man's action, unlike explanation of natural events, does not seem to require the existence of laws or law-like statements of the same *kind* as natural regularities.

We shall return to this point after examining Hume's attempted explanation of human actions.

[1] This point is due to Donald Davidson, "Actions, Reasons, and Causes," *The Journal of Philosophy*, LX No. 23 (1963).

e) *Rejection of metaphysical causation*

The two definitions of 'causation' serve Hume quite well in his attempted rejection of various metaphysical notions of causation.

First to be attacked is the causal maxim: "'Tis a general maxim in philosophy, that whatever begins to exist, must have a cause of existence." (T. 78)

He argues that the statement is not analytic "either demonstrative or intuitive" (T. 172) since if it were its denial would be self-contradictory which it is not. He then argues that various arguments produced by Hobbes, Clark, Locke and Spinoza to demonstrate the necessity of cause are fallacious and sophistical. He concludes "that when we exclude all causes we really do exclude them, and neither suppose nothing [Locke] nor the object itself [Spinoza] to be the causes of the existence." (T. 81)

Second, he argues then that if the Principle of Causation is not analytic, that is, "is not from knowledge or any scientific reasoning, that we derive the opinion of the necessity of a cause to every new production," then "that opinion must necessarily arise from observation and experience." (T. 82)

But all that experience suggests is "that such particular causes must necessarily have such particular effects" (T. 82) but not that necessarily every thing whose existence has a beginning must have a cause, hence the maxim is neither analytic or a factual statement.

Further, since "necessity" in a final analysis is subjective "there is no absolute nor metaphysical necessity, that every beginning of existence shou'd be attended with such an object." (T. 172)

Hume's excellent refutation of the causal maxim, as we observed worried Kant. Kant thought that the causal maxim being a paradigm-case of metaphysics and metaphysical statements having the same structure as the maxim – we have to conclude that either metaphysics is a delusion or Hume's analytic-syntatic dicotomy is defective.

Now Hume immediately after rejecting the causal maxim raises a totally different question, namely: "*Why we conclude, that such particular causes must necessarily have such particular effects, and why we form an inference from one to another?*" (T. 82)

This is the first, but not the only statement, of the so-called "Problem of Induction" which is stated here in an oblique way and in the form of a question about the principle of causal inference. At this juncture Hume states that perhaps the Principle of Causal

Inference, (which is a subclass of the Principle of Induction), like the Causal Maxim, admits of the same kind of treatment (roughly neither reason or experience can support either the Causal Maxim or the Principle of Induction.)

f) *Causal Explanation of Action*

(Reason in animal – choice and cause)

Hume's definition of causation serves him also (1) to dismiss the four types of Aristotelian causation: "All causes are of the same kind." He does not give any serious reason for reducing final causes (and by that I do not mean metaphycal final causes) to constant conjunction between two sets of events.

He also dismisses (2) the traditional distinction between *moral* and *physical* necessities. He states that as there is only one type of causation "there is but one kind of *necessity* and that the common distinction betwixt *moral* and *physical* necessity is without any foundation in nature" (T. 171).

And why so? Because, once again by his own stipulation 'necessity' is the name of that determination of the mind to pass from cause to the effect or vice versa due to constant conjunction of events.

The serious consequences of the reduction of final cause to constant conjunction and moral necessity to physical necessity will appear later in his work. The reduction is the stepping stone for seeing a kind of determinism which is operative both in the "natural" as well as in "the moral world."

Since Hume regards motives and inclinations as causes for human action, "The same experienced union has the same effect on the mind, whether the united objects be motives, volition, and actions, or figure and motion" (E. 91), the distinction between intention and cause, and with that the line between the man and animal is reduced to a vanishing point.

And Hume in fact argues that there is no *essential* distinction between man and animal – but only differences in degree, which is another attack on the rationalists and about their metaphysical view about the nature of man and animal – for example, Descartes. [Reason in Animals]

Under the title "Of the Reason in Animals" he goes on to argue that "beasts are endow'd with thought and reason as well as we" (T. 176) for the following reasons:

1. Actions are external happenings.
2. Since in our own case, our actions are causally connected with "reason and design,"
3. We infer that animals do have motive and reason. "We judge their internal likewise to resemble ours."

A distinction then is made between instinctive behaviour, "those actions of animals, which are of a vulgar nature," and learned behavior, "those more extraordinary instances of sagacity, which they sometimes discover for their own preservation."

As an example of the first kind, "a dog that avoids fire and precipices," and an example of the second, "A bird that chosses with such care and nicety the place and materials of her nest... with all the precaution that a chymist is capable of in the most delicate projection." (T. 177)

Both sorts of animal behavior or "action" (no distinction is made here) whether habitual, instinctive or deliberate (again no clear distinction is made among these concepts) are like human behavior. Both man and animal are engaged in inferences from the given to the unknown, and such inferences are "natural" which means "non-rational," rather "irrational."

In the *Enquiries* the same view is expressed. But in a footnote, as an afterthought, he provides some answer to a would-be questioner. "Since all reasoning concerning facts or causes is derived merely from custom, it may be asked how it happens, that men so much surpass animals in reasoning, and one man so much surpasses another? Has not the same custom the same influence on all?" (E. 107).

He then lists nine facts which supposedly demarcate a Newton from a brute. These could be summed up as follows: man is able to expand his experience by using language, reading books, generalizing from experiences and by forming rules for inference and prediction. "The forming of general maxims from particular observation is a very nice operation."

[Choice and cause]

Since both man and animal patterns of behavior are similar and since both have reason for their behavior and since "reason" in one sense is the same as causal inference and since there are no "moral necessities" or "final causes" we may be able to explain man's action by discovery of the causes of his action.

Here we are confronted with a dilemma which Hume was aware

of and sought to remove. It is called the dilemna of Free-will and Determinism.

On Hume's theory our action like animal behavior is explainable by an appeal to a causal law. But if this is a case, there would be no place for claiming that some of our actions are intentional actions which are caused by the agent and directed towards a goal, and no sense in ascribing responsibility or moral-worth for a sub-class of our intentional actions. We are not responsible for the biological side of our nature. Why then are we held accountable for some of our actions?

Hume in an ingenious manner argues that there is no incompatibility in ascribing responsibility and moral worth to an agent and in explaining his action. He argued further that in fact moral assessment of an action presupposes the operation of causal factors. Hume's arguments on this issue is persuasive and many contemporary philosophers followed, defended and developed his argument. What is questionable is Hume's insistence that all causes are of the same type, viz. efficient, and hence all explanations are explanations *via* covering law of efficient type – the doctrine which was examined and rejected by Socrates when he argued in *Phaedo* that no amount of causal explanations about physiology of his body or other physical factors could explain his political actions (and action of the Athenians) which led to his imprisonment, his refusal to escape and his determination to face the death penalty without an appeal to his freely chosen moral goals which is the final cause and ought to be the final court of appeal.

In Part III Section 1 of the *Treatise* entitled *Of Liberty and Necessity*, Hume produced various arguments against the libertarion thesis that human actions are not coverable by causal laws and free choice is incompatible with causation. Here is a skeleton of his arguments:

1. He starts by assuming that the concept of freedom is linked up with that of volition. The assumption, perhaps, is due to the fact that philosophers often had been concerned with "freedom of will" and tradition posited that the will is a faculty. So the assumption is made. The next is define what is meant by 'the will.'

2. Now Hume tries to define 'the will' and he does it by an appeal to his general criterion of meaning. Thus we are not surprised that 'will' is defined as

the internal impression we feel and are conscious of, when we knowingly give rise to any new motion of our body, or new perception of our mind. (T. 399)

3. According to his analysis of "Necessary Connection," necessity consists of *constant union* of events and *inference* from this union.

4. If then he can show that *actions* are constantly conjoined with *volition* or with other events, he has shown that actions like other events are caused.

Further, if he can show that knowledge of such causal connections or laws fully explain our actions, he has proven that there is such a thing as the Science of Man similar to the Science of Nature. Note that he does not have to show that every action is caused in order to prove that actions are caused. We do not have to prove either that every event has a cause, in order to believe that events are explainable in principle.

5. He then proceeds, "I shall first prove from experience, that our actions have a constant union with our motives, tempers, and circumstances, before I consider the inference we draw from it" (T. 401).

He points out certain observed and explainable uniformities in our actions.

We not only observe, that men *always* seek society, but can also explain the principles, on which this universal propensity is founded. For is it more certain, that two flat pieces of marble will unite together, than that two young savages of different sexes will copulate? (T. 402)

He points out in an oblique manner to many uniformities basic to civilization, such as rearing and teaching children, etc.

6. Knowledge of uniformities, either in natural or human affairs, is a license-ticket for inference. Hume argues that there are such uniformities and such inferences in both domains:

The *union* betwixt motives and actions has the same constancy, as that in any natural operations, so its influence on the understanding is also the same in *determining* us to infer the existence of one from that of another. (T. 404)

An example is given to show the similarities between natural and moral uniformities and inferences made from them.

A prisoner... discovers the impossibility of his escape, as well from the obstinacy of the goaler, as from the walls and bars with which he is surrounded, and in all attempts for his freedom chooses rather to work upon the stone and iron of the one, than upon the inflexible nature of the other. (T. 406)

Here it is assumed that the will of the duty-minded prison guard is constantly conjoined with his action of guarding the prisoner, in the same way as certain properties of material objects, for example, their inpenetrability, are constantly conjoined with some other properties, for example, their weight. So one may say that his will causes his action as his heart causes the circulation of his blood.

7. What do we mean then when we talk about "free-will" or "liberty'," when we ascribe it to some of our actions and deny it to others?

He does not try to define this concept in the *Treatise*. Here he only states what "liberty" or "free-will" are not. But in the *Enquiries* a definition is given. Free-action is not definitely a chance action. "What the vulgar call chance is nothing but a secret and concealed cause." (T. 130) We might not know what causes an event, but this does not mean "negation of necessity and causes."

Thus if by 'liberty' we mean chance-action, not only are we talking nonsense, but also we could not mean that. Since if we do, then it follows that no man is ever accountable for his actions, "nor are men more accountable for those actions, which are design'd and premediated, than for such as are most casual and accidental." (T. 411)

The ascription of moral, political and legal responsibility to an agent, or moral assessment of actions presupposes that such actions are caused by the agents' will, that is, they are voluntary actions and not just happening or coercive actions.

Hence if we are ever morally responsible for any action, those actions are caused by our volition, and if they are not caused so, then we are not morally responsible for them. "'Tis only upon the principles of necessity that a person acquires any merit or demerit from his actions; however, the common opinion may incline to the contrary." (T. 411)

Hume does pride himself on discovering that the doctrine of causation or determinism of action is compatible with the doctrine of free-action, which is likewise compatible with morality and moral exhortation.

8. However, to say that some of our actions are caused by our volition is not to say that our will itself is uncaused. Volition itself is not the end of the causal chain. Why should it be "that all actions of the will have particular causes." (T. 412)

Here then begins his search into the psychological causes of our motives, cravings and impulses. They are such agents as Pride and Humility.

9. In the *Enquiries* Hume provides a definition of 'liberty' which

is meant to be self-consistent and consistent with "plain matter of fact," namely:

> By liberty, then, we can only mean *a power of acting or not acting, according to the determations of the will,* that is, if we choose to remain at rest, we may: if we choose to move, we also may. Now this hypothetical liberty is universally allowed to belong to every one who is not a prisoner in chains. (E. 95)

It seems that Hume's position on this issue fits the description of the "soft-determinist." Human actions, like animal behavior and like physical happening are explainable in terms of causal laws. We call an action free if it is caused by our will and some of those actions are those for which we are responsible, praiseworthy or blameworthy.

Hume's general thesis: that human actions, like other natural events, are explainable, and that explanation and prediction of action is not incompatible with our ability to make a genuine choice and with the ascription of responsibility, seems plausible. However, the following subsidiary assumptions are questionable, if not muddled or mistaken:

1. That there is an event such as the will or intention or even motive of the same nature as color or pain (impression).

2. That such supposed events are constantly accompanying our actions. This by itself violates his rule 8 according to which the dispositional property of an object is not the cause of the occurrence of that property. Thus the cause of the obstinacy of a prison guard in preventing the prisoner's flight cannot be his obstinacy. He was obstinate all the time but did not move until the prisoner made his move.[1]

3. That the relation between will or intention or motives and actions are causal, similar to other causal relations among natural events.

4. That the supposed will itself is caused, in the same manner by some proceeding events.

5. That there is one sort of explanation, i.e., causal, and hence to explain action we should cover it by a causal law.

6. Finally, Hume is unable to reduce moral necessities to physical necessities and final causes to the efficient causes.

On the other hand, the explanation and prediction of actions by appeal to final causes is often adequate, whereas the supposed ex-

---

[1] This point is due to Irving Thalberg, "Hume's Concept of Moral Necessity," *The Indian Journal of Philosophy*, IV, (1964).

planation of the same kind of action in terms of efficient cause and by appeal to law or law-like statements vitiate ascription of moral responsibility and worth.

Moral laws, as Kant insists, are different from physical laws, and to act in accordance with them is not to act as if we are their victims.

3. THE PROBLEM OF INDUCTION

The root of inductive inference is what Russell calls "animal inference," i.e. a transition from a sense given to unperceived datum; without reflection and as a result of habit formation. The animal, as Russell puts it,

...experiences fa.ga', fb.gb', fc.gc'... and fd. On occasion of experiencing fd, he believes 'there is now a y such that gy', but he is unaware of the causes of his belief. When, in the course of evolution, he becomes an inductive logician, he notices the causes and says they are grounds. Since they are not, he might just as reasonable accept 'there is now a y such that gy' as a basic proposition; it is simpler than the inductive principle, and also more likely to be true. In this respect, therefore, the animal is to be preferred to the logician. This is a vindication of Hume.[1]

This supports Hume's description of causal inference in so far as the inference is "natural," i.e. non-philosophical. But Hume is also that inductive logician who, perhaps for the first time, states the Principle of Induction and showed its incoherence.

A. The Principle of Induction

The issue of induction in Hume is closely connected with the issue of causation, and sometimes confusedly so. Hume, after the analysis of the concept of causation, asks a fundamental question:

Since it appears that the transition from an impression present to the memory or senses to the ideas of an object, which we call cause and effect, is founded on past *experience*, and on our remembrance of their *constant conjunction*, the next question, is whether experience produces the idea by means of the understanding or of the imagination; whether we are determin'd by reason to make the transition, or by a certain association and relation of perceptions. (T. 89)

Hume is in effect asking what is the principle of causal inference, if there is one, which permits us to make a move from a given to a hidden datum.

Hume first states the metaphysical Principle of Causation, then replaces it with the non-metaphysical and hence in principle

[1] Bertrand Russell, *Inquiry into Meaning and Truth*, London: Allen and Unwin, 1948, p. 244.

verifiable version, and lastly replaces the Principle of Causation with a broader Principle of Induction. These moves are not obvious, but it is there and we should note them.

The metaphysical principle of causation is "the opinion of the necessity of a cause to every new production." It is the old Causal Maxim.

The First Version: This maxim, then, is replaced with the Causal Principle "But as I find it will be more convenient to state question in the following: *Why we conclude, that such particular causes must necessarily have such particular effects, and why we form an inference from one to another?*" (T. 82)

The Second Version: Here the reference to causation is dropped and the problem is stated in general terms and this is the Principle of Induction: "*that instances, of which we have had no experience, must resemble those of which we had experience, and that the course of nature continues always uniformly the same.*" (T. 89)

The Third Version: Here the reference to uniformity of nature is dropped, "*that instances of which we had no experience, resemble those, of which we had experience.*" (T. 89)

The Fourth version: "I wou'd renew my question, *why from this experience* we form any conclusion beyond those past instances, of which we have had experience." (T. 91)

The Fifth version: "*that instances of which we have no experience must necessarily resemble those, of which we have.*" (T. 104)

In the *Abstract* and the *Enquiries*, however, the principle is stated in causal context and with temporal reference, i.e. resemblance of the future instances to the past.

All reasonings concerning cause and effect, are founded an experience, and that all reasonings from experience are founded on the supposition, that the course of nature will continue uniformly the same. We conclude that like causes, in like circumstances, will always produce like effect. (A. 15)

and

All inferences from experience suppose as their foundation that the future will resemble the past, and that similar powers will be conjioned with similar sensible qualities. (E. 37)

a) *Is the principle justifiable?*

Hume not only formulates and states the Principle of Induction but also with unmatched originality and insight proves (in a sense any philosophical thesis could be proven) that no justification of the Principle is possible.

For justification is providing reason for beliefs, and reason is concerned with methods of inferences, and inferences very broadly are either deductive (he calls it "demonstrative") or inductive (he calls it "probable," "causal," "experimental"), and Hume proves that no reason, of either kinds, could support the Principle of Induction, the principle which itself is the principle of non-demonstrative reasoning.

b) *Deductive justification*

We observed that for Hume demonstrative reason is reason concerned with (A) Relations, or what in the *Enquiries* is called "Relations of Ideas" and such relations are discoverable from "mere ideas" and nothing else. A paradigm example of this sort of reason is reason used in mathematics. (He does not consider syllogistic deductions except by implication as tautologies).

(α) Let P and Q and S stand for three different conceptual sentences. If now we deduce S from (P ∧ Q) and our deduction is correct we could claim that "Necessarily {(P ∧ Q) → S}," and this is because to assert P and Q and to deny S is logically absurd, or implies contradiction.

(β) Let then P and Q and S stand for three different empirical sentences reporting three sorts of events. We can easily see that no matter how many times these events occur together and none occur without the other two, it does not follow that "Necessarily {(P ∧ Q) → S}." Give P and Q, it is only probably that S.

To prove the principle of induction by deduction we have to use (α), but we cannot. Since we want to show roughly that a certain chain of events is continuous, that is uniform throughout, we have to substitute empirical sentences for our variables, and if we do so we have to employ schema (β), and if we use (β) we shall never be able to demonstrate the Principle of Induction. Hume presents this argument in various forms:

There can be no *demonstrative* arguments to prove that instances... (The Principle of Induction), we can at least conceive a change in the course of nature, which sufficiently proves, that such a change is not absolutely impossible. (T. 89).

The strongest probability about the continuity of a chain of events is still a probability.

There is no probability so great as not to allow of contrary possibility; because otherwise it wou'd cease to be a probability, and wou'd become a certainty. (T. 135)
For if such an inference ("the motion of one body from the impulse of another") may be drawn merely from the ideas of body, of motion, and of impulse, it must amount to a demonstration, and must imply the absolute impossibility of any contrary supposition. Every effect, then, besides the communication of motion, implies a formal contradiction: and 't is impossible not only that it can exist, but also that it can be conceiv'd. (T. 111)

The same argument on the impossibility of the justification of the principle of induction by deductive reason is repeated in the *Enquiries*.

c) *Inductive justification*

If the principle of induction cannot be supported by deductive reason, the only other kind of reason that we can appeal to is induction (and let us mention at this very point that various other methods which are used for the solution of the problem, such as probablistic, pragmatic, "The Principle of Limited Independent Variety," etc. in one way or other presupposes induction).

But then to use induction in support of the Principle of Induction is to commit the vicious circle fallacy. The inductive method itself rests on the assumption that "instances of which we had no experience, resemble those of which we had experience." If we justify this assumption by saying that it worked well in the past, or that it was the only successful method that suited our aim for prediction and forecast in the past, and hence it should work in the future, then we are using the very assumption we are trying to prove.

So says Hume:

Probability is founded on the presumption of a resemblance betwixt those objects, of which we have had experience, and those of which we had none; and therefore 'tis impossible this presumption can arise from probability. The same principle cannot be both the cause and effect of another. (T. 90).

Thus inductive probabilities could not support the principle of Induction. "Shou'd it be said that we have experience that, that the same power continues united with the same object, and that the like objects are endow'd with like power, I would renew my question, *why from this experience we form any conclusion beyond those past instances, of which we have had no experience.* If you answer this question in the same manner as the preceding, your answer gives still occasion to a new question of the same kind, even in *in finitum* which clearly

proves, that the foregoing reasoning had no just foundation."
(T. 91)

Finally a quote from the *Enquiries*:

All our experimental conclusions proceed upon the supposition that the future will be conformable to the past. To endeavor, therefore, the proof of this last supposition by probable arguments, or arguments regarding existence must be evidently going in a circle, and taking that for granted which is the very point in question. (E. 36)

Hume is right, the principle of induction, if there is one, could not be rationally supported.

It seems that Hume won his case: No justification either deductive or inductive could be given for the Principle of Induction. The move from the given to unperceived data is not a rational move.

Reason can never satisfy us that the existence of any one object does ever imply that of another; so that when we pass from the impression of one to the idea or belief of another, we are not determin'd by reason, but by custom or principle of association. (T. 97).

Let us now consider an attempt justification of induction on pragmatic ground and construct a Humian kind of objection to it. This kind of justification is hinted at by Hume himself: "If we believe, that fire warms or water refreshes, 'tis only because it costs us too much pains to think otherwise." (T. 270)

Make Hume's assertion stronger, viz., that if we do not rely on well supported, inductively strong regularities, we shall perish (and by that I mean regularities which are captured by laws of science, or law-like statements which support counterfactual and are inductively confirmed by their instances).

Wait then for the confirmation of this assertion. Suppose that it is fully confirmed. But then you should note that no finite number of confirmation statements could ever establish the thesis that if we do not rely on inductively strong regularities we *shall* suffer death.

And this is simply because, by Hume's stipulation, we are forever barred to move from the present and the past to the future. When we wait for the event whose occurrence confirms our thesis, and when such events actually occur, we make it part of the past and then argue that events in the past-future could never point to events in the future-future. It is like saying that tomorrow will be doomsday – and when finally tomorrow comes without the doom, we say we meant by 'tomorrow', 'tomorrow,' and not today.[1]

[1] The point is due to F. L. Will, "Will the Future Be Like the Past?" *Logic and Language* (C. A. Flew, ed.), second series.

For the sake of argument take the thesis and negate its consequent that, if we do not rely on inductively strong regularities we shall not perish (by not heeding to them). Wait for the confirmation of the thesis. You shall see again that even if every one was a lucky fool – they discarded regularities and endured, no finite number of such episodes could support the thesis that they *shall* survive and *will* not suffer as a consequence of discarding inductive regularities.

Moving in either direction by trying to prove the probability of two mutually exclusive consequence of discarding inductively strong regularities is hopeless.

In each case we are using induction to show what will happen if we behave counter-inductively.

It follows that since such pragmatic accounts of the justification of induction is a species of the inductive justification of induction, we have to face Hume's charge of moving in a vicious circle.

We have to be aware, though, that if the Principle of Induction is neither confirmable or disconfirmable, there might be something wrong with the principle itself or with the demand for its justification, or both. This issue we shall consider in the last part.

B. Beliefs (Rational and Irrational)

Now, the main question is this: that if the Principle of Induction could not be supported by any reason, and if any inductive inference, i.e. any move from the given, *via* established regularities, to unperceived data, is nonrational, then what would be the demarcation line between beliefs which are supported by the experimental sciences, historical knowledge and commonsense beliefs based on experience, and beliefs which are mythological, anthropomorphic, wishful, biased, or, worst, theoretically untestable?

Of all the major philosophers, either the empiricists or rationalists, Hume is the most insistent proponent of the view that there is a great divide between rational or irrational beliefs, and all this despite his sceptical arguments about the very foundation of rational beliefs.

Hume himself is well aware of this dilemma, a dilemna which is the outcome of his own philosophical outlook. From the sceptical point of view, the credential of all our beliefs, even our belief in the validity of conceptual knowledge (see Scepticism with regard to Demonstrative Sciences) are seriously questioned and rejected. From the positivistic outlook a desparate attempt is made to save *bona fide* knowledge from annihilating scepticism by distinguishing it from irrational beliefs.

The intention of the great secular philosopher is obvious. He is a staunch enemy of every irrational belief. But his success is equally dubious. Could he defend the positive sciences and empirical knowledge with success, while at the same time, and often in the same section makes the most shocking announcement against the credibility and efficacy of reason – that "reason is and ought to be the slave of passion," that at best it is "a wonderful instinct in our soul" and is "nothing but a species of sensation"?

a) *The nature of belief*

In order to draw the line between rational and irrational beliefs, we should know the nature of belief. Hume tries to provide an analysis of certain epistemological concepts such as Knowledge, Probability or Belief in terms of certain relations between the knower or believer and certain relation between ideas and impressions.

Thus "Knowledge" is defined as the assurance arising from the comparison of ideas (T. 124) and though it is contrasted with "opinion or belief" which traditionally is limited to probabilities, the Platonic contrast between knowing and believing is not drawn with regard to their subject matter, but only in regard to our confidence about them.

There are various analyses of belief, and there is a tension and uneasiness with regard to this concept in Hume's books.

An opinion, therefore, or belief may be most accurately defin'd. *A lively idea related to or associated with present impression*... We join belief to the conception and are persuaded of the truth of what we conceive." (T. 96–97). "We may establish this one part of the definition of an opinion or belief, that '*tis an idea related to or associated with a present impression*". (T. 93)

That belief arises only from causation. (T. 107)

That an opinion or belief is nothing but an idea that is different from a fiction, not in the nature, or the order of its parts, but in the *manner* of its being conceiv'd. (T. 629). (He confesses, however, that he doesn't know how to explain this *manner*.)

In the *Abstract*, he says that the author of the *Treatise*

proceeds to explain the manner or feeling, which renders belief different from a loose conception.... He calls it sometimes a *stronger* conception, sometimes a more *lively*, a more *vivid* or *firmer*, or more *intense* conception. And indeed, whatever name we may give to this feeling, which constitutes belief, our author thinks it evident that it has a more forcible effect on the mind than fiction and mere conception. (A. 20)

In the *Enquiries* once again he tried to draw some distinction between fiction, or fictitious and serious belief. He says here that various descriptions of belief are

intended only to express that act of the mind, which renders realities or what is taken for such, more present to us than fictions, causes them to weigh more in thought, and gives them a superior influence on the passions and imagination. (E. 49)

Belief is something felt by the mind, which distinguishes the ideas of the judgment from the fictions of the imagination. (E. 49)

We observed that there is no theory of proposition and judgment in Hume's view of logic. Neither is there a corresponding theory of truth, which may provide a criterion for asserting or denying truth-value to propositions.

The lack is understandable. Within the framework of idea-impression, there cannot be any correspondence between our ideas and their *persishing* and non-recurring impressions, or coherence, among our vivid or faint ideas.

Hume is well aware of this problem and tries to overcome it without resorting to such stuff as Descartes, Berkeley's notion of God, or Locke's theory of the material substance.

The theory about belief then is invented to account for our true or false judgments. The theory would achieve its purpose if it can be shown that our true beliefs are those ideas which are related to, or caused by, impressions, and false beliefs are those which are not so related. This is not an open option for Hume. (Once an impression is gone, we cannot bring it back and link it to its idea.)

But then if we drop the object of belief and concentrate only on the psychological side, i.e. *lively, strong, vivid, firm conceptions*, we have to show that every true belief is vivid and strong and every false belief is "loose," dim and shaky, and Hume argues that this is definitely not the case.

Every chimera of the brain is as vivid and intense as any of those inferences, which we formerly dignify'd with the name of conclusions concerning matters of fact, and somtimes as the present impressions of the senses. (T. 123)

Hume boldly and with honesty unmatched among classical and modern philosophers faces the dilemna which is inherent in his system:

Shall we, then, establish it for a general maxim, that no refin'd or elaborate reasoning is ever to be receiv'd? Consider well the consequences of such a principle. By this means you cut off entirely all science and philosophy.

You proceed upon one singular quality of the imagination, and by a p'arity of reason, must embrace all of them. And you expressly contradict yourself;

since this maxim must be built on the preceding reasoning. . . What party then, shall we choose among these difficulties? If we embrace this principle and condemn all refin'd reasoning, we run into the most manifest absurdities. If we reject it in favour of these reasonings, we subvert entirely the human understanding. (T. 268)

Despite his scepticism with regard to the rationality of the Principle of Induction, with regard to reason, to the senses, etc., Hume chooses the party of reason and disavows the party of unreason; and he gives two different kinds of answers to his own sceptical thesis.

The first sort of answer to scepticism is that scepticism does not yield conviction. The human animal like other animals could not sustain his beliefs in certain regularities. We project our experiences into the future and past, back and forth, without either being aware that an inference is made or knowing the principle of it.

Most fortunately it happens, that since reason is incapable of dispelling these clouds, nature herself suffices to that purpose, and cures one of this philosophical melancholy and delirium. (T. 269)

But though the psychological explanation of the formation of beliefs is an answer to the question how we come to believe what we do believe, and why we cannot suspend some of our natural beliefs, it is not an answer to the question why some of our beliefs are credible and others are not.

Hume's psychological explanation of concept formation and belief formation in terms of sense-experience and the association of ideas, though speculative and descriptive, is in line with the conditioned reflex, stimulus response theories of learning. Hume was modest enough to say that he made a little contribution to the advancement of knowledge. "Perhaps we are still in too early an age of the world to discover any principles which will bear the examination of the latest posterity." (T. 273)

Nonetheless, psychology could not replace logic. Hume bypasses psychology and delves into the logic of inductive belief, which is the second answer to scepticism and to his question concerning the distinction between rational and irrational beliefs.

b) *The logic of belief*

We have noticed that 'belief' or 'opinion.' as Hume often uses them interchangeably, is a name for a strong conviction that something is a case. It is like an assertion sign ' ⊢ ' in Frege's which accompanies true sentences.

But since there is no theory of truth (empirical truth) in Hume's system, we do not know the truth condition of a sentence. We know that 'opinion' or 'belief' so used is distinguished from fiction or imagination, and that the statements of belief, being about matters of fact and existence, are not demonstrable. We know also that Hume is fully aware that the strength of a belief is not the measure of its truth. Kierkegaard's "Prince of Faith" believed that it was the Lord's voice which ordered him to kill his beloved son. "The Prince of Denmark," however, questioned the authenticity of his father's voice.

> The spirit that I have seen
> May be the devil: and the devil hath power
> To assume a pleasing shape...

Hence

> the play's the thing
> Wherein I'll catch the conscience of the king.

To separate true belief from fictious, Hume tried to link true belief with something external to it.

> We shall afterwords have occasion to remark both the resemblances and differences betwixt a poetical enthusiasm, and a serious conviction. In the meantime, I cannot forbear observing that the great difference in their feeling proceeds in some measure from reflexion and *general rules*. We observe that the vigour of conception, which fictions receive from poetry and eloquence, is a circumstance merely accidental... and that such fictions are connected with nothing that is real. (T. 631)

Let us then consider the subject of probability which is concerned with the formation and reliability of our empirical beliefs, and "general rules," which by its use "the understanding corrects the appearances of the senses."

c) *Probability and general rules*

There is no doubt that Hume was very much concerned with the epistemic foundation of inductive logic and with empirical and subjective probabilities.

The subtitle of the *Treatise* is "An Attempt to Introduce the Experimental Method of Reasoning into Moral Subjects," and the title of Part III of the *Treatise* is "Of Knowledge and Probability." In this part, after a brief contrast between knowledge and probability, Hume engages in various discussions of probability, chance, philosophical and unphilosophical probabilities and general rules.

We should note that probability for Hume has to do with our inference concerning "likelihood" of occurrences of events in the future. Hume has nothing to say about *a priori* and *mathematical* theories of probability.

The root of the issue is Bacon. Bacon was aware that though experience is the foundation of science, in explaining the phenomena we have to by-pass passive observation and engage in experimentation. To establish laws and make predictions by appeal to laws, we should resort to a better method than "induction by simple enumeration." To discover nature's secret we should torture and interrogate her. To that purpose Bacon tabulated some rules which he thought are basic for experimental enquiry.

Hume sees himself as following Bacon and other British philosophers who were concerned with the methodology and epistemology of science. He sees clearly that animal inference, i.e., the unreflective move from the given to the unperceived, due to the experienced conjunction of events, is not an infallible method of inference or a sufficient method in experimental inquiry.

Russell's example of the chicken who constantly was fed by the farmer until in the slaughter house saw that it was dead wrong is to the point. The chicken was a poor inductivist. To rectify induction by simple enumeration we need some rules.

We should remember that Hume's interests in stating the rules of inductive inference and explaining the logic of belief is in line with his other interest, i.e. his belief that there is no foundation for the Principle of Induction itself.

Despite his concern with scientific methodology and his positivistic bent, Hume through all his works is sure that he has shown that there is no "logic" and no "foundation" for inductive inference (E. 38–39) and that he has shown also that "not reason" but habit, or "instinct" is what causes us (human and animal) to make inductive, or causal inferences.

Albeit there are criteria by which we may demarcate strong inductive from poor arguments, or belief from loose-conception and fiction (to use his usual expressions).

We can sum up Hume's views as follows:

1. Probability or likelihood are regarded to be of two kinds: (a) chances (b) causes.

There are both random events and events which follow a certain discoverable order. But randomness does not imply negation of cause. It implies that we can say nothing at all about the order of events, because all the alternatives sequences, or all possible order of causal relations are equally probable. So by 'chance' we do not mean absence of cause. "That what the vulgar call chance is nothing but a secret and conceal'd cause." (T. 130)

However, our belief about equal or less or more chances of occurrence of an event is roughtly proportionate to our degree of knowledge about the chain of causes of which the event in question is the effect.

2. Thus the issue of probability of chances falls within the issue of probability of causes. The increase in the frequency of the occurrence of events or the "conjunction of objects" increases our belief about the probability of future occurrences.

When we transfer the past to the future, the known to the unknown, every past experiment has the same weight, and that 'tis only a superior number of them, which can throw the balance on any side. (T. 136)

As the probability increases there will be a point when we can claim certainty and speak of 'proofs' rather than 'probability'. And we can speak of 'proofs' about "those arguments which are deriv'd from the relation of cause and effect, and which are entirely free from doubt and uncertainty." (T. 124) Though "the gradation... from probabilities to proofs is in many cases insensible." (T. 131)

3. Contrary experiments, however, weaken probabilities and our belief in them. Thus though my inhaling is constantly followed by exhaling, my belief about the probability of continuous breathing decreases by observing death.

4. Even if we arrive at a very strong probability or a full-proof, the contrary of every probable statement is possible.

5. Frequency of events is not the only foundation of inference. We may correctly establish a causal relation, with one crucial experiment, and make inferences from that causal law. We can infer from "one single experiment, when duly prepar'd and examined." (T. 131)

This is "what natural philosophers, after Lord Bacon, have affected to call the *experimentum crucis.*" (E. 129)

But this is only because we *tacitly* project that experiment into the future (and the past).

Thus for Hume, the inference from one experiment is made on

the assumption that there is a law which is covering the events, although we might not know that law.[1]

We find in some cases, that the reflexion produces the belief without the custom; or more properly speaking, that the reflexion produces the custom in an oblique and artificial manner... 'Tis certain that not only in philosophy, but even in common life, we may attain the knowledge of a particular cause merely by one experiment, provided it be made with judgement and after a careful removal of all foreign and superfluous circumstances. (T. 105)

6. The General rules (Mill calls them "Canons of Induction") may help us eliminate superfluous circumstances and reveal causal connections.

These rules "by which we ought to regulate our judgment concerning causes and effects... are form'd on the nature of our understanding, and on our experience of its operation in the judgment we form concerning objects. By them we distinguish the accidental circumstances from the efficacious causes." (T. 149)

With a pronounced reluctance, fearing all along rivalry with "scholastic headpices and logicians," Hume states some "rules by which to judge of causes and effects" and concludes

Here is all the *logic* I think proper to employ in my reasoning, and perhaps even this was not very necessary, but might have been supply'd by the natural principles of our understanding. (T. 175)

Hume observes that since the co-presence of any two or more events or sets of events is possible, that is since in nature there is no contradiction, "nothing hinders them (objects) from having that constant conjunction, on which the relation of causes and effect totally depends" (T. 173); we need some rules by which we may establish causal relations.

The eight following rules are partly a restatement of conditions of ascription of causal relations to events and partly a device to eliminate possible rival theories, "the superfluous or accidental circumstances," and arrive at a theory which enables us to explain and predict "efficacious causes."

[1] Popper objects that though "Hume admits, even a single striking observation may be sufficient to create a belief or an expectation – a fact which he tries to explain as due to an inductive habit. . . . But this, I contended, was merely his attempt to explain away unfavorable facts which threatened his theory; an unsuccessful attempt, since these unfavorable facts could be observed in very young animals and babies." But Hume does not always talk about animal-inference. He is also concerned with inductive inference and experiment and gives reasons why we do make inferences from one experiment. Popper refers to rule 4, in the *Treatise*, and yet objects that an animal may learn from a single experience without "postulating a vast number of long repetitive sequences." Karl R. Popper, "Hume's Explanation of Inductive Inference," *Conjectures and Refutations*, New York, N.Y.: Basic Book, 1962, pp. 42–46.

We shall note that though Hume's rules are about the discovery of causal laws and though few scientific laws are stated in terms of causes and effects, Hume is not oblivious to inductive inferences which are not causal but drawn from "collateral" relations. Here are the rules:

1. Spatio-temporal contiguity of causes and effects.
2. Priority of the cause to effect.
3. Constant union of the causes and effects. (This he considered to be essential).
4. Projection and transferance of causal relations into the future and the past, on the ground that "the same cause always produces the same effect." This is the Principle of Causation, and is the source of scientific reasoning.
5. When different events produce the same effect, there must be a factor common among those events and that factor is the cause.
6. Since like causes produces like effects, the difference between two resembling effects is due to a different cause.
7. Concommitant variation between sets of events is an indication of the presence of a causal relation. The final elimination of an element in a set followed by the absence of an element in another set, or the introduction of a new element followed by the presence of an element, with due care, does reveal a causal connection. "We must, however, not to draw such a conclusion from a few experiments."
8. Finally, another eliminative rule which deserves attention:

An object, which exists for any time in its full perfection without any effect, is not the sole cause of that effect, but requires to be assisted by some other principle, which may forward its influence and operation. For as like effects necessarily follow from like causes, and in a contiguous time and place, their separation for a moment shows, that these causes are not compleat ones. (T. 175)

I quoted the whole rule which is by no means clear. The principle, however, is stated in a better form in an early part:

'Tis establish'd maxim... that an object, which exists for any time in its full perfection without producing another, is not its sole cause; but is assisted by some other principle, which pushes it from its state of inactivity, and makes it exert that energy, of which it was secretly possest. (T. 76)

The principle is meant to support the old thesis of temporal priority of cause by denying co-temporality of cause with its effect.

It could be interpreted as follows:

An object possesses some essential properties which define that object. We say sugar is sweet and soluble in water or tin is a fusible metal. We mean by that if certain conditions were satisfied the properties mentioned will be perceived. We may say that these properties are dispositional properties of the objects.

Now these dispositional properties themselves are not the cause of the events which will occur if the conditions were satisfied. Hence to say what caused the sugar to dissolve in water, or tin to melt is not to say because sugar is soluble or tin is fusible, but that because the sugar was dropped into the water, or the tin into fire. The sugar is soluble and tin is fusible in principle. (Solubility and fusibility are the essential properties of the objects after all) and then under certain conditions they exhibited these properties.

If such language, e.g. 'essential properties,' does not suit Humian epistemology, I don't know what other interpretation could be offered for the principle which, though defended by Hume, is taken as a philosophical maxim ennunciated by others.

The upshot of the introduction of these rules is that we may rise above the level of making induction by simple enumeration both in "natural philosophy" and "the science of man."

> There is no phaenomenon in nature, but what is compounded and modify'd by so many different circumstances, that in order to arrive at the decisive point, we must carefully separate whatever is superfluous, and enquire by new experiements, if any particular circumstance of the first experiment was essential to it. These new experiments are liable... so that the utmost constancy is requir'd to make us persevere in our inquiry... If this be the case even in natural philosophy, how much more in moral, where there is a much greater complication... (T. 175)

d) *Irrational beliefs*

In conformity with philosophical tradition, Hume wages a battle against the bewitchment of our intelligence by the trick of imagination (Wittgenstein said this of *"language"*).

Plato, banished the poets and dramatists from the Ideal State because they were dangerously mad, though divinely inspired. Bacon allocates to them a region in which their mind may escape the bondage of nature. Hobbes pities their "decaying sense," i.e. imagination, and Humes calls them "professional liars."

Hume repeatedly speaks of "imagination" as the main cause of our false, or fictitous beliefs, and contrasts it with *reason*, with *experience* and with *judgment*. It is the imagination that makes us go beyond experience, "to bestow on external objects the same emotions, which it observes in itself, such as the Peripatetics ideas of *sympathies, antipathies*, and *horrors of a vacuum*. . . trivial propensity of the imagination" (T. 224). It is the imagination which gives us religion:

> Examine the religious principles, which have, in fact, prevailed in the world. You will scarcely be persuaded, that they are anything but sick men's dreams: Or perhaps will regard them more as playsome whimsies of monkies in human shape, than the serious, pastime, dogmatical assertions of a being, who dignifies himself with the name of rational. (*Natural History of Religion*, p. 98)

At the end of Book I of the *Treatise* he reveals his preference for science and philosophy which he contrasts with "systems and hypotheses of superstition." The former, i.e., science and philosophy, "contents itself with assigning new causes and principles to the phaenomena which appear in the visible world" while a system of superstition (religion) "opens a world of its own and presents us with scenes, and beings, and objects, which are altogether new." (T. 271)

Both scientific and religious hypotheses transcend the given data of the sense, "since 'tis almost impossible for the mind of man to rest, like those of beasts, in the narrow circle of objects."

However, if it is asked which guide we have to choose, Hume answers:

> We ought to deliberate concerning the choice of our guide, and ought to prefer that which is safest and most agreeable. And in this respect I make bold to recommend philosophy, and shall not scruple to give it the preference to superstition of every kind or denomination. (T. 271)

Though this echoes Epicurius, there are more serious reasons for our choice between the alternatives.

Poets, those "liars by profession – endeavour to give an air of truth to their fictions." (T. 21). Children and fools commit anthropomorphism, indulge in fantasy and wishful thinking. "But what excuse shall we find to justify our philosophers in so signal a weakness?" (T. 225)

The contrast between imagination and reason or experience does not settle the issue of the nature of irrational and rational belief. Scientists and artists both use their imagination and there is truth in the arts as well as conjectures in science. What would be art which does not tell us some truth, or the science which only mirrors nature!

Despite the mockery of the imagination, Hume does make an

attempt to distinguish *in* imagination the principles which led us to correct inference and those which led us astray.

I must distinguish in the imagination betwixt the principles which are permanent, irresistable and universal such as the customary transition from the causes to effects and from effects to causes: And the principles, which are changeable, weak and irregular.... The former are the foundation of all our thoughts and actions, so that upon their removal human nature must immediately perish and go to ruin.... For this reason the former are received by philosophy, and the later rejected.

"One who concludes somebody to be near him, when he hears an articulate voice in the dark, reasons justly and naturally, tho' that conclusion he deriv'd from nothing but custom.... But one, who is tormented, he knows not why, with the apprehension of spectres in the dark, may, perhaps, be said to reason, and to reason naturally too. But then it must be in the same sense, that a *malady* is said to be natural as arising from natural causes, tho' it is contrary to health." (T. 225)

I quote in full to show Hume's desparate attempt to separate rational and irrational beliefs by stating their respective causes. But this won't do.

To see the difference, he ought to tell us the ground and not the causes of our beliefs. This he does, when he goes into the methodological issues of probability and general rules (as we already observed).

He does it again when in the essay on miracles and in the *Dialogues* he considers the question of methodology. The method may give us the criterion by which to determine a belief rational. The causal explanation does not.

Hume's psychological explanation of irrational belief reminds us of Freud's attempt in *The Future of an Illusion* to do the same. According to Freud, religious beliefs are roughly a response to certain needs – needs which reveal the helplessness of mankind in his historical infancy as a race and as an infant.

"Our science is not an illusion" he concludes but religion is! But why! Doesn't science also respond to those very same needs? This violates Hume's principle of same cause, different effect! It is simply a case of genetic fallacy.

Hume, however, does not stop with such an explanation. Take his treatment of miracle. According to Hume, miracle is not only an unexplained event; it is "a transgression of a law of nature by a particular volition of the Deity, or by the interposition of some invisible agent." (E. 115)

Now Hume argues that since there are well-confirmed regularities which are "agreeable to the laws of nature" we should not give up belief in such regularities upon a mere testimony of an agent who claims (a) that these laws are violated and (b) that violation is due to an act of a supernatural agent.

Note that he does not say that nature is uniform throughout so that our probable beliefs can never be questioned, revised, or be flatly false. "Nothing is esteemed a miracle, if it ever happens in the common course of nature." (E. 115), but that a mere testimony to the contrary is not enough to shake our tested beliefs and establish another such that we connect that supposed violation to supernatural agents.

He argues further that we should test the alleged testimony. The testimony concerning the alleged events, he believes, are not trustworthy, since "no testimony is sufficient to establish a miracle, unless the testimony be of such a kind, that its falsehood would be more miraculous than the fact, which it endeavours to establish." (E. 115).

Now the probability that the reporter is deluded, superstitious, suffers from wishful beliefs, exceeds the probability that (a) well-confirmed laws of nature are violated and that (b) they are violated by supernatural agents.

It was argued by Broad that there is an inconsistency in Hume's argument about miracles and Hume's argument about causation.

Hume has told us that he can find no logical ground for induction....
All that he professes to do is to tell us that we actually do make this transition and to explain psychologically how it comes about. Now this being so, I cannot see how Hume can distinguish between our variously caused beliefs about matters of fact, and call some of them justifiable and others unjustifiable....
Hence the enthusiast's belief in miracles and Hume's belief in natural laws (and consequent disbelief in miracles) stand on precisely the same logical footing.[1]

The ciriticism is justified if we obliterate from Hume's writing the part on probability and general rules in which Hume tried to draw a line between well-established inductive beliefs and mere fictitious ones (see Part B, sections a, b, and c). We should distinguish be-

---

[1] C. D. Broad, "Hume's Theory of the Credibility of Miracles," *Proceedings of the Aristotelian Society*, XVII (1916–1917).

tween Hume's scepticism with regard to foundation of *Induction* and his arguments about the logic of inductive beliefs.

Broad complained further that "the first reported exception (to the laws of nature) was, to anyone who had not himself observed it, in precisely the same position as a story of a miracle, if Hume be right." This again misses the point. The testimony is not only that a law is violated, but also that a miracle has occurred, and miracles, as we observed, are a violation of a law of nature "by a particular volition of the Deity... etc."

Lastly, to appreciate Hume's support for the rationality of inductive belief, note the following assertion expressed by Philo in the *Dialogue*:

> That a stone will fall, that fire will burn, that the earth has solidity, we have observed a thousand and a thousand times, and when any new instance of this nature is presented, we draw without hesitation the accustomed inference. The exact similarity of the cases give us a perfect assurance of a similar event and a stronger *evidence* is never desired nor sought after. But wherever you depart in the least, from the similarity of the case, you diminish proportionably the evidence. (D. 116)

4. MATTERS OF FACT

A. Contrast with the basic proposition and conceptual statement

Our knowledge about the world from the most basic and rudimentary such as belief in the existence of unperceived objects, and in our personal identity, to the most complex and sophisticated such as historical belief or belief in the laws of nature, according to Hume is knowledge about matters of fact and existence.

What, we may ask then, is "Matters of Fact" or Matters of Fact and Existence," as the two concepts are often conjoined?

The structure of our knowledge, according to Hume is built upon certain indubitable beliefs about some perceptually given data or relation of data.

Some singular statements about these data or their relations (and Hume is not clear about this disjunction) express what is directly known to us. They are the stuff of which our knowledge is built, since the rest of our knowledge, both mathematical and empirical, is based on inference from these premises. These statements are quite similar to what some logical empiricists called "Protekollsatz" and what Russell called "Basic Proposition."

Hume does not have a special name for these statements, but they exist in his system, and they have a very important function.

Among the seven philosophical relations, subdivided into contingent and necessary relations, some are known "at first sight, and fall more properly under the province of intuition than demonstration." (T. 70).

To apprehend these relations there is no inference or reason involved and that is because "when both the objects are present to the senses along with the relation, we call *this* perception rather than reasoning, nor is there in this case any exercise of the thought, or any action... but a mere passive admission of impressions thro' the organs of sensation." (T. 73)

There are only two kinds of relations which we may discover by inference from what is immediately given to the senses, namely: *Proportions of quantity or number* (among necessary relations) and *Causation* (among contingent relations).

Now our empirical knowledge is based on causation. "Causation gives us information about events which we do not see or feel," (T. 74) and such knowledge is about matters of fact and existence.

Hume, both in the *Treatise* and the *Enquiries*, speaks about "Matters of Fact," though in the *Enquiries* Matters of Fact replaces contingent relations, (B) Relations, and the expression "Relations of Ideas" replaces necessary relations, (A) Relations of the *Treatise*.

In the *Treatise* the following statements are made:

All reasonings from causes or effects terminate in conclusions concerning matter of fact; that is concerning the existence of objects or of their qualities. (T. 94)

Reasoning concerning causation, and concerning matters of fact (are not demonstrable). (T. 95)

When the mind forms a reasoning concerning any matter of fact, which is only probable, it casts its eye backward upon past experience, and transferring it to the future. (T. 141)

The relation of cause and effect, which is the only one that can assure us of matter of fact. (T. 193)

The operations of human understanding divide themselves into two kinds, the comparing of Ideas, and the inferring of matter of fact. (T. 463)

An inference concerning a matter of fact is nothing but the idea of an object, that is frequently conjoin'd or is associated with a present impression. (T. 636)

In the *Enquiries* he repeats the same, contrasts it with relations of ideas, adjoins it with "real existence" (E. 26) and with "moral reasoning." (E. 35)

To sum up:

1) Statements expressing matters of facts are not basic propositions, but are inferred from them.

2) The inference or derivation is causal rather than logical.

3) Existential and universal statements which appear in the empirical sciences are matter of fact statements.

4) Every matter of fact statement is probable, since its denial is logically possible.

5) Such statements are contrasted with fictitious statements.

6) Finally, matters of fact are contrasted with matters of tests.

B. Contrast with the optative assertions (the Is and the Ought)

Our ethical judgments, according to Hume, are fundamentally expressions of our wishes, whether universal (wishes of all or most men on all or most occasions) or particular (wishes of a man in all or some occasions), and the expression of a wish is neither demonstrable, probable nor have truth-value. We may call such expressions "Optative."

In the *Enquiries* some attention is paid to universal sentiments or wishes and the manner of conformity of expressions of our wishes to these universal sentiments.

Thus he writes:

> General language... being formed for general use, must be moulded on some more general views, and must affix the epithets of praise or blame, in conformity to sentiments, which arise from the general interests of the community. (E. 228)

There are occasions when our moral judgments express not our personal wishes but accord with certain standards, though those standards themselves are at the bottom expression of universal wishes.

> When a man denominates another his enemy, his *rival*, his *antagonist*, his *adversary*, he is understood to speak the language of self-love, and express sentiments peculiar to himself, and arising from his particular circumstances and situation. But when he bestows on any man the epithets of *vicious* or *odious*, or *depraved*, he then speaks another language, and expresses sentiments in which he expects all his audiences are to concur with him. He must here, therefore, depart from his private and particular situation, and must choose a point of view, common to him with others, he must move some universal principle of the human frame, and touch a string to which all mankind have an accord and symphony (E. 272)

Various reasons are given for the thesis that ethical expressions are fundamentally expressions of our wishes and that such expressions do not have truth or probability value.

1. We use reason in order to discover the truth value of either conceptual or factual relations. If there are such relations either in the realm of facts or ideas, then we may assign truth-value to their expressions. But there are no such relations with regard to our ultimate wishes.

> Reason is the discovery of truth or falsehood. Truth or falsehood consists in an agreement or disagreement either to the *real* relations of ideas, or to *real* existence and matter of fact. Whatever, therefore, is not susceptible of this agreement, or disagreement, is incapable of being true or false, and can never be an object of our reason. (T. 458)

2. In constructing our moral judgments we do consider some matters of fact or conceptual issues which are relevant, but fact alone cannot determine the goodness or wickedness of an action. For example, both Plutarch and Dante in passing judgments on Brutus' deed considered Brutus' relation to Caesar, Brutus' argument against tyranny, his motives, his past actions, etc. Also they considered the same with regard to Caesar. Concerning these matters there was no disagreement between them.

But Plutarch praised Brutus' deed, while Dante damned it, and each made the praise or blame, not according to their own personal wishes, but in accordance to two incompatable value systems, the system of Roman Republic was not the same as the Italian Catholic.

Since reason is the discovery of truth, actions are neither rational or irrational (in that restricted sense of "reason").

> Actions may be laudable or blameable, but they cannot be reasonable or unreasonable. (T. 458)

3) If reason alone were efficacious in determing the goodness of an action, an appeal to reason alone would be sufficient for arriving at a moral judgment. But the discovery of certain facts about such actions as *parricide, ingratitude,* or *incest,* Hume says, does not by itself tell us whether such actions are right or wrong. We know that such actions are sometimes committed by animals or other living beings, without being assessed as right or wrong.

4) Moral conflict, when it does not contain factual components, is a conflict of wishes and wishes may express our "passions." The conflict then is not between passion and reason, but between different kinds of passions, and this conflict may exist both in the same person (among his passions) or between one man and another or one nation and another nation.

Hume's wont for dramatic pronouncements against the rationalist reappears again in the following:

> We speak not strictly and philosophically when we talk of the combat of passion and reason. Reason is, and ought only to be, slave of the passions, and can never pretend to any other office than to serve and obey them. (T. 415)

Immediately after this dramatic announcement, Hume explains his meaning. There are two senses when "any affection can be call'd unreasonable... *First* when a passion... is founded on the supposition of the existence of objects, which really do not exist" such as a wishful hope for the eternal life, or fear of damnation.

Second, "When in exerting any passion in action, we chuse means insufficient for the design'd end, and deceive ourselves in our judgment of causes and effects."

However, "where a passion is neither founded on false suppositions, nor chuses means insufficient for the end, the understanding can neither justify nor condemn it. 'Tis not contrary to reason to prefer the destruction of the whole world to the scratching of my finger. 'Tis not contrary to reason for me to chuse my total ruin, to prevent the least uneasiness of an *Indian* or person wholly unknown to me." (T. 416)

5) Finally Hume exposes the fallacious deduction of deriving optative from certain alleged existential statements about God, or from certain factual statements, for example, psychological statements.

> In every system of morality, which I have hitherto met with, I have always remark'd, that the author proceeds for some time in the ordinary way of reasoning, and establishes the being of a God, or make observation concerning human affairs; when of a sudden I am surpriz'd to find, that instead of the usual copulations of propositions, *is*, and *is not*, I meet with no proposition that is not connected with an *ought*, or *ought not*. This change is imperceptible; but is, however, of the last consequence. For as this *ought*, or *ought not*, expresses some new relation or affirmation, 'tis necessary that it shou'd be observ'd and explain'd, and at the same time that a reason should be given, for what seems altogether unconceivable, how this new relation can be a deduction from others, which are entirely different from it. (T. 469).

Since of late, there has been some controversy on this issue I quoted the whole passage lest we may see what Hume himself says. We should note that Hume, contrary to general opinion, does not say that one cannot deduce *the ought* from *the is*, but only that if it is deduced "the new relation... shou'd be observ'd and explain'd."

Hume himself in an earlier passage quoted made such a move, i.e., "Reason is, and ought only to be the slave of passion." He argued that since reason is a method or means of discovering conceptual or factual relations, and since we do in fact often employ reason to discover means in fulfilling our wishes, it is a misuse of 'reason' if we speak of reason alone and by itself to dictate what we ought to wish.

To employ reason for that office is to misapprehend its function, and since it is irrational or unphilosophical to use it in such a manner, we ought not do that.

Hence to argue, with some recent authors, that Hume is wrong since we do correctly, derive 'the ought' from 'the is', *viz.* by saying "He is a medical doctor, therefore he ought to try helping his patient" or "He is a judge, therefore he ought to be impartial," is to miss the point. These examples are quite compatible with Hume's own observation about the office of reason and its correct employment in moral dispute.[1]

Note also that Hume, in accord with traditional syllogistic logic, regards syllogistic inference valid if the conclusion is entailed by the premises. Hence he argues that the "imperceptible" move from 'is' to 'ought' violates the old principle that an "entirely different" and "a new relation" is not deducible from the premises unless the premises explicitly or implicitly contain that conclusion.

Lastly, note that Hume is fully cognizant of the relevance of Matters of Fact to moral issues. Indeed, the main body of Book II and III of the *Treatise* and a major part of the *Enquiries* is concerned with the study of human values, ethical, political and aesthetical, in relation to psychological, historical and sociological data.

We have not however concerned ourselves with Hume's discussion of morality and relation of wishes to various passions, which falls outside our project.

C. Scepticism with regard to the External World

In the *Treatise* Hume makes some puzzling statements about the existence of material bodies, or the external world, that is, about the existence of entities which are outside "the internal" or "the mental world," as he sometimes calls it.

We shall note that the problem of existence of any entity, be it material or mental, is a part of the general problem of how we come to believe in Matters of Fact and Existence, and this is the old

---

[1] Consider also the following statement in Hume's essay "Of the Original Contract," "If the reason be asked of that obidience, which we are bound to pay to government, I readily answer, became society could not otherwise subsist."

problem of how an inference is made from the given to what transcends the given, and what is the rational ground, if any, of such an inference.

It is once again the problem of inductive inference which appears here in a particular form, i.e., what is the ground for our belief that something transcending the given, i.e., an unperceived material object, exists?

Hume's sceptical arguments appear in detail in the *Treatise*, "Of Scepticism with Regard to Senses," and in summary form in the *Enquiries*, "Academical or Sceptical Philosophy."

In the following we shall provide an outline of his argument.

1) We believe that material objects, or "the external universe" exist while not perceived. We cannot choose not to believe this, because we are psychologically conditioned even "before the use of reason" to believe that the existence of the external world does not depend on being perceived by us. "Nature has not left this to his (Sceptic's) choice, and has doubtless esteem'd it an affair of too great importance to be trusted to our uncertain reasoning... 'tis in vain to ask, *whether there be body or not?* That is a point which we must take for granted in all our reasonings." (T. 187)

Without any reasoning, or even almost before the use of reason, we always suppose an external universe, which depends not on our perception, but would exist, though we and every sensible creature were absent or annihilated. (E. 151)

2) The question which is asked by Hume is not the ontological, i.e. of what there is, but epistemological:

"*What causes induce us to believe in the existence of body?*" Now if we are able to reduce such a belief to what we know by acquaintance, the belief is vindicated, if not, the belief is not, strictly speaking, rational.

3) Hume then considers and rejects various arguments given for the rationality of this belief. He offers first an analysis of the phrase "belief in the existence of body." It means what we (i) believe that an object *continues* to exist, while it is not present to the senses. Or it means (ii) that an object is *distinct*, that is, *independent* from the preceiver, and has *external* position. And if that is the case the proof for the continuance of the existence of an unperceived object is the proof for its distinctness and independence.

Now given that the only data that we can possibly have are, roughly, sense-data, that perceptions are the sole entities that we can ever have, we cannot even form or conceive an idea of anything different from perception (T. 67). Hence, by "external object" we could not mean anything which "specifically differed from our perceptions." (T. 188). So by the rule of the game by "object" we mean "perception."

But then, it is absurd to argue that the senses cause us to believe that perceptions continue to exist when they are not sensed or perceived.

For that is a contradiction in terms, and supposes that the senses continue to operate, even after they have cese'd all manner of operation. (T. 188)

Therefore "the senses" give us no notion of contin'd existence, because they cannot operate beyond the extent in which they really operate." (T. 191)

4) The question then is, if not *sense*, what other faculty induces us to believe that perceptions have a continued and distinct existance? Two other faculties were considered, *reason* and *imagination*.

5) We may solve the problem by making a commonsense distinction between sense-data and the material object, for example, between the material apple and the seen, touched, tasted and smelled apple – on the ground that the material apple is one object which is spatio-temporally locatable even though some of its states may change; whereas the impressions, as Hume states, are many 'internal, flitting and perishing existences." (T. 194).

But then Hume objects that to ascribe identity or sameness to various and distinct impressions is a vulgar confusion. (We shall see on the next issue, *Personal Identity*, who is really confused about the concept of identity.)

The perceived apple is all that is given, and as long as we keep our mind on it, we shall never arrive at the material apple, "as long as we take our perceptions and objects to be the same we can never infer the existence of the one from that of the other." (T. 193)

And this is also true by the rules of the game.

6) The next faculty considered is *reason* and by that he means "reason" employed about matters of fact and that simply is causation. But the causal inference is a move from sense-data to other sense-data, even if we posit objects we cannot move from sense-data to objects.

7) *Sense* and *reason* both being eliminated, Hume considers the last faculty, i.e., *imagination*. Before he considers the role of the imagination in making us believe in the continuance of the un-

perceived object or perception, Hume raises another question: We do not attribute a distinct and continued existence to all of our impressions (not to pain and pleasure, etc.) but only to certain classes of impressions. Such attribution may be due to "a peculiar constancy" and "a coherence" of those impressions.

Coherence, or the regularity of appearance of certain classes of impressions, or their constancy, is supposed to be a mark of distinction between objects and other internal impressions, such as pain, However, upon examination, we discover that *interrupted* perceptions are really different. We assume our *interrupted* perceptions, due to their resemblance, belong to the same family. We talk about the *same* sun which appears every day only because various impressions of it closely resemble each other. But the resemblance of discernable impressions does give us only the fictitious notion of identity. Where we discover resemblance among certain family of impressions, we feign identity and speak of the *same* object.

The thought slides along the succession with equal facility, as if it consider'd only one object; and therefore confounds the succession with the identity. (T. 204).

The guilty faculty is imagination. "The imagination tells us that our resembling perceptions have a contin'd and uninterrupted existence, and are not annihilated by their absence." (T. 215)

8) Nonetheless, it is logically possible that perception exists unperceived, though it seems that such a supposition is in principle unverifiable. And this is because "What we call a *mind* is nothing but a heap or collection of different perceptions, united together by certain relations, and suppos'd, tho' falsely, to be endow'd with a perfect simplicit identity. Now as every perception is distinguishable from another, and may be consider'd as separately existent; it evidently follows, that there is no absurdity in separating any particular perception from the mind, that is, in breaking off all its relations, with that connected mass of perceptions, which constitute a thinking being." (T. 207)

Hence "the supposition of the contin'd existence of sensible objects or perceptions involves no contradiction." (T. 208). This nicely proves that it is logically possible that perception exists without being perceived.

But not only within "the doctrine of philosophers," that is, within the theory of phenomenalism, or within the Lockian theory of Idea, the assumption of the existence of an unperceived idea or impression is not logically absurd; but even within the frame of ordinary language wherein the distinction is made between impressions and objects, such an assumption is self-consistant. "This table, which is present to me, and that chimney, may and do exist separately. This is the doctrine of the vulgar, and implies no contradiction." Nonetheless, Hume at the same time states that this assumption is unverifiable.

Thus the attempted reduction of our belief in the existence of the external world, like the reduction of our belief in the uniformity of nature or in inductive inference to the immediate data of experience, has failed. At the same time it is argued that withholding such beliefs is psychologically impossible.

In the *Enquiries*, in a passing reference to Berkeley, he writes that Berkeley's arguments "though otherwise intended, are in reality, merely sceptical [since] they *admit of no answer and produce no conviction*." (E. 155)

This observation may be applied to his own arguments with regard to the rationality of our belief in the existence of unperceived objects.

Obviously the problem is so set that its solution is logically impossible. That is, the question what reason do we have to believe that some of our perceptions have *distinct*, independent and continuous existence, could not be answered if at the same time we are asked to believe that (1) the only stuff that we can ever know is what is immediately given to our senses (2) that every impression is different from the other and so though impressions may be similar they can never be identical and (3) that any inference from the given to what transcend the given is forbidden.

Nonetheless, there are some merits to Hume's theory. Hume inherits from Descartes, Locke, Berkeley and Malebranch the contagious belief that:

'Tis universally allowed by philosophers, and its besides pretty obvious of itself, that nothing is ever really present with the mind but its perceptions or impressions and ideas, and that external objects become known to us only by those perceptions they occasion. (T. 67)

But unlike these philosophers, Hume did not try to fill the gap between the given and transcendent by some metaphysical stuff. On the contrary, Hume produced strong arguments against these philosophers who made various moves to fill the gap. We did not go into Hume's critical arguments against such theories (such as causal or representative) but we should mention the gist of his elaborate criticism which appears in two sentences in the *Enquiries*.

The mind has never anything present to it but the perception, and cannot possibly reach any experience of their connexion with objects. The supposition of such a connexion is therefore without any foundation in reasoning. (E. 153)

D. *Scepticism with regard to Self and the Problem of Personal Identity*

Hume begins with the fact that we do believe that one's mind is continuous throughout the life. We do certainly speak of the present as well as the past and future states of our mind. The question is what is the foundation of our belief in something which transcends the given.

It seems thus, that the problem is similar to the problem of our belief in the existence of unperceived objects or belief in the necessary connection of events. However, as we shall see, Hume confesses that this problem is unsolvable. For the other two problems, he found at least a psychological solution, but this kind of maneuver does not work here.

The problem appears in the *Treatise* and the *Appendix* to it. He drops the whole issue from the *Enquiries*. First Hume states and rejects the metaphysical theory of mental substance.

We have already observed how the Cartesian notion of mental substance is rejected. Using the first kind reduction, Hume argues that it is assumed that mental substance is something invariable, simple and enduring "to which our several impressions and ideas (are) supposed to have a reference." (T. 251)

But he says there is no impression of such an idea since such a bottom-rock stuff does not appear to us when we dig deep into our selves and look for it.

For my part, when I enter most intimately into what I call *myself*, I always stumble on some particular perception or other, of heat or cold, light or shade, love or hatred, pain or pleasure. I never catch *myself* at any time without a perception, and never can observe anything but the perception. (T. 25)[1]

However, there is no objection to use 'self' as a class-name for certain impressions and ideas provided that we don't ontologise the class[2]. To ontologise about the class is to assume that the class is

---

[1] Kant, without referring to Hume produces the same kind of reason against Rational Psychology e.g., "For in what we call soul there is a continuous flux, and nothing permanent." *Critique* P. 309.

[2] As a matter of fact Hume sometimes speaks of "lively-conception of our own person," (T. 317) or of self "as the immediate object of pride," (T. 329) or even-carelessly of "the idea, or rather impression of ourselves,"! (T. 317)

some special entity. Hume comes very close to saying that the class is a fiction though its members may not be. This he says both with regard to physical as well as mental substances.

In the *Abstract* there appears a brief counter against the Cartesian notion of the Self. The self or "the soul" is "a system or train of different perceptions... and all united together, but without any perfect simplicity or identity." (A. 24)

Reference is made here to Descarte's notion of "thought" as an essence of the mental substance. Hume, following Berkeley's criticism of abstract general ideas, objects that thoughts as such are not a name for anything. There are of course particular thoughts, but no abstract general idea of thought.

Descartes maintained that thought was the essence of the mind; not this thought or that thought, but thought in general. This seems to be absolutely unintelligible since everything that exists is particular, and therefore it must be our several particular perceptions that compose the mind. I say *compose* the mind, not belong to it. The mind is not a substance in which the perceptions inhere. (A. 25)

But to argue against the metaphysical notion of self or of its essence is not the end of the issue, and Hume makes some attempt to give an account of "what he calls himself."

The first kind of reduction proves that the metaphysical idea of self is not derived from sense-data. The second kind of reduction should tell us what is the justification for our belief that there is something continuous, simple and invariable "thru the whole course of our lives" which we call 'self.'

If we are able to discover some empirical data expressable by basic propositions, then we could claim that the belief is justifiable, if not we may be forced to conclude that our belief is a fiction or a figment of the imagination.

In the following I will present Hume's arguments:

1) In order to understand the issue of personal identity, we should first note how the concept of identity is analyzed at the beginning of the *Treatise*.

Identity is one of the seven philosophical relations. It also belongs to the class of contingent relations and moreover belongs to a class of those immediately given relations and is "apply'd in its strictest sense to constant and unchangeable objects... of all relations the most universal being common to every being... whose existence has any duration." (T. 14)

It is contrasted with difference of number (T. 15) or with

numerical difference. "Two objects, tho' perfectly resembling each other, or even appearing in the same place at different times, may be numerically different." (T. 69)

We ascribe an identity to an object notwithstanding the interruption in our observation on the assumption that "if we had kept our eye or hand constantly upon it, (the object) it wou'd have convey'd an invariable and uninterrupted perception." (T. 74)

The assumption based on a move from the given to what transcend the given and is due to causation: "nor can we otherwise have any security that the object is not chang'd upon us, however much the new object may resemble that which was formerly present to the senses." (T. 74)

This kind of an identity seems to be a "loose sense of identity" since it is ascribeable to an object in spite of change in the state of that object.

2) In fact later two different senses of identity are recognized: A. Strict 'identity'. "We have a distinct idea of an object that remains invariable and uninterrupted thro' a suppos'd variation of time; and this idea we call that of *identity* or sameness." (T. 253) B. Loose sense of 'identity'. "We have also a distinct idea of several different objects existing in succession, and connected together by a close relation." (T. 253)

But we often confuse A with B. The careless use of these two different senses of identity is explainable. The semantic confusion has a psychological explanation. The resemblance of variable and different impressions, or various stages of an object "renders its passage as smooth as if it contemplated one continu'd object. This resemblance is the cause of the confusion and mistake, and makes us substitute the notion of identity, instead of that of related objects." (T. 254)

There is another analysis of identity (though Hume calls it 'equality') which seems to have no bearing on the issue of identity or sameness of an object, i.e. the idea of identity used in arithmetic. A definition of identity is given in terms of one-one correlation between two number sets. "When two numbers are so combin'd, as that the one has always an unite answering to every unite of the other, we pronounce them equal; and 'tis for want of such a standard of equality in extension, that geometry can scarce be esteem'd a perfect and infallible science." (T. 71)

The last part of the paragraph indicates that when empirical relation is an issue this criterion of identity is not to be used.

3) We ascribe identity to (A)-object and (B) to Self. Self may be divided into (1) our thought or imagination and (2) to our "passions or the concern we take in ourselves." And Hume says that he is only concerned with the ascription of identity to (1), i.e., our thought or imagination. Note that this restriction very much clouds the issue. There is more continuity in felt passion, emotion, habits and custom, than thought or images. In fact according to Hume himself habits or custom or determination of our mind to pass from one event to another are what makes inference possible. If there are such things, then they should have continuous existence or duration, otherwise they cannot perform their supposed function. And if they are part of the Self, they should be accounted for in its analysis. Hume's summary dismissal of this part of Self perhaps is responsible for his feeling that perhaps there is something "we only *feel* a connexion," but we cannot find any connections among distinct perceptions.

4) Hume makes another distinction between (A) numerical identity and (B) 'specific' or qualitative identity.

He says again that we often do not realize that there are various kinds of identities and we confuse them. For example: we hear a *noise* "that is interrupted" and we talk about the *same* noise, though numerically and strictly speaking they are different. We talk about the *same church* "without breach of the propriety of language" (T. 258) though it is rebuilt many times. We even talk about things which may change its parts entirely, *viz.* "the same river" or "the same ship," even though the river changed its path and the ship is rebuilt plank by plank.

Hume rightly indicates that in each case we use a different criteria for sameness. In the case of the noise "the cause," in the case of the church "relation to the inhabitants of the parish," in the case of the river "the nature of a river," in the case of the ship "the common end" is the same.

5) The ascription of identity to different and distinct perceptions of the mind like ascription of identity to a material object is fictitious. We take once again resembling perceptions "different perceptions, which succeed each other with an inconceivable rapidity, and are in a perpetual flux and movement," to be one identical entity.

6) However, in this case, the difficulty is augmented since here the imagination "is not able to run several different perceptions into one, and make them lose their characters of distinction and difference, which are essential to them." (T. 259) That is, the members of the class which we call Self, seems to be so different in types that imagination is unable to unite them by creating a fiction of identity out of so many adverse and dissimilar members.

He compares the self "to a republic or commonwealth, in which the several members are united by the reciprocal ties of government... And as the same individual republic may not only change its members, but also its laws and constitutions; in like manner the same person may vary his character and disposition, as well as his impressions and ideas, without losing his identity." (T. 261)

7) He asks: could there be "something that really binds our several perceptions together?" Do "we observe some real bond among his perceptions?" (T. 259)

8) If there is a relation which unites the perceptions of the mind, we should ask what kind of relation is it which makes identity out of diverse perceptions.

The relations are contiguity, resemblance and causation. But spatiotemporal contiguity is "irrelevent to the mental world." We are left with either resemblance or causation. Now knowledge of both relations presupposes memory. We may attribute personal identity to ourselves, because of certain resemblances or causal connections among our perceptions. We cannot do this, however, without the memory.

9) However "memory is a faculty by which we raise up the images of past perceptions." Memory "does not so much *produce* (T. 260) as discover personal identity." (T. 262)

Even if we say, mistakenly, that memory causes our idea of personal identity, we should note that we extend our identity beyond our memory. We talk about ourselves when young or an infant without remembering every episode which happened to us. The puzzle is left unsolved.

In the *Appendix* we observe the extent of Hume's puzzlement. He says again that he cannot catch himself – when the net is cast only some perceptions are caught. But then the problem arises

But having thus loosen'd all our particular perceptions, when I proceed to explain the principle of connexion, which binds them together, and makes us attribute to them a real simplicity and identity, I am sensible, that my account is very defective. . . . If perceptions are distinct existences, they form a whole only by being connected together. But no connexionx among distinct existences are ever discoverable by human understanding. We only feel a connexion. But all my hopes vanish, when I come to explain the principles that unite our successive perceptions in our thought or consciousness. . . . In short, there are two principles, which I cannot render consistent, nor is it in my power to renounce either of them, *viz. that all our distinct perceptions are distinct existences, and that the mind never perceives any real connexion among distinct existences.* (T. 636)

These two principles, as such, are not however inconsistent unless we assume, as he does, that

our perceptions either inhere in something simple and undivided, or did the mind perceive some real connexion among them. . . (T. 636)

Hume's rejection of mental-substance is successful, though his concept of identity when employed with regard to the self is incorrect, and his search for the principle of unity is in vain.

We do not need a principle in order to lump together our experiences as ours and separate them from experiences of others, or separate some of our perceptions as our own and others as belonging to the external objects.[1] Though if everything in the world is perception including our body as well as our mind (as Hume believes), then we do need some criteria to account for their separation and for their individuation.

Hume rightly observes that there are several critera of identity. He notices that we do classify things in various ways and for different reasons. But then he rejects these various criteria of identity. There is no reason, however, to suppose that "several different objects existing in succession" could not, and should not be classified as "the same" provided that we take care and change the unit or the class name. As such numerical identity and diversity are not incompatible given that we pay due attention to their types.

Berkeley observed that "we call a window one, a chimney one, and yet a house in which there are many windows and many chimneys, hath an equal right to be called one, and many houses go to the making of one city."

We do call a succession of many points, one line, and so on. Neither diversity among the parts of an object, or in Hume's language "the specific identity," is incompatible with numerical identity – the identity of the whole object. On the contrary, the change in parts presupposes numerical identity.

---

[1] The objection is Strawson's and is sound as such, though in Hume's framework there is a need for the Principle of Unity. "Persons," in Vol. *Concepts, Theories and the Mind-Body Problem*, H. Feigl, Ed., University of Minnesota Press, 1958.

We talk about the change occurring in the *same* object. We see the same sun which rises every morning and not a different and novel sun, though the sun is a bundle of moving particles and though we see it in different times and places. We say, "It is the same sun," because, among other reasons, there is a spatio-temporal continuity among various stages of the appearance of the sun. And if this is true about the sun, it is also true about a person, though we may use other criteria to establish identity of a person.

Such criticism of Hume, however, may not touch his problems – and this is because in criticizing his arguments the critics went beyond his system.

Hume, despite his rejection of metaphysical systems, has a system – a system which begins and ends with experience. However, Hume never claimed that his conceptual frame is a description of experience as it is actually described by our ordinary language. Hume's system is partly descriptive and partly prescriptive (Strawson).

Hume's basic conceptual tools are the very ones used by Descartes, Locke, Berkeley and others, though he often sharpened and modified these for his own purpose of supporting experience. Hume's system, notwithstanding various dilemnas and puzzles (which were known to him), is essentially consistent. Hence in order to solve or dissolve these puzzles, we should check his basic premise. And this I will attempt to do in connection with his sceptical argument with regard to induction. I believe that if we can show how the acceptance of certain simple premises is the main source of the puzzle of induction, we can also show in an oblique way why Hume was puzzled about the existence of the external world and about personal identity; since it is the puzzle of induction which generated the two other mentioned problems.

5. EVALUATION OF HUME'S PROBLEM OF INDUCTION

Hume is known to be the discoverer of the problem of induction, the problem which in our time has been challanged by Russell, Keynes, Nicod, Broad, Reichenbach and many other important philosophers. Some believe however that no one has yet solved the problem. It has been argued by others that the problem is muddled and various attempts have been made for its dissolution. There was yet another drastic move to be made. Being dissatisfied either with solution or dissolution, we are advised that we should leave the problem alone, on the ground that induction is not used in science.

Thus it seems that we have here another scandal on our hands analogous to Kant's discovery of the scandal of the absence of any proof for the existence of the external world.

It is surprising that despite the undeniable importance of Hume's problem of induction, no one so far as I know has examined in detail Hume's premises of the problem.

I shall argue that (1) only if we accept Hume's premises, may we claim that the principle of induction, as Hume showed is not justified, or even is not justifiable by appeal to any rational method, and (2) if we accept his premises we have to conclude that not only can we not rationally justifiy our claim that we know something about the future events but also that we know anything about present and past events, that we have any deductive or conceptual or historical knowledge.

If that is the case, that is, if we have no reason to believe that we do know something about the immediate present, then we cannot even state these premises, much less know that they are true which is necessary for stating the problem.

It follows that if the premises are not statable or meaningful, and if the conclusion is not derivable without those premises, then there is no argument and no problem which stands in need of solution or dissolution.

In this respect my argument is in line with the dissolutionist conclusion. But it goes much further – since it shows that Hume's premises are not statable, and if so, they cannot be false.

In the following I will first give a sketch of Hume's problem, second, I shall examine the premises of his problem and third, I will comment on Hume's rejection of the principle of the uniformity of nature as a main argument brought fourth for justification of induction.

A. A sketch of the Problem

Hume, as we observed, states the problem of induction in various ways. Here, I quote a version which I take to be paradagmatic:

> I wou'd review my question: *Why from this experience we form any conclusion beyond those past instances, of which we have had past experience.* (T. 91)

Hume then assumes that if any reason could be given in answer to his question, it would be by an appeal to a "principle":

that instances, of which we have had no experience, must resemble instances, of which we have had experience, and that the course of nature continues always uniformly the same.

Less generally stated the principle is:

like causes produce like effects.

The principle is the principle of induction, and Hume argues that it cannot be supported by reason. Hume's arguments could be restated and simplified in the following form: Reason is a method of making inferences from premises to conclusion. Inferences are either deductive or inductive. If we then make a deductive move from true premises which state some facts about the present or the past to a conclusion which expresses future states of these events, we are making a mistake since given that our premises are true the conclusion may turn out to be false.

And this is simply because no premise about the present or past, be it true or false, could entail a conclusion about the future.

On the other hand, if we make an inductive move from true premises which state some facts about the present or the past to a conclusion which express the future states of these events, we are again making a mistake – the mistake of assuming that we can, without circularity, support the Principle of induction by a use of the inductive method. We cannot claim in this case that our conclusion is probable, since probability itself is based on the assumption of uniformity of the course of events.

It follows accordingly that neither deductive or inductive justification of the principle of induction is possible.

Hume does not consider other kinds of support or arguments for the Principle. But it could be shown that other arguments are essentially species of deductive or inductive supports of the principle, and thus if Hume is right, there is no reason to believe in the principle of induction, the principle which supposes to be the principle of rationality.

Hume's Premises

The premises "instances, of which we had no experience, must resemble instances, of which we have had experience" or "from this experience we form any conclusion beyond those past instances," is stated in such a general form which does cover every inductive inference from what is given to what transcends the given. It covers thus (a) the inference from the given, to what is hidden in the past, which is called "retrodiction," (b) the inference from the given to what is hidden in the future, which is called "prediction" and (c) the inference from the given to what is hidden – the hidden may be properties of "natural kinds" or events which are concomittant with the given.

Hume gives many examples of (a) type, such as the inference drawn from a latter received to its writer, from a machine found in a desert island, to one who left the machine (E. 26), and from historical records and testimonies to historical and observed events.

Numerous examples are also provided for (b) types of inferences, such as from an initial motion of one billiard ball, to its course, its impact, and its final position, and from various causes to effects and vice versa.

There are also some examples of (c) type inferences, such as from the solidity of an object to its weight or from the light of a fire to its heat. He calls properties of natural kinds, "collateral," "heat and light are collateral effects of fire, and the one effect may justly be inferred from the other." (E. 27)

I do not claim that Hume here is making a distinction among various kinds of inferences. He was mostly concerned with causal inference, which involves a temporal co-ordinate. Nonetheless, Hume puts the problem of induction in such a general form which covers all inductive inference, including ones which are not causal and so need no temporal-coordination. The inference from the law of gravitation which states that there is a force proportional to the mass and inversely proportional to the square of the distance acting between two bodies, is not a causal inference, though we do make inference from this law. Such an inference may be brought under (c), i.e. inference from the given property of an object to the hidden collateral properties of the same. Thus the complaint that Hume's explanation does not fit those laws of science which are stated in the form of functional relations rather than causal, is not just if we pay attention to what he says about inductive inferences which are not causal.[1]

---

[1] The point about "Natural Kinds" is due to H. H. Price. However Price writes that: "Hume often seems to think that all inductive generalizations are causal, and those who make it their business to refute him nearly always think so. Certainly, in the *Treatise*, he first introduces the Problem of Induction in a causal context. But it is not true that all inductive generalizations are causal. Some concern concommitances and sequences." "The Permanent Significance of Hume's Philosophy," *Philosophy*, XV (1940).

The Given: We do draw inferences from the given to the hidden regardless of the spatio-temporal properties of the hidden. When we move from the given to the future or to the past or to co-present hidden events, we are making an inductive inference.

But what is the nature of the given which should be captured by our premise? Hume actually speaks about two classes of the given, without making a distinction between them

First he says "the only existence, of which we are certain are perceptions, which being immediately present to us by consciousness command our strongest assent, and are the first foundation of all our conclusions." (T. 212)

Second, he writes about certain *relations* which "are discoverable at first sight... fall properly under the province of intuition... in none of them the mind can go beyond what is immediately present to the senses." (T. 69–73). These are resemblance, contrarity, degrees of quality (among necessary relations) and identity and relations of time and place (among contingent relations).

Thus, for Hume "perceptions" are (and by that here he should mean "impressions" which are a sub-class of perceptions, and not ideas since ideas are derivative and may be mistaken; "When we pass from a present impression to the idea of any object, we might possibly have separated the idea from the impression, and have substituted any other idea in its room" (T. 87)):

1. "immediately present"
2. "command our strongest assent"
3. "the first foundation of all our conclusion"

which comes very close to the following:

1. Sense-data are the given
2. Sense-data are indubitable
3. Statements about sense-data are the premises of all empirical and also conceptual knowledge.

In the same way Hume's statements about some relations could be interpreted as the following. Certain relations among sense-data (let us call our data 's' and 'y'), such as:

1. "x resembles y"	Resemblance
2. "x is to the left of y" and "x is later than y"	Place and time

3. "x is darker than y"   Degree in quality
4. "x is y"   Identity
5. "(∃x) ∧ —(∃x)"   Contrarity

are immediately given relations of sense-data and are indubitable.

It is also clear that our knowledge about these relations are non-inferential, unlike our knowledge about mathematical and causal relations which are inferential.

We shall see that in each case Hume is wrong. There cannot be any knowledge about what is immediately given or knowledge about any relation between two or more sense-data.

B. The Myth of the Given and the Problem of Induction

Thoughts without contents are empty, intuitions without concepts are blind. (Kant) What has to be accepted, the given, is – one might say – forms of life. (Wittgenstein)

The first part of Kant's statement is compatible with Hume's principle of meaning and that principle was used by Kant with due recognition of indebtedness to Hume. However, it is the second part of Kant's injunction which was not considered by Hume, and which could have saved him from his "philosophical melancholy and delirium."

The premises of the Principle of Induction states, as we observed, that there is (1) "this experience" and also (2) "those past experiences" and the conclusion is (3) "there will be, or there were similar experiences of (1) and (2) types."

(1) and (2) are supposed to be unproblematic and our knowledge about them is regarded to be non-inferential and indubitable. Only our claim to know (3) is supposed to be inferential and hence dubious.

Now in order that I report or express (1) (or 2), i.e., talk about "this experience" or "those past experiences" of mine, I should be able to describe or name that experience. I cannot merely use the given. I should be able to use its name. Some knowledge of semanitc regularities, not to speak of syntactic regularities, is necessary in order that I describe my experience, let the experience be as simple as seeing a letter.

In short, I cannot talk about my experience without being able to conceptualize it. However, to be able to conceptualize my experience is to go already beyond it and to go beyond it is to make an inductive inference.

Now imagine that I cut all my cultural surroundings and invent my own private language and try to express my experience of the moment by employing that language and not the one I learned from my culture. Even so limited, in order to use this language I should be able to make an inference, i.e. that such given data belongs to such a given set of concepts.

As Hume himself observed, passing from "a present impression to the idea is not absolutely safe, for we might possibly have separated the idea from the impression, and have substituted any other idea in its room." And if this is the case, we have no *reason* to use any concept at all and we are back in the position of the old sceptic who wiggled his finger in place of talking.

Hume never fully recognized the implication of the above quoted statement which appears under the suggestive title "Of the inference from the impression to the idea."

He only pays slight attention to the processes of language-learning. For example, he writes that when "a particular idea is commonly annex'd to such a particular word, nothing is requir'd but the hearing of that word to produce the correspondent idea; ... In this case it is not absolutely necessary, that upon hearing such a particular sound, we shou'd reflect on any past experience and consider what idea has been usually connected with the sound. The imagination of itself supplies the place of this reflection." (T. 93)

In the *Enquiries* he notices that an animal associates or infers from an "arbitrary sound, that you mean him than any of his fellows." (E. 105)

These are fine observations with regard to linguistic habits. But description of such animal inferences does not tell us on what principle we make such inferences or that whether these inferences are reasonable.

Russell observes that "most object-words are condensed induction; this is true of the word 'dog,' as we have already had occasion to notice. We must avoid such words, if we wish to be merely recording what we perceive. To do this is very difficult, and requires a special vocabulary."[1]

But why "most object-words"? Indeed, if we have any word and not a mere sound, and if we are able to use it, we have to pass from the given (phoneme) if we want to use it as a word.

[1] Russell, *Ibid.*, p. 152.

In short, if we are able to speak about "this experience" and "those past experiences" we are already transcending the given – we are using not only our senses but our memory, and if we have no reason to transcend the given, we could not ask "why from this experience we form any conclusion beyond" it. To have an experience requires not only having perceptions, but also requires cognition that something is experienced.

The given is a myth, and exposed as such by no less a philosopher than Kant. He observed that in using a concept in our judgment about the raw material of experience, we make experience intelligible. When we apply a concept we unify or "contract" many presentations given or remembered and the unifying function of concepts is quite different from the passive apprehension which perception is.

It was Kant's insight to recognize that

No knowledge is possible without a concept, however obscure or imperfect it may be, and a concept is always, with regard to its form, something general, something that can serve as a rule.[1]

Thus we cannot speak of "this experience" much less about "those past experiences" which are Hume's premises and wonder about our reason to conclude that "there *will* be similar experiences," which is the conclusion of the Principle of Induction.

Speaking of *this* and *those* experiences are of the same nature as speaking about future similar experiences. In each case we have to transcend the object of our present, past and future experiences if we wish to speak about them.

I have tried to connect the myth of the given with the problem of justification of induction. The myth, as I already said, is exposed and induction, is said to require no justification. It was not recognized, though, that unless the given is not a myth, we cannot even state what is the problem which requires justification.

C. The Assumption of the Uniformity of Nature

Lastly, let us consider Hume's argument that the inductive inference from the given to the hidden is made on the unjustified assumption that nature is uniform.

---

[1] Kant's *Critique of Pure Reason*, Max Muller (tr.), New York, N.Y.: Macmillan Company, 1949, p. 87.

He states this assumption in various forms:

The course of nature continues always uniformly the same,
That the future will be conformable to the past,
That like causes produce like effect. (E. 25)

The assumption, if ever, is made to justify any induction – is so general that it is almost empty of any empirical content, and it is so because we cannot refute the assumption under any condition.

Let us note that as a matter of fact when certain theories in modern physics replaced the classical theories no one denied that nature is uniform.

More fundamentally, since any set of events could in principle be covered by a law no matter how random are those events, it is utterly uninformative to claim that nature is uniform throughout.

In this respect the assumption of the uniformity of nature is similar to the assumption of teleological order of nature. It was Hume's insight to note that "the religious hypothesis" or the argument to the effect that the universe has a purposive order, or a design, is vacuous, since "any change is compatable with the design."

The question that we need to ask is whether we do as a matter of fact make such an assumption in order to support our inductive inferences. The assumption is tantamont to inferences by induction through simple enumeration. But as a matter of fact we do not assume that any regularities are projectable but only certain well-confirmed regularities. Space scientists did not simply assume that the moon has an atmosphere or is composed of the same minerals or geological structure as the earth. They however projected certain regularities about its orbit or its distance from the earth.

To the question why do we assume that certain regularities are projectable and others are not, the answer could be given (though the question and answer are too general), that of course the projectable ones are confirmed and non-exceptional regularities (and if exceptions, easily removable). Now if a Humeian type of objection arises that it does not follow that these confirmed regularities will be confirmed in the future, we may say of course it does not deductively follow that these regularities will hold in the future, though it is rational to believe and expect continuity of such regularities. On the other hand, not to believe in them and to act upon such negative beliefs is exactly what we mean by saying that such beliefs and actions are irrational.

The interesting problems about the types of projectable regularities and calculation of objective and subjective probabilities are problems within the domain of inductive logic and should not be confused with the pseudoproblem of justification of induction.

In this respect the problem is similar to the justification of certain specific theorems or rules of inference within a deductive system, though there is no problem about justification of deduction as such.

POSTSCRIPT

After writing this chapter I came across the following passage which supports my arguments against psudo-problem of justification of induction; "This consideration of the fact that theorises or expectations are built into our very sense organs shows that the epistemology of induction breaks down even before having taken its first step. It cannot start from sense data or perceptions and build our theories upon them, since there are no such things as sense data or perceptions which are not built upon theories (or expectations, that is, the biological predecessors of linguistically formulated theories). Thus the 'data' are no basis of, no guarantee for, the theories: they are not more secure than any of our theories or 'prejudices' but, if anything, less so." Pp. 368–399.

[Popper's address to the Third International Congress for Logic Methodology and Philosophy of Science, reprinted under "Epistemology, without knowing subject" in *Studies In Logic*, III. Edited by Van Rootselarr & J. F. Stall. North Holland Publishing Company. Amsterdam, 1968.]

Hume on pure and applied geometry

Antony Flew in his book on Hume and also in a review, attributes a view to Hume which is too good to be true. He claims that Hume,

> Besides restoring pure geometry to its place alongside the other two elements of the trinity [Algebra and Arithmetic] in the *Inquiry* also sketches the account of applied mathematics.

Then, after citing some quotations from Hume, which supposedly warrant this interpretation, he goes on to say,

> Brief and incidental though it is Hume's account of the relations between pure and applied mathematics is already sufficient to indicate the great potential as a tool of analysis of the dichotomy which it is here employed to illustrate.[1]

The same conviction is expressed in his review. He writes:

> Hume is interpreted as holding a view much more like that of J. S. Mill than anything favoured by any logical empiricist. For the *Treatise* this interpretation seems to be substantially correct. The question is whether Zabeeh does justice to the suggestions of better things to be found in the first Inquiry... Zabeeh is encouraged in this interpretation [that definitions of geometrical terms "are not verbal definitions" but "rather descriptions of physical space" (p. 142)] by his belief that Hume refuses "to distinguish between pure and applied geometry." (p. 143). This, surely, is just mistaken. It ignores Hume's seminal account of the nature of applied mathematics.[2]

Not withstanding such announcements, Flew is well aware of other statements in the *Enquiries* which would violate such interpretations. However, instead of giving up his unwarranted interpretation, Flew, in both places, (the book and the review) talks about Hume's *backslidings* towards the position of the *Treatise* (a

---

[1] Antony Flew, *Hume's Philosophy of Belief*. A Study of his First Inquiry (New York: the Humanities Press, 1961), pp. 62–6.
[2] Antony Flew, Review of "Hume: Precursor of Modern Empiricism," by Farhang Zabeeh, *Ratio*, vol. V, no. 2, Dec. 1963.

view which supposedly is similar to Mill's or Kant's). Flew continues:

This account has such an up-to-date ring that it is tempting to attribute rather more to him than is warranted by the actual text. Thus Reichenbach maintained that Hume "arrives at the result that all knowledge is either analytic or derived from experience: mathematics and logic are analytic, all synthetic knowledge is derived from experience" (Reichenbach, p. 86). If *analytic* and *synthetic* are to be employed – wastefully, but perhaps none the less wisely – as mere synonyms for *necessary* and *contingent*, or for *a priori* and *a posteriori*, then the only though considerable objection to this statement is that Hume does not in fact in this connection mention logic at all. In such a usage to speak of a synthetic *a priori* would indeed be obviously contradictory. But if the words are not used simply in this uneconomical way it may be more doubtful whether it is really correct to attribute to Hume the view that mathematics contains no synthetic elements. For even if we continue for the present, as we have been doing so far, to ignore certain important backslidings towards the positions of the *Treatise*, it is by no means unequivocally clear that Hume really would have disagreed with Kant in saying that mathematics is not all analytic, in Kant's sense of that term.[3]

The same awareness is expressed in the review. "Of course there are both elsewhere in the first *Enquiry* and probably in the suppressed essay on geometry also, backslidings towards the position of the *Treatise*."[4] However, a few pages later in his book, despite the awareness that Reichenbach's interpretations, and perhaps, his own, may be too cavalier, he ends up his chapter on *The Great Divide* by saying,

On the relation between pure and applied mathematics his remarks though brief and often overlooked are both basic and illuminating.

In the following, I would like to argue that:

First, Hume's important distinction between relation of ideas and matters of fact in the *Enquiries*, is the same dichotomy which he already made, and made use of, in the *Treatise*, i.e. the dichotomy between necessary and contingent relations. Both relations have their relata as ideas which owe their existence to their antecedent impressions. Hence, there is no reason to believe that this dichotomy in the *Enquiries* enables Hume to separate pure from applied geometry.

Second, even if we give up the desire to make a coherent theory out of Hume's statements, and take some of his statements to be inconsistent with the main theses of his works, I still believe that the two paragraphs cited by Flew from the *Enquiries* do not entitle him to draw his conclusion.

---

[3] Ibid.
[4] Ibid.

My own interpretation of Hume's view in the *Enquiries*, despite neglect of one paragraph, still seems to be a correct one – a view which is based on the fact that Hume does distinguish between necessary and contingent statements without violating his principle that all ideas in the last analysis are cashable in terms of sense experience. Hume's view is not similar to Mill's but is quite similar to that of Locke, who holds that mathematical concepts are known to us by experience, while mathematical truths are analytic and instructive. Flew does not see this alternative which is previously indicated by Pap and reached by myself and hence falls into the trap. This is why he mistakenly believes that I make Hume sound like Mill.

In the *Treatise*, Hume divides philosophical relations into two classes which we call Necessary and Contingent. The former described as those "depend entirely on ideas," are "invariable, as long as our ideas remain the same," are "discoverable from mere ideas" (T. 69, 74, 89). He is referring to this class of relations when he uses expressions such as "real relations," "inseparable and inviolable connection," and even "necessary relation." An important member of this class is "proportions of quantity and number."

In contrast, contingent relations are described as those which "may be chang'd without any change of ideas," depend, "on a hundred different accidents, which cannot be foreseen by the mind," are "never discoverable merely from their ideas." Concerning such relations, he says, "We receive information from experience and not from any abstract reasoning or reflexion" (T. 69). An important member of this class is causation.

Now we have to remember all along that though philosophical relations are divided into necessary and contingent, the relata in each case are ideas and all ideas are derived, if not copied, from impressions. Hence, in the *Treatise*, Hume while separating the empirical sciences from purely deductive sciences (algebra, arithmetic, and geometry) does not and cannot (on that frame of reference) distinguish between pure and applied geometry.

In the *Enquiries*, Hume drops altogether the discussion of philosophical relations and, with that, the troublesome distinction between separable and inseparable relations. Instead, he substitutes new expressions for his old relations, i.e. instead of "inseparable relations' 'he simply uses the expression "relations of ideas," and for "separable relations" he substitutes "matters of fact, and real existence." However, these new expressions were also used in the *Treatise*, viz., "Reason is the discovery of truth or falsehood. Truth or falsehood consists in an agreement or disagreement either to the *real* relations of ideas, or to *real* existence and matter of fact" (T. 458), also "The operations of human understanding divide themselves into two kinds, the comparing of ideas, and the inferring of matter of fact" (T. 463).

In the *Enquiries* again, Hume allocates the sciences of algebra, arithmetic and geometry as belonging to the class of relations of ideas. In neither of the two books, however, logic is classed with mathematics. But in the *Enquiries* geometry regains its status as an exact science, the status which was denied to her in the *Treatise*.

Once again we should remember that Hume in the *Enquiries*, no doubt unwisely, does not give up his introspective chase after the genesis of all ideas. He still insists that all of them, without exception, are somehow derived from impressions. (He uses different expressions: "copied," "derived," "borrowed," "suggested"). So he writes,

All the ideas of quantity, upon which mathematicians reason, are nothing but particular, and such as are suggested by the senses and imagination (E. 158), and "The great advantage of the mathematical sciences above the moral consists in this, that the ideas of the former, being sensible, are always clear and determinate, the smallest distinction between them is immediately perceptible, and the same terms are still expressive of the same ideas, without ambiguity or variation." (E. 60).

So, after all, mathematical ideas like any other ideas are sensible, though certain relations of ideas are not necessarily sensible, but perhaps intelligible.

Flew offers two evidences for his conviction. He cites those famous statements which have puzzled many commentators.

All the objects of human reason or enquiry may naturally be divided into two kinds, to wit, *Relations of Ideas*, and *Matters of Fact*. Of the first kind are sciences of Geometry, Algebra, and Arithmetic; and in short, every affirmation which is either intuitively or demonstratively certain. *That the square of the hypothenuse is equal to the square of the two sides*, is a proposition which expresses a relation between these figures. *That three times five is equal to the half of thirty*, expresses a relation between these numbers. Propositions of this kind are discoverable by the mere operation of thought, without dependence on what is anywhere existent in the universe. Though there never were a circle or triangle in nature, the truths demonstrated by Euclid would for ever retain their certainty and evidence (E. 25).

I believe that Hume by making this assertion does not imply that Euclid arrived at his theorems by deducing them merely from the axioms, postulates, and definitions of *The Elements*, but rather, given certain geometrical ideas, "the truths demonstrated by Euclid," e.g. the mentioned theorems in the quotations, "for ever retain their certainty and evidence." It is important to notice that Hume in that passage is talking about "truth" and "evidence for proposition which expresses relation of ideas," and not about "ideas," i.e. relata. Only a few pages later Hume, when contrasting empirical and deductive inference, maintains that:

> After the constant conjunction of two objects – heat and flame, for instance, weight and solidity – we are determined by custom alone to expect the one from the appearance of the other. This hypothesis seems even the only one which explains the difficulty, why we draw, from a thousand instances, an inference which we are not able to draw from one instance, that is, in no respect, different from them. Reason is incapable of any such variation. The conclusions which it draws from considering one circle are the same which it would from upon surveying all the circles in the universe. But no man, having seen only one body move after being impelled by another, could infer that every other body will move after a like impulse. (E. 43).

Can we imagine that Hume who in the same book when rejecting the Cartesian metaphysico-deductive systems that, "we must assure ourselves, by a chain of reasoning, deduced from some original principle, which cannot possibly be fallacious or deceitful" (E. 150) – by saying that, "neither is there any such original principle, which has a perogative above other, that are self-evident and convincing: or if there were, could we advance a step beyond it?" (E. 150), at the same time telling us that the axioms and postulates of Euclid are self-evident and his theorems informative? Hume does refer to geometrical theorems as informative and to syllogistic arguments as empty (E. 163).

Such assertions (and many others) led me to conclude that:

> By making this assertion, he does not want to imply that "though there never were a circle or triangle *even for Euclid*" the geometrical truths discovered by him would forever retain their certainty and evidence, but that once Euclid observed a geometrical figure and discovered certain relations, "the conclusions which [he] draws from considering one circle are the same which [he] would form upon surveying all the circles in the universe."

No doubt, as Laird and others had already noticed "This tamer view [division between relations of ideas and matters of fact] is difficult to reconcile with Hume's phenomenalism. No doubt Hume was unable to provide a secure shelter for the apodictic nature of mathematical truths in his framework of "internal and perishing impressions" and their pale and bloodless shadows viz. "The less forcible and lively [perception] are commonly denominated

Thoughts or Ideas" (E. 18). But as Pap maintained a long time ago, and Flew never considered as an alternative, "A sensationalist might maintain that all the concepts that constitute a given proposition are derived from experience and might nonetheless admit that the proposition itself is *a priori* in the sense of requiring no empirical verification in order to be assertable as true. Thus Hume the sensationalist, admitted that *a priori* knowledge is possible in mathe-mathematics, which is conversant "exclusively about "relations of ideas" and not about "matters of fact.""[5]

Let us now consider the evidence which entitles Flew to draw the inference that Hume, not only recognized pure geometry (in that famous passage) but that he also recognized the existence of applied geometry ("applied" is contrasted with "pure"). Flew does not quote the passage in full. The whole passage is the following:

> Nor is geometry, when taken into the assistance of natural philosophy, ever able to remedy this defect, or lead us into the knowledge of ultimate causes, by all that accuracy of reasoning for which it is so justly celebrated. Every part of mixed mathematics proceeds upon the supposition that certain laws are established by nature in her operations; and abstract reasonings are employed, either to assist experience in the discovery of these laws, or to determine their influence in particular instances, . . . Geometry assists us in the application of this law (E. 31).

None of Hume's commentators before Flew took notice of this passage. However, I still think that Flew is wrong to assume that here Hume, by talking about "mixed mathematics," is recognizing that there exists something like pure geometry. I think Hume in this passage is talking about the application of euclidean geometry in classical mechanics. From the fact that geometry may be "taken into the assistance of natural philosophy," it does not at all follow that when it is not applied then we have pure geometry.[6]

[5] Arthur Pap, *Elements of Analytic Philosophy* (New York, the Macmillan Company, 1949), p. 98.

[6] It seems that Hume repeats not only the opinion, but also the very words of Lock'es in Book IV, Chapter IV, Paragraph 6–7 of *An Essay Concerning Human Understanding*, e.g.,

The mathematician considers the truth and properties belonging to a rectangle or circle only as they are in idea in his own mind. For it is possible he never found either of them existing mathematically, i.e. precisely true, in his life.

Is it true of the *idea* of a triangle, that its three angles are equal to two right ones? It is true also of a triangle, wherever it really exists. Whatever other figure exists, that it is not exactly answerable to that idea of a triangle in his mind, is not at all concerned in that proposition.

All the discourses of the mathematicians about the squaring of a circle, conic sections, or any other part of mathematics, concern not the existence of any of those figures: but their demonstrations, which depend on their ideas, are the same, whether there be any square or circle existing in the world or no. In the same manner, the truth and certainty of moral discourses abstracts from the lives of men, and the existence of those virtues in the world whereof they treat: nor are *Tully's offices* less true, because there is nobody in the world that exactly practices his rules, and lives up to that pattern of a virtuous man which he has given us.

CHAPTER SEVEN

Summary and Conclusion

We began in Chapter One our analysis of Hume's principle of meaning by discussing his dominating passion to wage war against metaphysics and theology, and his pronounced intention of freeing the human mind from the tyranny of superstitions and dogmas "of every kind or denomination." To do this, Hume states we should know the limit and extent of the human mind, and this can be accomplished by study of the *Science of Man*. We saw that an important part of this science is what Hume calls "logic," and logic for him consists mainly of what we call epistemology and semantics. We interpreted Hume's inquiry into the scope and limit of the human mind as an investigation into the nature of the expression of thought. In this interpretation we were inspired by the views of Carnap, Moore, Ryle and others. We noted that Hume's critique of metaphysics is based mainly on the principle of the priority of impressions to ideas. This maxim itself is not intended to be an article of inquisition, as alleged by *Reid*, but rather is a generalization from experience open to revision and weakened by exceptions. We then carefully examined both the nature and application of this principle, and the occasions on which Hume applies it. We demonstrated how the concepts of material and mental substances, or the theory of the ultimate qualities of mind or matter, together with the suppositions of Deity and a future state, went under a "new microscope" and were cut to pieces by Hume's razor. But the search for a criterion of meaning led us to criteria other than the known principle of priority, which Hume often employs to determine the significance of a concept. We found that on some occasions Hume uses a principle akin to the verifiability criterion of meaning. He does indicate, for example, that "the religious hypothesis" is indeed an empty theory, not because the terms employed in the theory do not stand for any sense-data, but because the theory lacks any observable consequences. We also discovered that Hume, in addition to the principle of priority of impressions to ideas, employs, without warning, when dealing with expressions of complex ideas, two other implied principles which we called *the criterion of the absence of contradiction* and *the criterion of propriety of usage*. He maintains, in effect, that an expression of complex ideas is not meaningful if it is self-contradictory. Besides the requirement that every term in an expression of complex ideas should denote a particular entity, the terms should also be used properly in the statements in which they occur, and one guarantee of this propriety is lack of contradiction. Then to our surprise we discovered in Hume's ethics, in his discussion on promises, an occasion on which he abandons his search for denotations. He tries to provide meanings for some expressions by establishing rules of procedure, knowing that at the same time these expressions do not stand for any impressions.

In Chapter Two we undertook to evaluate Hume's main principle of meaning, and carefully examined the relation of impressions and ideas and words and impressions. We interpreted Hume's maxim of the priority of impressions to ideas to be a semantical principle in disguise. In view of this fact we had occasion to correct James' and Laird's judgments and we cited Russell's attempt to explain away Hume's own exception to his principle. Then we showed the inadequacy of Hume's thesis by finding three main difficulties in his theory, i.e., the difficulty with the recurrence of an impression, with the privacy of impressions, and with the attempt to determine the meaning of expressions by tracing the origin of our ideas.

In Chapter Three we tried to formulate another significant principle which was used and mentioned on many occasions in Hume's works. We observed that Hume shares the view of modern empiricism in seeing a fundamental cleavage between analytic and synthetic judgments. In the *Treatise*, by making the distinction between relations which depend on relata and relations which are independent of their terms, and in the *Enquiries* by making the distinction between relations of ideas and matters of fact, Hume showed his full awareness of the different nature of truths. We gathered all Hume's assertions on this issue and showed that the so-called principle of atomism is also employed by him to distinguish analytic from synthetic truths. Then we pushed forward our inquiry and found that for him the ultimate ground for what is analytic or synthetic is our ability or inability to conceive certain arrangements of ideas. The examination of Hume's theory of analyticity led us to consider his views on logic. We showed the undesirable consequence of Hume's endeavor to substitute psychology for logic, and criticized, not the distinction which he makes between analytic and synthetic truths, but the psychological grounds for such a distinction.

In Chapter Four we provided a historical setting by a brief review of the central theses of empiricism, which were promulgated, though in different language, by Locke, Berkeley and Hume – namely the conviction that all knowledge is based on experience. We found that to establish this general conviction the empirical philosophers employed a method, called by Locke the "historical plain method," which is a retrospective procedure of finding evidence for our beliefs by looking back to the original source of our ideas. It is claimed that we can know the limit and the scope of human knowledge by using such a procedure. The predominating purpose of the empiricist in advocating the retrospective method was to free mankind from fruitless metaphysical speculation. We realized, however, that empiricists, in their endeavor to establish an empirical basis for knowledge by such a method, displayed an undue hostility towards the demonstrative sciences, especially towards syllogistic logic, which they associated with scholasticism. Having expounded the general principle that all knowledge is derived from experience, the empiricists were faced, from the outset, with the problem of accounting for the derivation of non-sensory concepts and the exactness of mathematical truths. The apparent non-sensory mathematical concepts and the recognized universality and exactness of mathematical truths were an anachronism for the old empiricists. Either they had to force all non-sensory concepts into the pigeon hole of sense-data and reduce all truths to empicrial truths, or were forced to admit that not all significant expressions stand for sense-data and not all truths are empirical. That is what we called "the empiricist dilemma." In order to see the full implication of this dilemma, we provided a brief comparison between the views of some of the rationalists and empiricists with regard to the nature of mathematical concepts. We called the position taken by Plato, Leibniz and Frege *The Platonic Position*. We took Berkeley's stand to represent roughly *The Formalist Position*, and we let Mill's theory stand for *The Phenomenalist Position*. Then we simply asked ourselves: How does Hume, consistent with his principle of empiricism, explain the meaning of mathematical truths? We observed, meanwhile, no unanimity of opinion among his critics on this issue (we cited as examples various views expressed by Kant, Windelband, Baumann, Metz, etc.).

In Chapter Five we examined in detail Hume's stand on the nature of deductive reason. In this examination, we first stated his argument against Platonism in mathematics. We then considered Hume's own theory of general ideas and showed the inadequacy of this theory, which again is mainly due to his preoccupation with psychologism. Third, we undertook to elucidate Hume's much debated opinion on the nature of mathematical truths. We distinguished, in analyzing this subject, two separate but often confused topics, viz., the nature of mathematical relations, and the nature of mathematical data. We found that Hume's view on the nature of arithmetical data is similar to that of Locke. But then with Frege's help we criticized his attempts to explain the meaning of number in terms of units. Then we considered carefully Hume's view on geometry, and proved that his view on geometry, despite its shortcomings, on all occasions is compatible with his principle of meaning. In the last part of this chapter we examined Hume's scepticism with regard to reason and pointed out that though his arguments in this section are inconclusive, and though some of his statements are contradictory to his pronounced view that knowledge and probability are quite distinct and separate, the argument itself is the logical outcome of his psychologism. We then attempted to answer, point by point, certain specific questions which we asked in the conclusion of this chapter. We tried to settle the divergent views of Hume's commentators on what is his real opinion on the nature of the mathematical sciences. We established that Hume definitely would not agree with any Platonic view of mathematics. It seems also that he did not consider any formalistic view akin to that of Berkeley; neither would he accept Mill's phenomenalistic view that the processes of the deductive sciences are altogether inductive, though he would agree with Mill that the axioms of arithmetic and geometry are known to us by experience. We admitted, however, that Hume's assertions on this score are ambiguous, and this ambiguity is responsible for the contradictory opinions of his critics. In the main, Hume's view is similar to Locke's, that mathematical truths are analytic and they are at the same time informative and instructive.

In conclusion, I argued that Hume's theory on the nature of mathematical truths does not fit his schematism, and this defect is the logical consequence of his main principle of meaning. He could not (and did not) explain the exactness and universality of the demonstrative sciences in the framework of his "internal and perishing" impressions which are "conjoined" together only by associative links. Perhaps this failure could be explained partly by his ignorance of the mathematical sciences,[1] and partly by his recognition that any non-sensory account of the basis of such sciences might give the victory to the metaphysicians and so weaken his polemic against the rationalists. But if mathematics is to be saved, his main principle of meaning, I suggest, shoud be altered. Otherwise there would be no place for "reason strictly so-called" in his theory of knowledge.

Finally in Chapter Six we discussed in detail the issues of the Foundation of Empirical Knowledge, the Nature of Causal Inference, the Problem of Induction, the Nature of Beliefs and Factual and Ethical assertions.

I argued that the myth of the Given, which was propagated by the classical empiricists, is the core of Hume's unsolved problems of the justification of Induction, of the Existence of the External World and of Personal Identity.

At this juncture I want to register my opinion that, though Hume, in the words of Russell, "represents, in a certain sense, a dead end: in his direction, it is impossible to go further,"[2] this is only true in so far as he speaks as a sceptic. Of Hume it could also be said that he opened a new avenue in philosophy. Despite all his failures, Hume, without scepticism, is a true precursor of modern

---

[1] Hume, unlike Berkeley, was ignorant of mathematical science. In one of his letters he tacitly admits his ignorance.

"I intended to print ... on the Metaphysical Principles of Geometry.... I happened to meet with Lord Stanhope ... and he convinced me, that either there was some Defect in the Argument or in its perspicuity ... and I wrote to Mr. Millar, that I would not print that Essay." *The Letters of D. Hume*, ed. Greig, vol. II, p. 253.

Laird mentions that "it is interesting to observe that the Hume manuscripts in Edinburgh contain two short disquisitions upon the foundations of geometry, neither of which appears to be in Hume's handwriting, and both of which are criticisms of Hume himself." Hume's *Philosophy of Human Nature*, p. 66.

[2] B. Russell, *A History of Western Philosophy*, p. 659.

empiricism. His two basic concepts, namely, the principle of priority of impressions to ideas, and the distinction between relations of ideas and matter of fact, stripped of his psychologism, became two known cornerstones of empiricism, i.e., the principle of verifiability and the principle of analyticity. Now, since Hume throughout his work avoided "that love of *simplicity* which has been the source of much false reasoning in philosophy" (E. 298) and since he did not take any "principles upon trust," principles which "are every where to be met with in the systems of the most eminent philosophers" (T. XVII), I trust that any improvement which has been made upon the essentials of his philosophy would be welcomed by him.

Bibliography

Austin, J. L., "Are There APriori Concepts?". Aristotelian Society Supp., Vol. XVIII.

Bacon, Francis, *The Philosophical Work of Francis Bacon*. John M. Robertson, ed. London: G. Routledge and Sons, Ltd., 1905.

Basson, A. H., *David Hume*. London: Pelican Philosophy Series, 1958.

Baumann, J. J., *Die Lehren von Raum, Zeit und Mathematik in der neueren Philosophie*. II Band. Berlin, 1869.

Berkeley, George, *The Works of George Berkeley*. A. A. Luce and T. E. Jessop, eds. London: T. Nelson, 1948.

Caird, Edward, *A Critical Account of the Philosophy of Kant*. Macmillan and Co., 1877.

Carnap, Rudolph, *Logical Foundation of Probability*. University of Chicago Press, 1950.

Church, R. W., *Hume's Theory of the Understanding*. London: G. Allen and Unwin Ltd., 1935.

Einstein, Albert. *Albert Einstein*. The Library of Living Philosophers, Paul Arthur Schilpp (ed.). New York: Tudor Publishing Company, 1951.:

Flew, Antony, *Hume's Philosophy of Belief. A Study of his First Inquiry*: New York: Humanities Press, 1961.

Frege, G., *The Foundations of Arithmetic*. Austin translation. Oxford: Blackwell, 1950.

Hampshire, S., "Scepticism and Meaning." *Philosophy*, Vol. XXV, No. 94.

Heath, T. L., *A History of Greek Mathematics*. Oxford: The Clarendon Press, 1921.

Holloway, John, *Language and Intelligence*. London: Macmillan, 1951.

Hume, David, *A Treatise of Human Nature*. Selby-Bigge edition (1st ed.). Oxford: Clarendon Press, 1951.

– , *Enquiries Concerning The Human Understanding and Concerning The Principles of Morals*. Selby-Bigge edition. Oxford: The Clarendon Press, 1951.

– , *Hume's Dialogues Concerning Natural Religon*. N. Kemp Smith, ed. Oxford: Clarendon Press, 1935.

– , *An Abstract of A Treatise of Human Nature*. J. M. Keynes and P. Sraffa, eds. Cambridge: University Press, 1938.

– , *The Natural History of Religion* in *Hume On Religion*. Richard Wollheim, ed. The World Publishing Company, Cleveland, 1964.

– , *The History of England*. Vol. V. Philadelphia: Porteve Coates.

– , *The Philosophical Works of David Hume*. T. H. Green and T. H. Grose, eds, London, 1874.

– , *Essays Moral, Political, and Literary*, T. H. Green and T. H. Grose, eds, Vol. I, London, 1875.

– , *The Letters of David Hume*. J. Y. T. Greig, ed. Oxford: Clarendon Press, 1932.

Huxley, Thomas H., *Hume with Helps to the Study of Berkeley*. New York: D. Appleton and Company, 1895.

Jackson, R., *An Examination of Deductive Logic of John Stuart Mill*. Oxford University Press, 1941.

James, William, *Principles of Psychology*. Part I, Vol. II, New York: H. Holt and Company, 1923.

Kant, Immanuel, *Critique of Pure Reason*. Max Muller translation. London: Macmillan Company, 1949.

—, *Prolegomena to Any Future Metaphysics*. P. G. Lucas translation. Manchester: Manchester University Press, 1953.

—, *Prolegomena to Any Future Metaphysics*. Mahaffy and Bernard translation. London: Macmillan and Co., 1889.

Körner, S., "On The Nature of Pure and Applied Mathematics." *Ratio*, Vol. II, No. 1.

Kruse, V., *Hume's Philosophy*. Translation by P. T. Federspiel. Oxford University Press, 1939.

Laird John, *Hume's Philosophy of Human Nature*. London: Methuen, 1932.

MacNabb, D. G. C., *David Hume, His Theory of Knowledge and Morality*. New York: Hutchinson's University Library, 1951.

Marhenke, Paul, "The Criterion of Significance", Presidential Address, Pacific Division of A.P.A., 1949.

Metz, Rudolf, *David Hume, Leben und Philosophie*. Stuttgart: Fr. Frommann, 1929.

Mill, John Stuart, *A System of Logic*. Eighth edition. London: Longmans, Green, Reader, 1872.

Moore, G. E., *Philosophical Studies*. London: Routledge and Kegan Paul Ltd., 1922.

Morris, C. W., *Foundation of the Theory of Signs*. International Encyclopedia of Unified Science. Vol. I, Number 2. Chicago, Illinois, 1928.

Mossner, E. C., *The Forgotten Hume*. New York: Columbia University Press, 1943.

Nagel, Ernest and Newman, James, *Gödel's Proof*. New York University Press, 1958.

Newton, *Optiks*, 4th (1730) ed. New York: Dover, 1952.

Passmore, J. A., *Hume's Intensions*. Cambridge: University Press, 1952.

Plato, *The Dialogues of Plato*. B. Jowett, Ed. New York: Random House, 1937.

Popkin, Richard H., "David Hume and the Pyrrohian Controversy." *The Review of Metaphysics*, Vol. VI, No. 1.

Price, H. H., *Thinking and Experience*. London and New York: Hutchinson's University Library, 1953.

Quine, W. V. O., *From a Logical Point of View*. Cambridge: Harvard University Press, 1953.

Reid, Thomas, *The Works of Thomas Reid*. William Hamilton, ed. Third edition. Edinburgh: Maclachlan and Stewart, 1863.

Ross, David, *Plato's Theory of Ideas*. Oxford: Clarendon Press, 1951.

Russell, Bertrand, *Mysticism and Logic*. Logmans Green and Company, 1921.

—, *Inquiry into Meaning and Truth*, London: Allen and Unwin, 1948.

—, *The Analysis of Mind*. London: George Allen, 1924.

—, *A History of Western Philosophy*. New York: Simon and Schuster, 1945.

—, *The Philosophy of Bertrand Russell*. The Library of Living Philosophers. Volume V, Paul Arthur Schilpp (ed.). Evanston, Illinois, 1946.

—, *Human Knowledge, Its Scope and Limits*. New York: Simon and Schuster, 1948.

—, *An Outline of Philosophy*. London: George Allen, 1949.

—, *My Philosophical Development*. New York: Simon and Schuster, 1959.

Ryle, Gilbert, *The Concept of Mind*. New York: Barnes and Noble, 1949.

Smith, N. Kemp, *The Philosophy of David Hume*. London: Macmillan and Co. Ltd., 1941.

Urmson, J. O., *Philosophical Analysis*. Oxford: Clarendon Press, 1956.

Weinberg, Julius Rudolph, *An Examination of Logical Positivism*. London: Routledge and Kegan Paul, 1950.

Windelband, W., *A History of Philosophy*. English translation by Tufts. Macmillan Co., 1901.

Wisdom, John, *Philosophy and Psycho-Analysis*. Oxford: Blackwell, 1953.

Wittgenstein, L., *Tractatus Logico- Philosophicus*. London: Routledge and Kegan Paul Ltd., fourth impression, 1945.

– , *Philosophical Investigations*. Translation by G. E. M. Anscombe. Oxford: Blackwell, 1953.

Index